Jill:

Beloved woman Thank you
for the Love and Joy That
Shines from your eyes When
you smile ♡

Terry McBride

THE HELL I CAN'T!

By

Terry McBride

Notice: This book is not intended as a medical manual, nor is it intended to diagnose, treat, cure, or prevent any illness. If you suspect you have a medical problem, we urge you to seek competent medical help.

Published by McBride Enterprises,
2753 E. Broadway
Suite 101-313
Mesa, AZ 85204
www.terrymcbride.info

Library of Congress Cataloging-in-Publication Data
McBride, Terry.
    The Hell I Can't! / by Terry McBride. 1st. ed.
    p. cm.
    LCCN: 2003097230

    ISBN 0-9745850-0-9 (hc)
    1. Self Help   2. Inspirational   3. Spirituality

Cover Design by Derek Gold, www.mezmotech.com
Book Design by Leslie Petrovich
Cover Photograph by Kevin Kassel,
www.kevinkasselphotography.com
Editor: Leslie Petrovich, www.lesliepublishing.com

Printed in the United States of America

To The Reader

This is a true story. However, with the exception of the names of my family members, Dr. Greenlee, and the University of Washington Medical Center, all names have been changed. I have used Dr. Greenlee's actual name because I wish to honor him for his deep character and caring. Likewise, I wish to acknowledge the University of Washington Medical Center as the truly remarkable facility it is.

To Karen, Kris and Sheri,
the three who went with me

SPECIAL ACKNOWLEDGMENTS:

To Leslie Petrovich, my editor
A woman of depth and ability who understood the vision of this book and was committed to bringing the whole story out of me. Thank you for your writing skills and the times you were willing to "go to the mat" and confront me with "that's close but you're not done yet." Because of you, I am a better writer, and this book is all I have dreamed it could be. And then you took care of all the details to get it in print; you are a great "full service book packager."

And Especially to my Wife, Kami Elliott McBride

Thank you for all you have done to become who you are. Thank you for your commitment to yourself and your relationship with God. Thank you for the countless hours where we explored how this story could be told.

You are my best friend and the smartest person I know. I had been waiting for you so we could finish this book together. I feel such peace and joy knowing I will spend the rest of my life with you by my side.

ACKNOWLEDGMENTS

To my mother, who taught me it was okay to be a dreamer and never gave up her vision of my perfect health.

To my brother Gerry, who was my first real-world example of not listening to what the experts said about being sick.

To Karen who went through the pain and terror with me and stood as a rock of love and understanding.

To Kris and Sheri my precious daughters. I live because you chose me as your father. You are my friends and teachers. You gave me the reason to pick myself up when I had given up doing it for myself.

To Kenneth and Elizabeth Breer, Karen's parents, who were there with prayers and support in so many ways. Thank you for opening your home and taking care of Karen and my girls all those days and nights when I was in the hospital.

To Beverly, Holly and Deborah for your commitment to love and your willingness to allow the form of it to change.

To Mike Murphy and Jerry Crossler two of the first who believed in me as a teacher.

To the nurses who, night after night, were there caring and doing for me what I couldn't do for myself. Thank you for your profession and your love.

To the doctors, residents and interns; many of you became my friends. Thank you for your dedication. I know you always did the very best you knew to do.

To Dr. Greenlee, the only one in this book I call by his real name. You were a shining star and without your caring and willingness to listen and believe, I might still be sick.

To: Malcolm Campbell, my "brother" on this glorious path. Thank you for all you have taught me and all you allowed me to teach you. What a joy it's been traveling with you these past twenty plus years.

To Sabrina Braham, my "sister," who always seeks past my words to what I am trying to say and helps me say it better. Thank you for your unconditional love and support.

To Rick Robertson, my other "brother," a scientist with the heart and understanding of a saint. Thank you for reminding me from a scientific point of view of the magnificence of our bodies and minds.

To Steve Wayne, the boy who came to work for me when he was seventeen and through the past twenty years has grown to be my "son." Thank you for your laughter, thank you for your wisdom, thank you for coming home from India and picking me.

To Alvin, Jeannie, Shannon and Cassidy Edge. Thank you for accepting me as part of your family.

To Roger Leslie, my writing coach. Your constant encouragement and guidance propelled me to complete the draft of my book. Thank you for your diligence and wisdom.

To Judy McKenzie. Thank you for the music that is your life and the music of your CD. Thank you for running my company. Thank you for holding the vision of what this book is to be. And thank you for bringing Michael McKenzie into my life.

To The Carpenter From Galilee. Thank you for being my friend. Thank you for your teachings that allowed me to find that facet of me that was not sick, not afraid, and from that place, create a life of health, love, joy and abundance.

TABLE OF CONTENTS

CHAPTER 1

THE BEGINNING

*M*y temples are screaming. Dr. Hedgewood is looking down at me in my hospital bed. His lips are moving, nothing registers. The roar of blood in my ears drowns out everything.

His face is a bright pinpoint; the other doctors standing around him are shadows. He leans over the bed and places a hand on my arm. The touch focuses me. "Terry, do you understand?"

I can hear the worry in his voice.

Understand? What, is he crazy? How can I wrap my mind around what he's saying? I'm twenty-four and he's telling me this operation will rob me of the use of one leg, probably both, and there's a good chance it will leave me sexually impotent and without the control of my bowels and bladder.

Understand? Hell, no! I don't want to understand. I don't want to believe that this E. coli bacteria is eating me alive. I don't want to believe that my life could be over. I want to unzip myself from this body and get out!

It started when I was twenty-two, with a simple accident on the job. Something I thought nothing of. Something that changed the entire course of my life. I was working a summer construction job as a "stake hop," helping to fine-grade the land at the main site for the new Boeing 747 plant near Everett, Washington.

Each day the routine was the same—fill in and level the ground to the height of the blue-topped engineering stakes. Beside each of these stakes was a three-foot-long guard stake with a blue ribbon tied to the top, used to locate the engineering stake when it got buried with excess dirt as the grader went by.

Dean, the grader operator I worked with, was the best on the job. He liked to run the line quickly with the grader in third gear. "Gives me a feeling of flow," he said. "I can get the ground to level more easily if it all flows together."

Other graders ran in first gear, slow enough for their stake hops to walk alongside them. But because I was willing to sprint to keep up with him, Dean consistently finished more rows than the rest of the crew combined. The boss liked the output, so he left us alone, and we did our job the way Dean wanted to do it.

There was about thirty feet between each set of stakes. With Dean's grader moving in third, I'd have to run to keep up with him. When we came to the first guard stake, I would plant my foot, bend down, reach over the grader's blade, and pull up the guard stake just as the grader passed by, burying the engineering stake. Then I'd lay down the guard stake to mark the buried engineering stake and sprint to catch up and pass him once again.

There were only two weeks left at work before I would quit and go back to school. I was eager to begin my sophomore year at the local community college without the added pressure of working. My wife Karen and I had decided I would not work during the next school year so I could spend more time with her and our one-year-old daughter Kris, who was and still is one of the lights in my life.

I didn't need to work when I went to school because I received money from the War Orphans' Program (my father had been killed in World War II). It was something like the GI Bill. This also meant Karen could stay home and be with our daughter.

Over the summer, Dean and I had been working six days a week, ten hours a day. Late one Saturday afternoon, only days before I was to quit, we had a couple more lines to run to finish our shift. I was hot and tired, ready to finish up. We were about two-thirds done with one of the rows when I sprinted after the grader as I had done so many times before. This time when I stopped and planted my right foot, I heard a strange popping sound when I bent over the blade to grab the guard stake. Searing pain shot through my lower back and legs. I stumbled and pitched forward toward the blade, barely catching my balance. I took a few steps back, then the pain dropped me to my knees. I leaned forward and buried my hands deep into the cool plowed earth, trying to catch my breath. My head was pounding so hard I couldn't think.

Dean finished the row, running over the remaining guard stakes. Then he turned around and saw me down the line on my knees. He turned off the grader and trotted back to me. When he saw I was in pain, he asked a stream of questions. "What happened, Terry? Are you okay? What are you doing on your knees?"

"Can't move," I gasped. "Something snapped."

"Are you bleeding? Did the blade get you?" he asked, looking me over.

"No, just a bad pain in my back." Wincing, I started to get up. Dean grabbed my arm, trying to help. Walking back to the grader, my lower back and legs felt like they were on fire.

"Just rest 'til the shift is over," Dean said. "We can find the blues for this line Monday."

I stayed in bed on Sunday, and by the end of the day, the pain was better. But it really hurt to bend over. On Monday I showed up for work, still hurting but not worried. I thought it was just a pulled muscle.

When Dean saw me walking toward him, limping and obviously in pain, he frowned. "Geez, Terry, you look great. I can see the day off did you a lot of good."

"Yep, fixed me right up." Then more seriously, "I'm sure I'll be okay once I warm up."

"Like hell you will. You cart yourself into the office and fill out an accident report. Then take the rest of the day off and go to a chiropractor. I'll give you the name of the guy that helped me when my back went out."

Encouraged by Dean, I left, hoping the pain would soon be over. It was a blessing that I had no hint of the ordeal that lay ahead of me.

During the remaining two weeks left of work, I made numerous trips to Dean's chiropractor with mixed results. Some days were better than others, but the anticipated relief didn't come.

School started, and the change to a sedentary lifestyle helped. I had more time to rest and give my back a chance to recover. I knew it was just a matter of time now.

For the next six months, I made regular visits to the chiropractor. Sometimes the sessions helped for awhile, but the hoped-for full recovery never came. My chiropractor finally referred me to an osteopath who prescribed painkillers and muscle relaxers, and treated me with physical therapy. After four months with no noticeable improvement, he referred me to Dr. Carlisle, an orthopedic surgeon.

By this time, the pain was a constant in my life—sometimes a dull throbbing, other times sharp red-hot spikes down my legs. I was tired of being tough, tired of being cranky, and I was tired of going to doctors' offices week after week with no relief. Even though the Labor and Industry insurance was paying the bills, I wanted a normal life back.

≈ ≈ ≈ ≈

When I showed up at Dr. Carlisle's office, he reviewed my history and the X-rays taken by the osteopath. He said he wanted his in-house X-ray technician to take a new battery of pictures. I agreed and waited while the X-rays were developed and he reviewed them. When I was shown back into his private office, Dr. Carlisle had the X-rays on his light box.

"Terry, these X-rays show why you've had so much pain. You've got a ruptured disk in your lower back," he reported.

"How do you fix it?"

"I've given that some thought. Your records show that you've had no relief from all the various therapies you've tried. I'm strongly recommending surgery for this reason: you're probably as strong as you're going to be. With school and then a job, the muscles supporting your back will probably become weaker. Then what would happen?"

"The pain would get worse?"

"Exactly. I believe you'll need to have a spinal fusion to gain any relief. And I see no reason to put it off."

"If it will eliminate the pain, I'm all for it!" I told him.

"Yes," he smiled, "it should eliminate the pain, and after a period of healing, you will be almost as good as new."

"What do you mean 'almost as good as new'?"

"Well, with a fusion, you'll lose some of the flexibility in your back, not a lot, but it won't be the same as it was before your injury."

"Okay, but are you sure this will eliminate the pain?"

"I really think it should because we'll be taking the pressure off that disk," he finished.

The surgery would take place a month before I started my junior year at the University Of Washington. I'd be in the hospital for two weeks, at home for another two, and then, wearing a specially fitted brace, I would start school on time. After six months, I would get rid of the brace. This sounded like a plan I could get behind. At this point, I would happily exchange the ever-present pain for an "almost as good as new" prognosis.

I was admitted to Smith Medical Center in Seattle the day

before surgery. That afternoon, they performed a myelogram. The procedure consisted of injecting dye into the spinal column through a lumbar puncture. Then a CT scan was performed to determine if the rupture went into the spinal column. Mine did not.

When I was brought back to my room after the procedure, Karen was waiting for me. I was in a room with three beds. To fit them in, they were in an odd arrangement. As you came into the room, there were two beds side by side with the heads of the beds against the back wall. Mine was on the left. Another bed ran alongside the front wall to the right of the door.

Karen giggled when she saw my six-foot-three frame in an old robe and hospital gown that barely reached down to mid-thigh.

"You think that's bad," I said, taking the robe off, "take a look at this!" I turned around and showed her my backside. With the exception of the strings tied at the back of my neck, I was exposed to the world. I got in bed, and Karen pulled up a chair beside me.

"Well, at least you have this nice little robe they gave you!" she teased.

"It's great, but you can see right through it."

Karen chuckled. "Yeah, it's old like this hospital. I bet there's a gazillion coats of paint on these walls. I heard this could be the oldest hospital on Pill Hill."

"Pill Hill?"

"You know, it's the nickname for this area because of all the hospitals."

I pulled Karen's hand to my lips and kissed it, thankful that she could make me forget why I was here. "Honey, I don't care if this place was built by Columbus in 1492. Right now all I want is to get rid of this damned pain."

Just then we heard a voice from another bed. "Yeah, well, it may be ancient, but it's sporting new linoleum, look." Karen and I looked down at the new floor, then smiled at the man in the bed against the right wall. He was in his mid-thirties, a big man with dark curly hair and a nice smile.

"Name's Dave," he said. "How're you doing? Let me introduce ourselves. Frank here is a platinum miner and bush pilot from Alaska. Me, I work at a hardware store. We've been here long enough to make friends. Glad to have you."

Frank's broad face was weather-beaten. He had at least thirty years on me.

"Nice to meet you folks," he said. When I asked why he was here, he replied, "Hurt my back one too many times. When the injuries finally caught up with me, I came down from Alaska for the specialists to figure out what was wrong and try to correct it with surgery."

At twenty-three, I was the "kid" in the room and something new for Dave and Frank to enjoy. I would learn soon enough about long, monotonous hours in a hospital bed.

"Frank, look at those two. Aren't they a pair?" Dave said.

"Cute as two bugs on a stump," Frank replied.

We had heard this kind of thing before. Karen, at just a half an inch over five feet, was dwarfed by me. She was petite and pretty with light brown wispy hair, while I was tall, rugged, and muscular with a swarthy complexion. We were certainly noticeable.

≈ ≈ ≈ ≈

That night my mom and stepdad and Karen's parents came by. I was expecting them to bring my daughter Kris; we had rarely been separated. But when they arrived, she wasn't with them.

"Mom, where's Kris?" I asked.

"We found out there's a hospital rule," she said. "No kids under twelve allowed."

"You've got to be kidding!" Disappointed, I turned to Karen.

"It's true, honey, I just found out myself," she replied. "Maybe I'll find a way to sneak her in."

I felt a void just thinking that I would not be able to see Kris for days or weeks because I had rarely been away from her.

Soon visiting hours were over and my family left with kisses, hugs, and predictions of a successful operation. When they were gone, an orderly came in to prep me for surgery. He shaved my lower back and hip area where the incisions would be. Dr. Carlisle had explained that they were going to take a piece of bone from my hip to use in the fusion.

Early the next morning, a nurse gave me a shot to relax me before surgery. The next thing I knew I was in the recovery room hearing my drugged voice saying, "I didn't think it would hurt this much."

That afternoon, Dr. Carlisle came by on his rounds.

"The fusion went well," he told me. "We trimmed the ruptured disk and took bone pieces from your right hip and placed them around the vertebrae on either side of the disk. The bone should grow and attach to each vertebra so they can't move independently of each other. This will take the pressure off the disk between them," he explained. "Everything looks good, Terry, just make sure you stay in bed and do what the nurses tell you, so you can get out of here as soon as possible."

For the next few days, I was given morphine every four hours. Even when I was awake and hurting, I didn't really care. Days crawled by in a haze. I slept most of the time and spent visiting hours in a dopey fog. Then one afternoon an attractive LPN came into my room when Karen was visiting and pulled the curtain around my bed for privacy. I looked at Karen, puzzled; she shrugged her shoulders.

"Hi, Terry," the nurse said. She was holding a huge plastic bag full of sudsy water with a tube attached to it.

"Hi," I said. Pointing to the bag, I asked, "What's that?"

"You haven't gone to the bathroom in the bedpan since the operation," she said. "So, this will give your system a little help."

I felt embarrassed talking with a girl my own age about whether or not I had gone to the bathroom. Then she explained what she was going to do, and I blurted out, "You want to put it where?"

I heard Dave and Frank chuckle.

She asked Karen to step out for twenty minutes. When Karen walked around the curtain, I glimpsed Frank and Dave holding their hands over their mouths so they wouldn't laugh out loud.

I had never had an enema before. "So, ah, what do you want me to do?" I whispered.

"Just lie on your side and let the water in. Hold it for a while, and the water will do the rest," she said.

When I started feeling uncomfortably full of water, I wanted to tell her "enough," but I wasn't sure it was proper. Besides, Frank and Dave were on the other side of the curtain. They'd hear me and probably laugh again—another reason to keep my mouth shut.

"Boy, you really took a lot," she said as she finished up. She told me to roll over on my back, bend my legs, and lift my bottom. Then she propped some pillows underneath my hips, situated a bedpan under my buttocks, and told me to hold the water in as long as I could. With that, she was gone.

I lay there with the middle of my body arched up, putting strain on my swollen abdomen. Every time I felt the urge and relaxed down onto the bedpan, the pan would press against my incision, and my body would tense up. By the time the nurse came back twenty minutes later, I was mad and hurting.

"This isn't working," I complained. "I'm not used to going to the bathroom in a bed. If I could just use the restroom, I'm sure everything will be fine."

"You know you can't get up," she said. "Just be patient. It'll come in time." She removed the pillows, set the bedpan nearby, and pulled the curtain back. Frank and Dave weren't laughing, but their smiles and twinkling eyes told me they were having fun at my expense. The nurse told Karen she could come back in and then went to get a shot for pain. Soon I was sound asleep, holding Karen's hand.

I awoke when dinner came. The second shift staff came on, and visiting hours ended. Shortly after Karen went home, another nurse came in.

"Since your bowels aren't cooperating, I'm going to give them a little help," she said. She too had a large plastic bag full of sudsy water. Was this déjà vu?

Had I not been on morphine or had I known more about hospital procedures, I might have figured out before it was too late that there was either a mix-up in the records or my first enema hadn't been recorded. I was confused, but I wasn't about to make a fuss in front of Frank and Dave. So I rolled onto my side as the nurse pulled the curtain shut.

When she was done she said, "Boy, you can sure hold a lot of water." Then she handed me a bedpan and walked away. No pillows, no explanations this time, just a smile and a disappearing act.

Now there was even more pressure, and my body gave me signals that it was ready to release its double dose. Little beads of sweat emerged on my forehead. I held my distended abdomen, searching for a solution. When I thought of the restroom, I moaned.

Looking up, I had an idea. Above me attached to my bed was a square metal frame. Two four-foot rods rose up at each end of the bed and were attached to a horizontal rod at the top. They were connected by a rod in the center, which ran the length of the bed. Earlier they had taken a little trapeze off the central frame because they didn't want me to get up. Feeling safe behind the closed curtain, I tossed a towel over the center rod, and holding it with one hand, pulled my body up. I carefully slid the cold stainless steel bedpan under my rear and tried to settle down on it. But as soon as the pan pressed against the incision site, my body tensed again. After several more unsuccessful attempts, I gave up.

I lay on my side with my knees up to take the pressure off. More cramping, more sweating. The thought of getting up and using the restroom consumed me. Finally, the nurse came back.

"Ma'am, I tried to use the bedpan, but there's no use. It hurts my incision too much. How about I take a quick run to the restroom?"

"No way, Terry," she said. "You're not allowed out of bed. Doctor's orders. Hang in there, it'll all work out," she assured me.

As she pulled the curtains back and left, I thought to myself, *damn it, I'm getting up anyway.* Then I remembered the surgeon's words: complete bed rest for several days after the operation to ensure that the bones fuse properly. I sighed, looking with yearning toward the door, knowing I would stay put. Before my resolve could be tested, I was saved by the evening's pain shot and sleeping pill. Soon I was dreaming fitfully.

By the middle of the night, I was deep in a crazy dream. I was sitting in a small rowboat in the middle of Puget Sound near the Seattle docks. A huge freighter was about to run over my little boat. It felt like others were with me, and I knew we would have to swim for it or be crushed. I stood in the bow of the boat and shouted, "Get ready to abandon ship, lads. We must swim for shore."

The boat was actually my hospital bed. Though sound asleep, I had pulled myself up with the aid of a towel over the bed frame and stood at the end of the bed/boat, gaining courage to jump.

Dave told me later that when I yelled "get ready to abandon ship, lads," he woke up and almost fell out of his bed when he saw me there. Worried, he asked, "Terry, what are you doing standing on your bed?" Getting no response from me, he turned to Frank, "Frank, wake up! You've got to see this!"

Thinking back, I can imagine why Dave was so surprised. It must have been quite a shock to come out of a sound sleep and see a naked man standing at the end of his bed with a catheter between his legs swinging in the breeze, babbling about jumping for safety.

Before he could say another word, I said, "It's now or never," and jumped. I was trying to make it to his bed, to safety—the freighter was capsizing my boat. I might have made it if the catheter going into my penis had been longer. But it wasn't.

In mid-flight, I ran out of tubing. The catheter, fastened to the bed, suddenly snapped in two at the middle, flew up and hit me squarely in my family jewels. With a blood-chilling howl, I landed on the edge of Dave's bed. Stunned, he grabbed my arms and held me, while I mumbled about swimming for shore.

I was dead weight, slipping from his grasp.

"What the hell are you doing?" he said, then grabbed hold of the back of my neck in an effort to keep me from slipping off and hitting the floor.

With my face pressed into the bed, I muttered, "Where's the freighter?" and began to come out of my stupor. Looking up at Dave, I was completely bewildered.

"Go back to your own bed before the nurse comes and you get into trouble," he insisted, obviously concerned.

Suddenly, I realized that I was completely out of bed. "As long as I'm up," I said, still foggy, "might as well sneak down the hall to the bathroom."

"Not a good idea, Terry," Dave said, trying to hold on to me.

Somehow I got away from him and grabbed my bed for support. Needing my glasses to see clearly, I slowly rounded the end of my bed to retrieve them from the nightstand. I heard Dave saying, "Frank, wake up. You gotta stop Terry, Frank. Wake up!"

On my way back around my bed, I stubbed my toe on the bedpost and started to fall. Grabbing the bed frame, I swung around to land on a chair against the wall. For a split second, it seemed like a great save, but when my backside rocketed onto the seat of the chair, pain lit up my whole lower back like a Christmas tree.

Panting, I tried to get up, but my legs would *not* move. With my right cheek barely on the chair, my bowels began to rumble. This sitting position was exactly what they had been waiting for. Squeezing my cheeks as tightly as I could, I considered my options. Then I did what any self-reliant twenty-three-year-old guy would do when sitting naked on a chair needing to get to a bathroom really, really fast and unable to get there himself. I yelled for help!

All the while, Dave was trying to rouse Frank. He kept repeating, "Frank, wake up, you've got to see this. Frank, wake up!"

My cries for help were answered almost immediately. I could hear one of the nurses running down the hall. I leaned toward the door and urgently whispered, "Hurry, hurry."

A small Philippine nurse barged through the door like a headmistress ready to punish someone for breaking the quiet of the night. I needed a loving, caring nurse, not a headmistress. She glanced around the dimly lit room and quickly recognized my shape in the wrong place. She grabbed my right arm, "What are you doing out of bed?" she demanded.

"Don't move me, just get me a pan!"

She ignored me. "Get back in bed NOW," she said louder.

I begged her. "Please listen to me. Get me a bedpan NOW or I'm going to lose it!"

She squared her shoulders and glared at me.

I turned to Dave and pleaded, "Dave, have you got a bedpan?" Instead of support, all I heard was laughter from his bed. I couldn't believe it! "Frank," he called, "wake up! You've got to see this!"

Meanwhile, the nurse had spread her sturdy little legs, and with her left foot planted firmly under my chair, she started pulling on my right arm to haul me up. In spite of her total determination, I simply weighed too much for her; all she managed to accomplish was to pull my right cheek off the chair.

"Oh, God, no!" I moaned, trying without success to stop the oncoming deluge.

My words were lost in the sound of gallons of water and whatever else was in me gushing out onto her leg, running into her shoe, then spilling onto the floor. As I looked down, I saw my broken catheter start flowing. Now I was also peeing on her foot.

"Stop it. Stop it!" she insisted. "What you are doing?" In

her very proper English she shouted over and over, "Stop it!" But she hung on to my arm through it all.

By this time Dave was hysterical with laughter, and I was mortified beyond belief. I hung my head, unable to stop the flow from either of my orifices. It just kept coming and coming. I wished I could crawl under a rock.

I don't know why that little nurse didn't just let go and step back. Perhaps she was afraid that I might fall off the chair. Maybe she was just in shock.

When the flow finally stopped, she stared down at her leg and shoe. "Why did you do that?"

Shaking my head, embarrassed beyond belief, I grabbed the bed frame, pulled myself up and, without saying a word, walked around the big puddle on the floor. As I eased myself back into bed, I heard heavy running steps approaching. A large woman, the shift leader, bounded through the door, stepped right into the middle of the mess, and slid into the side of my bed, pushing it into my nightstand on the other side and knocking off a glass, which shattered on the floor. "My God," she said, looking around dazed. "What happened?"

"He pooped all over my leg," the little Philippine nurse said accusingly, pointing to her shoe.

That was it! I pulled the covers over my head, still hearing Dave's laughter and attempts to rouse Frank, then I promptly passed out.

≈ ≈ ≈ ≈

The next morning, I awoke to vague memories of the night's events. Trying to shift positions, I realized I couldn't move. Now what? I could feel a lump under my back, as if the sheets had crumpled into a knot. Carefully lifting my head, I looked down to find a wide cotton belt around my waist that attached to a strap on each side of the bed. Fastened to the belt was a small padlock securing the buckle. They were taking no chances!

"Dave tells me you had a big shindig last night," Frank

chuckled, "and you didn't even invite me. What kind of a room-mate are you?" he asked, grinning from ear to ear.

Dave started laughing again. "I tried to wake you. It was a hell of a party!"

I was a big hit, all right. No one had seen that much action on the ward in years. People smiled when they walked by our room. Staff who weren't associated with us stopped in just to say "hi." Dave was all too happy to retell the whole story for each new visitor.

From Dave's point of view, it had been frightening to wake up suddenly with a large naked man standing on a bed not four feet from his own, carrying on about a freighter and the need to swim for shore. But then to have this lunatic jump for his bed was too much.

I'm sure he embellished some as he described the look on my face when, while I was in midair, the catheter broke and snapped back to hit me. I felt even worse when I learned that the broken catheter had sprayed his bed and the walls behind him. The entire room had to be sterilized, just another element of that evening to shake my head over.

When Dr. Carlisle came in that morning on his rounds, he was his normal, reserved self. I thought he'd never bring up the subject. Finally, I could stand it no longer.

"I'm real sorry about last night," I said with my eyes down. "Do you think I ruined the fusion?"

"I'm sure it's okay, Terry. I doubt if you damaged anything. There are two metal screws holding it all in place. The complete bed rest is just a precaution, standard procedure," he said.

I let out a breath I didn't realize I was holding and said, "Thank God!"

"I've decided you can use the portable bathroom while you're up for lunch," he said with a widening grin, "but the rest of the time I want you lying flat. Is that understood?"

"Yes, sir. I really didn't mean to . . ."

"Of course."

He ordered the "posse belt" removed, and I promised him I wouldn't get up again, except at lunch.

He walked out the door, was gone a few seconds, then popped back in. "Terry," he said, "I've been in medicine for over twenty years, and I don't think I've ever heard anything as funny as what happened last night. Thanks for that. And don't worry, you're going to be just fine."

I lay back and closed my eyes, relieved and happy. I was going to get the "posse belt" off, I could get up to go to the bathroom, and I hadn't hurt anything. I couldn't wait to tell Karen everything that had happened, knowing she'd get a big laugh out of it.

That night the little Philippine nurse came into my room and said, "How do you like my new shoes?" She smiled briefly, turned, and left. I knew the morphine slowed me down, but nothing registered with me.

I asked, "Frank, Dave, what was that about?"

Frank smiled. "Maybe her old pair wouldn't come clean."

Then I connected it all, and my face turned bright red again. Oh, was I ever ready to get out of here and go home!

CHAPTER 2

THE STAKES GET HIGHER

Dave was released, and Tommy moved in from the next room. He was a few years older than I and had also undergone a spinal fusion in his lower back around the time I had mine. For the first few days, we all got to know each other better as we laid around while Frank told us true-life adventure stories about being a platinum miner and bush pilot in Alaska.

On the sixth day after my surgery, I got a green light to get up for a little while to do more than just sit on the pot during lunch.

Karen's eyes lit up when I told her. "That's great, honey. Means you're really doing well. Think they'd let you walk to the lobby to see Kris?"

"I doubt it, and damn it, the hardest thing about this hospital stay is not being able to spend time with her." I looked over at the window and had an idea.

"Honey, could you take a look out the window? How far down is the street?"

Karen looked puzzled but went to the window. "Not far. It's

just an alley between the buildings," she said as she turned back.

"Great. Maybe I could see Kris from there. You think your parents would mind bringing her to the hospital?"

Karen saw the excitement in my eyes and smiled. "Why not? It's a great idea."

I listened to Karen making arrangements with her parents on the phone. Hanging up, she turned to me beaming.

"They're on the way. They'll call from the lobby."

It seemed like a year passed until the phone finally rang.

"I'll go down and help them find the alley," Karen said, as she planted a kiss on my cheek and left.

Shuffling slowly over to the window, I opened it and in a few moments, saw the car turning in below. As soon as Karen got out of the car and hiked Kris into her arms, I called, "Kris, Kris."

I will never forget the look on her face when she heard my voice. Looking up, the instant she saw my head poking out of the second-story window, her mouth flew open in a brilliant smile. She spread her small arms out wide as if to say, "Hi, Daddy!" My heart leapt with joy. I knew it would be a moment I would never forget.

Bending out the window was probably not what they meant by "getting up." It was painful and exhausting. Still, we played with each other as best we could, and I kept it up for as long as I was able. Grudgingly, I said good-bye to my little angel, blew her a kiss and crawled back into bed, filled with peace. Just a few more days and I'd be home with my family. I couldn't wait to finally close the book on this injury.

≈ ≈ ≈ ≈

One evening when it came time for lights out, Tommy called over to Frank and me.

"Hey, guys, have a drink of whiskey with me."

"You got whiskey?" Frank asked, rising on his elbow, showing a wide grin.

"See, my doctor got me a pint of whiskey 'cause I'm allergic to the sleeping medications they've got here. I'm supposed to take a few swigs at bedtime. Helps me sleep, you know," he said.

Now, generally I avoided whiskey. When I was fifteen celebrating New Year's Eve, I got drunk for the first time —wasted was more like it. I was sick for a week. Throughout repeated trips to the john, I promised God that if He would let me live, I'd never drink whiskey again.

I'm not sure it was the promise that kept me from whiskey; I had broken other promises. I think the real deterrent was the smell of hard liquor, which always triggered sickening body memories from that week. I still drank, but I stuck to wine or those foofoo drinks that didn't smell of booze.

"What about you, Terry?" Tommy asked.

Wanting to be one of the boys won out over my old memories. "Yeah, sure."

"Good. Go find some paper cups," he said.

I went off to the bathroom, returning with three cups. Tommy poured the whiskey. I passed one to Frank, then took my own. Soon, we were laughing over our efforts to come up with the best toast. Suddenly, the head nurse burst into our room. *Uh oh, her again*, I thought, the same shift leader who had slid into my bed a few nights before. I hadn't seen her since that night, but deep inside I suspected she had pegged me as a troublemaker.

Tommy blurted "Busted!" Frank quickly downed his whiskey, and I yanked my cup behind me, spilling it all over my hospital robe. *Now I'm really in trouble*, I thought. She took in the situation and settled her gaze on me. Since I was the one out of bed, I felt the need to explain. But before I could gather my words, the nurse smiled briefly at each of us and said, "If you boys are going to break the rules, don't make so much noise doing it." Then she left, closing the door softly behind her.

While still standing in the middle of the room trying to

figure out what to say, I felt myself trembling. God, I hated being so helpless and dependent, and always afraid I was going to get in trouble. I downed what was left of my share and went back to my bed. I crawled in, said "good night," and pulled the covers over my head.

As I lay there I kept reminding myself that in only another week or so, I would be released. I thought about how good it would feel to be in my own home with Karen and Kris.

Mornings were the best. Kris always woke up full of joy and delight. We would get her up and bring her back to snuggle with us in our king-sized bed. No matter what the night was like, she greeted each day with an unbridled enthusiasm about being alive, and it was infectious. Karen and I would find ourselves overcome by her excitement for life as we watched her explore her world and discover the wonder of it.

I imagined getting out of the hospital, free from pain, back home with my wonderful family, back in school, making something of myself. I kept telling myself it was all going to work out fine, just as my doctor said it would.

Each succeeding day got better. Most of the pain from the surgery was gone, and I experienced no pain from the ruptured disk. I wouldn't go as far as saying my stay there was fun: there was no privacy, and every time I used the bathroom, I had to tell them when and how much. The staff constantly monitored what I ate and how much water I drank. It was still an old hospital that smelled and looked like an old hospital. Nevertheless, Frank, Tommy, and I made the best of it and, except for the therapy, for the most part the staff left us alone.

As part of our exercise program, Tommy and I "raced" up and down the hall. Actually, because we both had new spinal fusions, the pace was more like a snail's crawl; our first attempts consisted of ambling down the hall like two old men, heads down, focused on moving each foot without losing our balance. Calling it a race just kept our spirits up; I certainly didn't push myself to win.

When I say I didn't push myself, I mean exactly that. I had

strict orders, and I followed them. Each day, an orderly would take me in a wheelchair down to the physical therapy room for a "workout." In this small gym, I worked with Phil, the physical therapy coordinator. He was a terrific guy who took the trouble to carefully explain what I needed to do.

"Terry, you want to always protect your back. So you don't want to bend over at the waist. Instead, use your legs to bend down. Go nice and slow, steady," Phil explained. "Don't push your body."

I listened and watched attentively as he showed me how to move, how to stretch. I was powerfully motivated to recover as quickly as possible. In other areas of my life, I shot from the hip, but when it came to regaining the strength of my back, I stayed focused on my target and did my part to have the least amount of limitation.

One day I asked Phil what he meant when he had mentioned, "You'll probably always have some lack of flexibility and movement."

He told me, "Because of the fused vertebrae, you can't expect it to be as good as it was before." But he would not quantify what he meant; he said it varied from patient to patient. Although I was intent on following his directions so I could minimize any limitations, I sensed that somewhere deep inside me there was turmoil that I was beginning to accept that I would never be whole again.

≈ ≈ ≈ ≈

I had been told I'd be in the hospital for two weeks, but I recovered faster than they expected and was released two days early with congratulations for healing so fast. I felt pretty good about that and vowed to faithfully follow my physical therapy program and take it easy.

Karen picked me up. As she drove, I talked nonstop, thrilled to be going home. By the time we arrived though, I was worn out. I took a nap and then spent the evening playing with Kris. I delighted in finally being able to hold her, touch her soft hair, smell her sweet baby scent. That night's sleep was bliss.

I had realized in the hospital that recovering from major surgery would take longer than I had expected. I tired easily and was much weaker than I could ever have imagined. Fortunately, I had two more weeks before I began my junior year at the University of Washington. I would only be taking three classes a day, and even though I was in pretty bad shape, I really believed the recovery process was going to work out fine. In a few short months, I expected to be "almost as good as new."

In the middle of the second night home, I woke up sweating, shivering with cold. Karen was immediately awake.

"My God, Terry, you're drenched."

Head pounding, I muttered, "I'm so cold."

She vaulted out of bed and came back with a blanket and a thermometer. My temperature was 102 degrees.

Early the next morning, Karen called Dr. Carlisle and described my symptoms. After a brief conversation, she put the phone down. The color had drained from her face. "Terry, he said to get you to the emergency room right now."

We dressed, Karen grabbed Kris, I grabbed an extra blanket, and we piled into the car.

Once in the emergency room, I was rushed into an examination room, and a nurse took my vitals. Soon Dr. Carlisle came in.

"That's quite a temperature you have, Terry. Let's see what we have here. Could you turn on your side, please?"

I did, shaking from chills.

"Looks like you've got swelling around the surgical site," he said, gently pressing around the area. "I'm going to extract some fluid so we can figure out what this is."

Inserting a needle with a large syringe attached, Dr. Carlisle extracted the fluid. "There's quite a lot of fluid here," he said. He walked around the table, rubbing his chin. "I'm concerned about that, Terry. It looks like you may have an infection in the surgical site. We better have you readmitted. I'll send the fluid upstairs to be analyzed, then we'll know what's going on."

I didn't care what happened. I was so overcome with severe chills, I was desperate for a warm bed.

Karen left to take Kris to her parents. I was soon back on the orthopedic wing in a private room as a precaution. By the time Karen returned, I was peacefully asleep, aided by hospital drugs.

That evening while making his rounds, Dr. Carlisle extracted more fluid from the swollen area. As he worked, he said, "Terry, the preliminary results show that you have a deep wound infection."

Shit! I thought. How was this possible? I had never been sick a day in my life before all this happened.

"I don't understand."

"Well, the bugs didn't get there through your skin. The tissue on the top of the surgical site has healed well and is perfectly healthy. The infection is deep and may have come from bacteria in your system. I'm not really sure," he said. "Everyone has bacteria floating in their bodies, waiting for an opportunity to grow. The immune system usually keeps them in check. Who knows."

"How will you find out?" I asked.

"Once the lab cultures come back, we'll know what specific bug we're dealing with, so we can give you the appropriate antibiotic before and after the surgery."

"Surgery?"

"Yes, we'll need to lance the site and put in a drain," he said. "We'll keep you on a broad-spectrum antibiotic for the next day or two, then do the surgery."

"Okay," I said, feeling very much *not* okay.

"Just relax and get plenty of sleep."

The next day, Dr. Carlisle walked in with a report in hand. His face was pinched as he sat down next to my bed. What was up? He never sat down.

With a soft voice he began, "You remember our talk before the spinal fusion, how I mentioned that any surgical procedure runs some risk of infection?"

"I guess."

"Well, somehow you were one of the unlucky ones. Your infection is caused by the E. coli bacteria," he explained.

"Okay." *What was the big deal?* I wondered. I had never heard of this bacteria.

"Tomorrow morning we're going to take you back into surgery. We'll open the original surgical site and insert a flat rubber tube into the incision, then stitch it in place. This will keep the wound open so the fluid from the infection can drain out onto a bandage. Do you have any questions?" he asked.

"Will this get rid of the infection?"

"It's possible the drain and the antibiotics will eliminate it. If they don't," he paused, "well, let's just wait and see." He took a deep breath and rose slowly.

"Dr. Carlisle, I'm just curious. What if it doesn't work?"

He looked at me, then over at the window. "We're going to need to wait several months to let the fusion heal. On the off chance you still have the infection, we'll have to do a major debridement."

"What's that?"

"A debridement is when we cut out all the infected material."

"Oh," was all I could say.

"The infection is a serious problem we need to deal with carefully. It'll make the whole undertaking of getting you back to good health a bit more involved. You'll have to spend a little more time in the hospital and have a few more procedures to get you on your way. But don't worry, it will all work out fine." He looked up at the clock on the wall. "Now you get a good night's sleep, Terry," he said and walked out.

It was puzzling. I sensed something was out of kilter, but Dr. Carlisle didn't seem overly concerned about the infection, and there was nothing in his words that suggested anything other than successfully achieving our overall objective, so I wasn't worried either.

I don't think I was smart enough to be worried. I had never been sick like this before. When I had health challenges in the past, my doctors always fixed me up. And I expected that to happen this time. I had faith in Dr. Carlisle and his abilities.

But as I lay in the dark room trying to sleep, his words kept replaying in my head. The more I thought about Dr. Carlisle's reassurances, the more irritated I got. I tried to remind myself to be grateful that I didn't have any more pain from the ruptured disk, but this surgery stuff was turning out to be a damned sight more complicated and inconvenient than I had ever imagined. In a place deep within that I was barely conscious of, I was becoming totally pissed off.

≈ ≈ ≈ ≈

When I awoke from surgery the next morning, I felt weak and groggy. As the days wore on, my temperature didn't go down. What was supposed to be a simple drainage procedure that would take a few days in the hospital stretched out into a twelve-day marathon.

Dr. Carlisle told me the procedure had gone well. Yet when the days piled up onto each other, my concern turned to despair. One morning after a nurse took my temperature and it was high again, I said, "I don't understand. Aren't I supposed to be getting better?"

"Things don't always go the way we want," she said without looking at me. "You'll just need to accept that."

More days dragged on, and further questions produced the same vague answers and platitudes. "Things just happen sometimes." "You've got to roll with the punches." "Hang in there." I felt more and more as if my life was spinning out of control. I knew the staff was concerned, but I wanted a solution, not meaningless drivel about accepting it all.

When I was finally released, I went home wearing my brace, carrying a bag full of bandages, tape, sterilizing material, syringes, and vials of antibiotics.

My bathroom began to look like a doctor's examination

room, and it smelled like one, too. Twice a day I had to change my bandages and monitor the drainage. Three times a day, I had to give myself an injection of antibiotics. The liquid was so thick and syrupy it required a large needle. The doctor wanted me to use only my hips, upper arms, and upper thighs as injection sites.

The first shot was an ordeal. I drew the serum into the needle like they demonstrated at the hospital. Then I sat on the bed looking at it. *This is impossible,* I thought. Karen walked into the bedroom just then and saw my downcast face and the needle in my hand.

"Want some help?" she asked.

"Nah, I think I can do it," I said.

"You sure?"

"You wouldn't mind?"

We decided to start with the back of my hip. Sitting on the bed, she held the needle out at hip height, bracing it with both hands. I backed up to her and when the needle touched my skin, she poked it into me. Reflexively, I flinched forward, and out popped the needle.

"Ow!" I yelled.

"You've got to hold still, honey."

"I know! I didn't mean to pull it out."

"Okay, let's do it again."

I backed up, and again when she poked me, I pulled forward. This continued two more times. With each new attempt, our conversation got more tense. Finally, on the fifth try I managed to stay put.

"About time," Karen said, as she slowly pushed on the syringe plunger. "My nerves are shot."

"Tell me about it," I replied.

≈ ≈ ≈ ≈

My recovery progressed as Dr. Carlisle predicted it would, and I was regaining a sense of control. Then one morning, three weeks after being released from the hospital, I noticed pieces of bone on the bandage as I changed it. The biggest one was about the size of my thumbnail. Holy shit! I thought. I hurried over to the phone and called Dr. Carlisle. Could some of the fusion be breaking loose? I wondered as I waited for him to come on the line.

"This is Dr. Carlisle."

"You're not going to believe this, Dr. Carlisle, but I just found some chunks of bone on my bandage." My voice was higher than I wanted it to be.

When I answered his questions about size and how much, he said, "Well, I half expected this, Terry. There's nothing to worry about. It's just some of the bone at the fusion site sloughing off. I knew there was a chance that this might happen. But don't be concerned, it will all work out fine."

His words did nothing to help the raw feeling in the pit of my stomach. The more we talked, the more I felt that he was over his head, that he had never dealt with this kind of an infection before. This alarmed me more than the bone fragments.

≈ ≈ ≈ ≈

In the midst of all this craziness, I started my junior year at the University of Washington. I had missed the first week, but my professors understood. I threw myself into my studies, making up for lost time.

Because I wasn't supposed to sit for long periods of time, my instructors let me take a seat at the back of the room and alternate between sitting and standing every ten or fifteen minutes. The incision and drains made wearing the brace even more uncomfortable.

Although the infection was a gigantic nuisance, I was determined to stay positive, convinced that the next surgery would eliminate it. Then I would only have to wear a brace for a few more months. Yes, there were some more hardships to endure, but I could take anything for a few months if it meant getting back to normal, or almost normal.

Ironically, it was better for me financially if I still had a problem to deal with. The state workers' compensation insurance was picking up the tab for the hospital stays and also paying me about $400 a month. When I wrote to tell them I was going to quit work when I started school, it didn't matter to them. As long as I was still dealing with the original injury that necessitated the fusion, they would pay me until my doctor said I could go back to work.

The weeks settled into a steady routine of going to school and doing regular maintenance on the drain. To keep the incision site open, each day I wet a long wooden Q-Tip with hydrogen peroxide and reaching back, slid the Q-Tip as far as it would go into the hole in my back. It was like cleaning a pipe so that the fluid would drain out easily, because as long as the fluid had a place to come out, I felt little or no pain.

I was glad my life calmed down and got back to some semblance of normalcy because the University of Washington curriculum was much more demanding than the community college I had attended.

After two months, even though the drains seemed to be open and draining well, I began to experience a dull, aching pain in my lower back. At my next scheduled visit, I mentioned the increased pain to Dr. Carlisle.

After a careful examination, he said, "Looks like the fluid is building up in a new area away from the drainage site. Excuse me a moment." He left the room and returned in a few minutes. "Terry, we're going to need to put another drain in your back. I've made arrangements with the hospital to readmit you."

Reeling, I started to protest, but he raised his hand.

"We have to open up this new area and let it drain."

Then an idea popped into my head. "If I have to go in again," I said, "why not do the debridement. You can cut out all the infected stuff and get it over with." I thought my idea was brilliant.

He sighed. "I wish I could, but the fusion hasn't healed yet.

We'll need to wait a few more months before the debridement is safe."

I was admitted for my third surgery the next week. I had spoken with my professors and gathered homework assignments. I was taking no chances; these things had a way of sprouting complications. But I was pleasantly surprised. This surgery was much less invasive; I was home after only three days.

Four months later, we scheduled the major debridement for spring break so I wouldn't miss much class time.

I checked into the hospital the day before the operation for tests. Dr. Carlisle had ordered X-rays to determine the extent of my infection, but the technicians were unable to get any good ones, although it was not for lack of effort.

The idea was to fill the infected area with a dye that would show up on an X-ray. I was delivered to Radiology and asked to lie on my side on the X-ray table. The technician filled a large eyedropper-type apparatus with the dye. When he tried to force the dye into the drainage site in my back, it kept squirting back out. After a few more attempts, he gave up.

That night Dr. Carlisle explained that without the X-rays, he didn't really know what he'd find. The next morning in surgery, he opened the previously cut areas around the fusion and drainage sites and found the infection had moved to my spine. He removed the infected tissues, then chiseled and scraped off the infected bone.

I woke up in Recovery to the smiling face of a nurse. I gave her a groggy smile in return.

"Hi, Terry," she said. "Everything went well. We'll be moving you into your room as soon as the orderly arrives with the gurney."

Fifteen minutes later, I was being wheeled down the corridor. When we went into the surgical wing instead of the orthopedic wing, I was puzzled.

"Ah, aren't we going back to my room?" I asked.

"Got orders to take you to Room 206," the orderly stated

matter-of-factly.

When we rounded the corner, I saw ISOLATION written in large red letters above Room 206. I looked around, bewildered.

The orderly opened the door and disappeared inside for a moment. I could hear another door being opened. He reappeared, rounded the gurney, and began pushing me into the room. I didn't know where to look first. We were going through a type of foyer or vestibule. Shelves were built into one side wall, laden with various items of hospital-green clothing. On the other wall was a bench with pegs above it. The wall in front of me was all glass, with a glass door. We passed through and were in my room.

"I'll be right back," the orderly said.

I looked at him retreating, as he closed the glass door behind him. For the first time, I realized he was dressed differently, in what I would soon learn was the isolation uniform: gown, rubber gloves, hat, mask, and shoe covers.

Soon he returned with another orderly. They stopped in the vestibule. With growing dismay, I watched the orderly take items from the shelves and cover himself from head to foot. Would this need to be done every time a nurse or visitor came into my room?

When he had completed the transformation, he opened the door and they entered the room. They transferred me to the hospital bed, set up the equipment, and left with the gurney, closing the inner glass door then the outer solid door behind them.

I lay there in the quiet, stunned.

Why was I here? Still heavily medicated from the surgery, I soon fell into an uncomfortable sleep.

When I awoke in the late afternoon, Karen was sitting in a chair nearby, dressed from head to foot in green.

"Hi," she said through her mask. "Like your new deluxe private room? I had to pull some major strings to get you this one."

"What am I doing in here, honey? It's creeping me out," I

said, still groggy.

"Hey, you're special, like I told you," she said, trying but failing to humor me. "Actually, they said this was just a precaution, to protect you. Dr. Carlisle ordered it, so maybe he can explain it when you see him."

Later that evening when Karen was gone, before my next shot of morphine, I was lucid enough to realize how truly frightened I was.

I was sick; I got that message loud and clear. It wasn't just the tubes attached to suction pumps coming out of my back, or the room and the precautions the staff and visitors had to take when they came in. More than anything, it was how the staff now approached me. They were hesitant, more careful, and they seemed to have more compassion.

A few days after the surgery, when I was no longer on heavy medication, Dr. Carlisle had a long talk with me. During every other visit, he was cordial, answered my questions, but mostly stuck to what he was going to do and what was expected from me. We weren't buddies, and he never volunteered much information. Until that day.

"It turns out that the infection isn't just in the soft tissues," he said. "It has spread to the fused vertebrae and to two others not involved in the fusion." He gauged my reaction—stunned silence—then continued. "I'm not sure how effective the debridement was, Terry. I couldn't see the other side of the spine to determine how far the infection may have spread."

He continued with more bad news.

"What you have is called osteomyelitis, which means infection of the bone. The normal remedy is to completely remove the infected bone and surrounding tissue, such as removing part of an arm or leg. In this case, we'll have to use other measures because we can't scrape too much off your spine."

I was so shocked I could barely breathe.

"Now, this E. coli bacteria is resistant to most antibiotics. We're going to start you on the most effective one we have.

But it's such a strong killer, you'll only be able to take it for two weeks at a time."

Dr. Carlisle no longer talked about weeks or months until my full recovery. His focus shifted to the procedures and precautions that must be taken now that the infection was in my spine, and my recovery changed from being a sure thing to something that was up for grabs. Even the success of the fusion was now in question because of the extent of infection in the two fused vertebrae.

I'm not sure it even registered with me consciously that my frame of reference was being shifted from "my back has a problem that will be over some time soon" to my back has a serious problem I will have to deal with for a long, long time," but that's what started to happen.

When Dr. Carlisle left, I was dazed. Teeth clenched, hands balled into fists, I looked around at something to punch. Why did I have to be a goddamn statistic—one of those unfortunate few who got infections during surgery? I was angry about being in the hospital again, angry and frustrated that I had to spend a large part of my day keeping drains open, messing with bandages and the many inconveniences of being sick.

Over the next few days, I realized that buried beneath the anger, I sensed a feeling of danger. And it wasn't just about whether or not this infection might be easily eradicated. At some level I sensed that life as I wanted it was getting lost. What I wanted was being shifted from center stage, and I was encouraged to focus on what others thought I should focus on.

I saw myself as strong and healthy. Others wanted me to change that perspective. They wanted me to focus on my illness. I felt like I was hanging onto the edge of a cliff by my fingers. Each time I heard a comment such as "things don't always work out the way you want them to," or ideas like "making the best of a bad situation," one more finger would be ripped away. With supposedly helpful suggestions like "accepting things as they are" or "there may be a lesson in here for you," I felt perilously close to losing my grip on what I wanted. These ideas weren't quite as limiting as facing reality, but they were in the same ballpark. The danger had something to do with believing what others were telling me about me. Although I couldn't get my mind around what it was, I knew without a doubt that the stakes of this game had gotten much higher.

CHAPTER 3

THE BOX

S pring break came and went, and I was still in the hospital. I was beginning to understand that this infection
could have ominous consequences that I would not walk
away from any time soon. With the first three operations, I
had recuperated on the orthopedic floor in a regular room,
recovering like everyone else—expecting to recover like everyone else. Now I was in isolation on the surgical ward.

My independence had vanished with the diagnosis of osteomyelitis. It seemed someone was constantly checking some
part of me and recording the findings on my chart. I could
never get away from my problem, and I hated that.

Every two hours, a nurse in sterile garb came in to check
my blood pressure, temperature, the tubes coming out of my
back, and the pumps sucking on the tubes.

Every six hours, I got a shot of antibiotics. The syrupy sub-
stance was administered through a long, thick needle. There
were only six places on my body with the necessary tissues
for this shot. Most nurses attempted to bring some gentleness to the painful procedure, inserting the long needle with
care and taking their time injecting it.

Nurse Richards was a different story. She had the build and manner of a drill sergeant. Cropped gray hair bristled around her angular face. Each time she marched into my room, I tensed. She'd stab the needle into the same general area, forcing the antibiotic mixture into my body as quickly as she could. Each shot left a bruise and lingering pain. I didn't complain at first. I had felt so drained, so vulnerable, I simply hadn't protested. But I decided the next time I saw her, I'd ask her to lighten up.

Later that afternoon, Nurse Richards stomped into my room with needle in hand. "Ma'am, before you start," I said, "could you ease up a little with that needle, maybe slow down some. It hurts when you inject it fast."

Her face darkened. "Don't tell me how to do my job, young man. You're acting just like a baby." Giving me no time to protest, she plunged the needle into my thigh and pushed with gusto. "Get used to it," she growled. "You're going to have this condition for a long time."

After she left the room, I turned on my side, bringing my knees to my chest. I squeezed my eyes shut, stomach churning, trying to forget the humiliation of being called a baby and a complainer. But her words kept repeating like an echo.

What did she mean by "you're going to have this condition for a long time"? I was young and strong and healthy. It might take awhile, but I'd be just fine. That old bitch could put a negative spin on anything, I decided.

Soon, however, my bravado slipped away. Long hours in my room gave me too much time to think. The subdued whooshing noise of the pump was a constant reminder that I had just had my spine scraped. I was on a cocktail of antibiotics that was having little effect. I had expected to be released from the hospital within a few days. That hadn't happened. It was what? ten or eleven days already with no release date in sight. If Karen hadn't faithfully come every day, I think I would have gone crazy.

I realized that until now, I had handled whatever life had

thrown my way. I was a fighter and a loner. I didn't like depending on other people. I rebelled against the rules, made up my own, and used my wits to make the system work for me. Sometimes I had paid a price, but it was a price I was willing to pay to do it my way. Now, I didn't know what the rules were. Stripped of any control, I felt like a caged animal, imprisoned by four gray walls, on view and monitored constantly. Day after day, I resisted a growing sense of fear, humiliation, and helplessness.

I closed my eyes, remembering times in my past when I felt like this. My father died a war hero two days after my birth. My mother constantly measured me against the memory of his greatness, and I was expected to make my star shine even brighter than his. And quite frankly, I felt unequal to the task.

I couldn't get away from Mom. Literally. As a teacher in my grade school, I felt her presence everywhere. We drove to school together every day, then we drove home together. Our conversations were often filled with reminders of my responsibilities and deficiencies.

"Terry, you've got big shoes to fill. You'd want your daddy to be proud, wouldn't you?"

"Yeah."

"You're so bright, just like him. But at your age, he was making excellent grades. Are you listening, Terry?"

"Uh huh."

"You could be making good grades, but you're not applying yourself. You're not even getting average grades. I expect better than this from you."

I must have heard conversations like this a million times as I grew up.

When I moved on to junior high school, Mom moved right along with me, becoming a teacher at my new school. The routine continued. Suffocated by her constant presence and pressure, I rebelled, resisted, and did anything but what she wanted.

My mother's patience ran out when I was fifteen. The school year had just ended. She had been unusually reserved for several days. I assumed my dismal grades might have been the cause, but something was strange about her, like the air between us was thicker.

One day I came in from outside to find her sitting quietly in the living room's dim afternoon light. She motioned for me to sit down.

"Terry, I've been doing a lot of thinking. I've tried everything I know to help you, but nothing I do seems to make any difference."

My Adam's apple did a dance up and down. I started to say something, but she raised her hand to silence me.

"You don't listen to me any more, and I'm tired of your constant rebellion. I had such high hopes for you, but now I just feel worn down." She stared at the floor. "You were born with so many natural talents, honey, but you seem hell-bent to thumb your nose at them."

She paused, taking a few deep breaths. I began to hear my heart throbbing in my ears.

"You remember the Cutlers? Their son Jerry? He was a grade ahead of you. Wasn't doing very well either. They decided to send him to this military school in Victoria, British Columbia. It's just a few hours away. I spoke with Mrs. Cutler yesterday. She said Jerry thrived in the disciplined atmosphere and is a changed boy."

My stomach began to cramp. This couldn't be happening. Maybe life was a struggle with my mother, but it was a well-choreographed dance. I had an endless supply of ways to whittle her down and get my way, to get out of trouble, to get her to smile even when she didn't want to.

"Ah, Mom . . . ," I broke in.

"No, hear me out, Terry. I've checked into this school, and I've made up my mind. You're going."

"No!" I blurted out.

"Terry, don't even start. I'm not going to discuss it with you. Before I'd know it, you'd have me changing my mind. I hate to use this cliché, but it's for your own good. I think a strong male environment could straighten you out, maybe give you the structure your father would've given you."

Over the next few days, she would not be dissuaded. I pulled every punch I knew to change her mind, but for once, she was immune to my manipulations. I was being sent to prison!

The day she drove me up to the military school, I was numb. My daily life was so filled with her, the thought of Mom not being there gave me shivers. It was weird—in spite of all my defiance, I suddenly realized how dependent I was on her. I blinked tears away when I thought of not seeing her for months, then felt a wave of rage that she was doing this to me!

When we arrived, she helped me settle in. While we were unpacking, I talked nonstop, hoping to prolong her stay. Finally, she said, "Walk me to the car, honey."

I looked around, desperate for something that would keep her there, an unfinished chore. But there was nothing. "Don't you want to stay for a while?" I asked.

"I wish I could, honey, but I want to get back to Seattle before dark. You know how I hate to drive at night."

A quick hug and she was gone. As I stood on the sidewalk watching her drive away, I felt ten instead of fifteen. Shocked to find tears streaming down my face, I ducked my head to my chin, swiped the tears away, and went back inside to go to my room.

Suddenly, someone bumped my shoulder and ordered, "What's your name, kid?"

"Terry," I mumbled, walking away. I felt something grab my arm.

"Not good enough, plebe. I want your surname!"

Looking up, I saw a large, muscular guy with a menacing scowl. Something snapped inside me. I saw red and moved into him, "It's McBride, asshole, now get your hands off me and leave me alone!" I pulled away and continued down the hall.

As I walked away, I heard: "You just made a big mistake,

jerk. Do you know what a prefect is? The head boy that can make your life hell? You're the asshole, and you're _mine!_"

The prefect kept his promise. When I didn't tow his line, I found myself in detention or getting hacks (swats from a five-foot cane while bending over, grabbing my ankles). One day, with a broad smile on his face, the prefect handed me a note from the headmaster demanding my presence. A tingle ran down my spine. What now?

Inside the mahogany-lined office, I sat down in front of his massive desk, concentrating on keeping my body still. The headmaster was an old, stern man with stooping shoulders and patches at the elbows of his ancient jacket. I sat across from him, armpits getting wet as he studied my file.

Sighing, he looked up. "Son, do you realize that you've received more hacks these first four months of school than anyone in our forty-seven-year history? You have also received more detention in this single week than anyone ever has."

I sat there defiant, waiting to hear what my next punishment would be.

"Young man," he said kindly, "don't you know that being mad at the world doesn't hurt the world? It only hurts you."

I looked at him, confused.

"I have no plans to discipline you today," he said. "You obviously punish yourself enough. I only ask that you think about who is actually getting the short end of the stick. Will you do that for me?"

I nodded, my voice failing me.

Back in my dorm room, I lay on my bed, every nerve tingling. The headmaster's words echoed in my head, stirring up memories of my stubborn refusal to play by their rules, and all the grief I'd brought on myself. Scenes flickered in front of my closed eyes: the times I got six hacks, barely being able to sit for days; the humiliating scoldings in front of other students.

At that moment, I made a decision. From now on, things would be different. The headmaster was right; I was the one getting hurt. I still wanted to do it my way, but I was going to be a lot smarter about it.

I slept well that night and awoke with a new attitude. I carefully devised a scheme to better my circumstances at the school.

Each Saturday afternoon, the prefects had a poker game. I called in a favor and got myself invited, pretending that I was a novice player. I knew they'd let me in the game, eager to take advantage of me. Actually, I was a pretty good poker player and usually was the big winner when we plebes played. Tapping into my winnings, I showed up with $26, a small fortune for a fifteen-year-old in those days. I played the naïve kid, happy to be included, staying in every pot and betting even when I didn't have good cards. And in short order, I lost my $26. I walked away from the game broke but happy. My plan was working; I was enthusiastically invited back.

On the next Saturday, I showed up with $40. With that kind of money, they were drooling. I acted anxious to please and to be "taught" by my superiors. I intentionally lost again, but only about half of what I had. More importantly, I concentrated on a little psychology to get these guys on my side. In line with my plan, I pretended to be nervous about my next play, squirming in my seat, fiddling with the cards. Then I pulled out a cigarette and started to light it.

"Hey, you can't do that here!"

I knew this. Although the prefects smoked at the poker game, as a plebe I wasn't allowed to smoke on campus.

"Oh, shit, you're right!" I said. "Man, I'm sorry, I forgot." I shrugged and put the cigarette away, then started biting at a fingernail, apologizing again. When the hand was over, I had stayed in the pot but lost. Then I pretended I was going to quit because I was so nervous.

After a moment, one of the prefects said, "What's it matter if Terry smokes here? I don't see any harm in it." The others looked around and then nodded their approval.

"Just don't think this gives you the right to smoke anywhere else, but as long as you're here with us, it's okay."

I gushed with thanks and lit up, inwardly celebrating.

Saturday after Saturday, I gained their trust and respect, finally becoming their friend. Detention and hacks were now an infrequent occurrence. Even so, as the school year ended, I was relieved when my mother said I would not have to go back. I couldn't pack up fast enough.

Back in Seattle, I finished high school with an unimpressive 1.9 grade point average and a few memorable scrapes with authority. One antic got me kicked out of school for the last two weeks and stripped of the privilege to go on our senior cruise.

Like most of my capers, it started out innocently. Part of our drama class was invited to another high school to perform a popular skit. Arriving that morning, we found we wouldn't be putting on the production until the assembly was gathered late that afternoon. With time to kill, a few of us went down to the beach. Boredom set in, and I asked if anyone wanted a beer. Eyes lit up, and my fake ID came out. Hours flew by as we drank. We returned to the high school rowdy and high and would have pulled it off if one of the boys hadn't gotten sick.

"Hey, you," a teacher said, "you look green around the gills. You been drinking?"

"No, sir," he lied, trying to act normal. Sweat popped out on his face. With his next breath, he grabbed his stomach. Vomit erupted from him and sprayed the front of the teacher's shirt.

Oh, were we busted! Right out of high school. Damn, I had really wanted to go on that senior cruise.

With high school completed, I moved to Idaho to live with my Uncle Larry and Auntie Lil. I worked as a laborer on a pulp mill construction site. It was mostly digging ditches, but good, hard work. I thought a few years of working outside in the elements would help me appreciate college and motivate me to study a little harder than I had in high school.

With this hard labor, I began to change, trimming down and getting muscular, exchanging bottle glasses for contacts. With money in my pockets, I felt like hot stuff. I bought a sports car, and my new persona was complete. I saw myself as a fighter, struggling against the "shoulds" and "have to's" that one is confronted with while growing up. I thought I could talk my way into or out of almost any situation.

When my aunt and uncle moved to Seattle for the next construction job, I followed them. I had been working for two years and knew I needed to get into college to avoid being drafted, a sure ticket to Vietnam. With poor grades in high school, a four-year university wasn't an option, so I enrolled at the local community college. During my first year, I met Karen, and we fell in love. We decided to get married when our first daughter made her presence known.

I suppose I knew with the responsibilities of a new family, I would have to straighten up. I had been doing better at school, but I wasn't really applying myself. To finish my education, get a good job, and "make something" of myself, I realized I needed to be more disciplined and accept the rules I had rebelled against for my whole life. And God, how I hated the idea of playing my life by somebody else's rules. Nevertheless, my love for Karen and our baby gave me the strength I needed to work toward that goal. Then fate stepped in and changed the course of my life when I injured my back.

≈ ≈ ≈ ≈

I heard the outer door open, and as I watched a nurse enter, I came back to the present with a jolt. I cursed, remembering I was in the hospital, incapacitated, sick and needy, surrounded by experts who were paid to tell me what to do. As always with experts, they started telling me what I could and could not expect. I don't think they consciously set out to speak to me about the limitations I should believe about myself, but that's what was happening.

It was slowly becoming apparent that this infection was

far worse than I wished to believe. And my nonchalant attitude got me into serious trouble once again.

On the third morning after the surgery, a nurse came in to give me a sponge bath. Ellen was twenty-four, petite, with strawberry-blonde hair, often pulled into a ponytail. She had an infectious smile and was a bright spot in my colorless days.

Each day Ellen and I had the same routine. She would wash most of my body, then leave a pan of water and washcloth for me to take care of my privates. But after about a week, I couldn't stop thinking about how good a long, hot shower would feel. One of the few perks of an isolation room was a private bath with a shower. It was out of the question, I was told, because they didn't want the drainage site to get wet. But I couldn't get it out of my mind, turning over every possibility until I came up with what seemed an ingenious solution.

When I expected to be left alone for awhile, I got out of bed, grabbed the IV stand with the pump hooked to it, and rolled the stand to the bathroom. Along the way, I snatched a stool. Putting the stool squarely in the shower, with the IV stand nearby, I hoisted myself up, draping the drainage tubes over the top of the stand. As I had imagined, I stood high enough that the water only hit the lower part of my body, I began to shower. Oh, it felt so good!

Suddenly the door flew open and Dr. Carlisle's presence filled the small space. I was so stunned I almost fell. "What do you think you're doing, Terry? Get out of there!" he demanded. "Do you want to cripple yourself for life?"

With shaking legs, I got down and dried myself off, only half listening to Dr. Carlisle grousing about hospital rules and procedures to safeguard me from danger. *Blah, blah, blah,* I thought.

I put on a clean gown, and got back into bed. "Terry, what would have happened if you fell? I don't think you understand the seriousness of your condition."

I looked at his worried face.

"You need to accept your limitations, Terry," he chided. "If you understood the risks, you wouldn't ignore our requests."

"What risks?"

"Your condition is very serious. You need to be careful so you'll have every opportunity to fight this thing, and an accident could set you back I don't know how far." He ran his fingers through his hair abruptly. "I wasn't going to tell you this until tomorrow, but, well, now seems like a good time. I've arranged for a specialist in chronic infectious diseases to be part of your care. I'll bring him by in a couple of days. Here's his card."

He handed me the card and walked to the door. "No more antics, okay?"

"Okay."

What had he said? Accept your limitations? Crippled for life? Chronic disease specialist? I was so used to being a healthy person, I could not understand something that could damage me forever. I thought I couldn't get more depressed, but I was wrong.

Later that afternoon, I pulled out the card and studied it: Dr. Howard, Chronic Infectious Disease Specialist. My eyes kept wandering over the word "chronic." What exactly did this mean? How did this apply to me?

When Karen came that afternoon, I showed her the card and pointed to the title.

"I'm going to be working with this chronic infectious disease guy, but I'm not sure what the chronic part is about."

"I don't know," she said.

"Maybe he helps people who have difficulty in dealing with infections."

Dr. Carlisle had already mentioned that, but it didn't really answer my question. I took the card back and looked at the word chronic again.

"Honey, I'd really like to look this up in a dictionary. Would you go find one?"

Moments later she came back. "Couldn't find a dictionary. Here's what it says in the thesaurus." She looked at me to make sure I was paying attention, then recited: "Constant, recurring, unceasing, persistent, never-ending, and ever present . . . do you want me to continue?"

I raised my hand. "Enough. I get the picture."

After Karen left that evening, I was on edge, unable to get comfortable. The walls seemed like they were closing in on me. My head began to throb as my thoughts got blacker and blacker.

Who did Dr. Carlisle think he was, bringing this new guy on board? How dare they decide what's going to happen to me, my inner voice screamed. I'll decide what's going to happen to me! I won't be put in the box they're creating for me. No way! I'm going to do the same thing my older brother Gerry did—thumb my nose at their ridiculous ideas.

In 1945, when my brother Gerry was five years old, he was diagnosed with diabetes. His doctors said he probably wouldn't live into his teens. He had other ideas. When he reached puberty, they said he would probably not live through his twenties, and if he did, he would have serious complications because of the disease. Gerry still didn't buy into their ideas.

At the time of this writing, he's had severe diabetes for over fifty-seven years, taking shots every day, and he is vitally healthy and active.

Gerry had a triple bypass at the age of sixty-two. I was with him the morning of his surgery when the doctor came in to check the veins in his legs, which they hoped to use in the bypass.

Before his examination, the doctor said, "I understand the physiology of diabetes and those veins will probably not be good enough to use."

"Don't bet on it!" Gerry retorted.

When the doctor checked his veins he was amazed. "These aren't just good veins, they're like the veins of a healthy forty-year-old."

He taught me early on that he was well because he refused

to be sick. "A good denial is just the flip side of a good declaration of the truth," he often said. No matter how hard Mom and the doctors tried to put him in the "diabetic" box, Gerry refused to go. Yes, he has diabetes, but there are no signs of it other than the need for insulin.

I figured if it worked for Gerry, it would work for me. I relentlessly refused to be sick. Sure, I had an infection in my spine, but that's all it was, an infection. In the past, I'd always gotten rid of any infection I had, so why should I expect anything different this time?

A few days after the shower incident, Dr. Carlisle brought in the promised specialist, Dr. Howard. I had decided I had no need for him and knew I wouldn't like him. He was a man of few words and sparse gestures. With dark hair, brown eyes and a ruddy complexion, he exuded good health. He spoke to me quietly, respectfully, answering my questions thoroughly. In the end, I couldn't help but like the guy.

"I'll be in charge of your care after you're discharged, Terry," he said. "My job is to assist you in keeping the drains open and monitor how your body deals with the infection and the antibiotic regimen." It seemed like he supported my intention to lick this thing, and I liked him all the more for that.

≈ ≈ ≈ ≈

Seventeen days after the surgery, I was finally discharged. Although I did my best to hold on to Gerry's well-honed denial system about disease, my resolve had been weakened. I was scared and I was worried.

Two days after being released from the hospital, I had my first appointment with Dr. Howard. I arrived on time, irritated to have to fill out pages of new-patient information. When I had completed the forms, one of the patients struck up a conversation. I didn't feel like talking, but I didn't want to be rude either.

"What are you seeing the doctor about?" he asked politely.

"Oh, I had a fusion several months ago, and somehow my

spine got infected." I noticed several other patients turned their heads toward us.

"What kind of bug are you infected with?"

"E. coli," I answered, turning in the direction of a tiny gasp that had escaped from one of the listeners.

"Oh," the man said, "well, now . . . ." He smiled awkwardly and turned away.

After that, the conversation just died. The room got heavy with tension. I caught other patients sneaking looks at me. I felt as if they were thinking, "It's too late for you, buddy, you're done for." Relief filled me when the nurse called my name.

≈ ≈ ≈ ≈

Eleven short days after my discharge, I was once again readmitted to the hospital. Would this ever end? This time it was because my temperature had started to go up again, and I was feeling more and more pain in my lower back and upper thighs. Confused because the drains from the previous surgery were still open and draining well, Dr. Carlisle probed, discovering a separate pocket of infection that was not draining. He did another simple procedure, cut more holes in my back, and inserted more drains.

Some of Dr. Carlisle's comments worried me. Apparently, he didn't think this area was infected the last time he operated. Even worse, he seemed concerned that the infection was still spreading even though I had good drainage. He never openly admitted any of his concerns. He just inadvertently made little slips here and there that led me to think he was becoming increasingly concerned.

Until now, it never dawned on me that the infection could spread. I knew more of the spine was involved than just the two vertebrae that had been fused, but it never registered that this infection could damage other parts of my body, too.

The fifth surgery was very simple, and I spent only four days in the hospital before being sent home with more bandages and instructions to make another appointment with Dr.

Howard. This time I decided not to have any conversations with other patients. But "the best laid plans of mice and men . . . ."

During my appointment, Dr. Howard checked the drains, asking me various questions about how I was doing, as he had during my first appointment.

"Terry, I'd like you to attend a meeting tomorrow night at my office," he said. "You'd get a chance to meet some of my other patients. They come together to discuss the problems and challenges they're facing."

Being fairly naïve, I assumed this meeting would encourage us to maintain a positive attitude, and I certainly needed that. "Sure, thanks. It sounds good," I said.

So the next night I showed up all bright and shiny with my best "I'm not sick" mindset.

That meeting rudely awakened me to the realm of chronic disease. Some attendees had been dealing with infections for years. Many years. This was my first real contact with a group of people facing the same health challenge I had. Almost immediately, I noticed that many of them really identified with their problems. They couldn't wait to talk about their specific infections and how long they had had them. They wore their sicknesses like a badge of honor that gave them their identity.

Throughout the meeting, no one seemed to be providing anybody else with hope. The ongoing discussion focused exclusively on how we might handle the diseases we had. Finally, I asked, "When are we going to talk about how to get rid of these infections?"

The lady next to me said, "You're new, aren't you?"

On my way home that night, I promised myself I'd never go back to that kind of meeting again. It was depressing, and I came away from it full of doubt and fear. I wanted to eliminate my disease, not learn to live with it.

Although I respected Dr. Howard, I was acutely aware of the box he wanted to put me in. I was also sensitive to the limiting beliefs of some of the other professionals I was working with. I'm not saying these beliefs were negative or bad; they were just limiting. But that's the way beliefs are. Any belief that states "this is the way it is" eliminates the possibility that it can be different.

Yes, compelling evidence did support that the box they wanted me to stand in really existed. Although I had to agree with some of their data, I was not going to lie down in this box and let them put a lid over me. Or at least that's what I was telling myself. I was busy getting on with my life, going to school, and being a married man with a family.

Over the nine months that these first five surgeries took place, there were many long days and nights filled with loneliness, fear, and doubt. And I learned quickly that other people didn't really want to know how devastating it is to be cut open time and time again, so I kept my mouth shut, sucked it up, and hoped for the best. But I didn't get what I hoped for. It just got worse.

CHAPTER 4

NEW HOSPITAL, NEW DOCTORS

One month after the fifth surgery, I completed my junior year at the University of Washington with the best grades I had ever received. Maybe I was growing up and finally applying myself. A month after that, the incisions healed and the drains closed. With hopeful anticipation, we started our waiting game to see if any signs of the infection would resurface.

With the help of Karen's parents as co-signers, we purchased a new Volkswagen Squareback, a small station wagon-like car. It was a long way from my sports car, which I had traded in for an old Rambler when Kris arrived, but it was still a fun car.

When a check arrived unexpectedly for some damages done to our car, we decided to take a vacation rather than fix the dent. The next day, we packed our camping gear and headed north to Canada. We felt we had the world by the tail and wanted to make the most of the last few weeks before school started.

At Vancouver, British Columbia, we turned east and went

through Banff and Jasper, then south into Glacier National Park. Kris loved to travel. Along the way, we sang songs and played games. In the afternoons, we stopped at city parks to fix lunch; in the evenings, we set up our tent and cooked dinner. As the days passed and I remained pain-free, we decided to extend the trip.

We proceeded on to Yellowstone, the Grand Teton National Park, then west into Yosemite. It was a hurry-and-drive trip, having lots of fun along the way. From Yosemite we headed down to San Diego and stayed with John, a school buddy of mine from my military academy days.

We left Kris with a lady who lived in John's apartment complex and took a day trip into Tijuana, Mexico. We bought a few blankets and other trinkets for Kris and family, and I picked up a genuine carved wood chess set.

Back in San Diego, we enjoyed a balmy evening lounging around the pool and playing with Kris.

"Isn't this something!" I said to Karen.

"It sure beats rainy days at home," she replied.

"How long has it been since your incisions healed?"

"Hmm, I think it's been at least three weeks now."

"No signs of the infection, no pain?"

"Nope." I looked up at the blue sky. "You think it could finally be over?"

"Looks like it to me. And why not? You've been taking real good care of yourself, and I think this vacation's helped you relax. Maybe that's all you needed."

I looked at Karen and smiled. She looked more beautiful than ever, and she was a beauty to begin with.

"Let's stay another day or two and go to the beach," I said. "Then we can take our time driving back to Seattle and get ready for the start of school."

≈ ≈ ≈ ≈

The next morning I woke up with an ache in my low back and my stomach tightened. "Honey, take a look at my back and tell me what you see."

"It's kinda swollen and red around the incision sites. Does it hurt?" she asked.

"Yeah," I sighed.

I could tell by the all-too-familiar dull pain that the infection was back. It wasn't going down my thighs yet, but it would be within a day or two. And that was serious pain.

"We better call Dr. Carlisle and get back," I said, deflated.

Within hours, we were packed and on the freeway. Except for a few naps at rest stops, we drove straight through the night and went directly to Dr. Carlisle's office the next day. He did a preliminary examination and gave me pain medication. When he saw the angry red swelling, he called the hospital and scheduled me for admittance the next day.

The next morning, I was checked into another private room. Soon Dr. Carlisle came in and used the same needle-and-syringe method to relieve some of the pressure, but that was only temporary and we both knew it. He told me he had scheduled surgery for the next day and left me alone in my room with my anger and resentment. It had been such a great few weeks with Karen and Kris. Now I was right back where I hated being, at the mercy of a disease I had no idea how to heal.

The following morning, Dr. Carlisle opened my back, intent on developing a good drainage system. He found the infection involved even more areas than before. He decided to do no more than put drains in where he could to minimize the pressure and sewed me back up.

I woke up late that afternoon back in my room. Dr. Carlisle came to see me that evening.

"I'm sorry to say the infection is gaining ground, Terry," he said softly. "You need to have more elaborate care than I can give you." He looked down at his hands. "I've been in consultation with some specialists at the University of Washington Medical Center. It's a teaching hospital. They've agreed to take your case. With your permission, I'll forward your medical records to them."

"Sure, I guess" I said, feeling a bit overwhelmed.

He looked at my frown and smiled. "This is good news, really. Well, I know the infection has spread, but this is a very special hospital. They're known for having the best doctors available. They can give your particular challenge the attention it deserves."

Dr. Carlisle went on to explain that the University Medical Center didn't take just any patient. To be accepted as a referral patient, one had to have a serious problem that presented a unique challenge. The staff consisted of some of the finest doctors in the country. He believed sending me there was the best he could do for me. A whole team would be involved in helping me.

I was released on the third day. The new drains helped ease the pain, so at least I was relatively comfortable. Mentally, I was a wreck. Dr. Carlisle signed my discharge papers, and we said our good-byes. That was the last time I ever saw him.

The next day, I went to the University of Washington Medical Center for my first appointment. I was impressed by the modern facility, a first-class operation. This place wasn't at all like Smith Medical Center. The people had a totally different attitude; they didn't act like they were doing me a favor by letting me be there. I was directed to the orthopedic clinic where I filled out a few forms. While waiting, I picked up a pamphlet and read:

Welcome to University of Washington Medical Center, offering world-class primary and specialty care to you and your family. University of Washington Medical Center is a teaching hospital of the University of Washington, nationally recognized for its outstanding patient care.

After a brief wait, I was shown into one of the examination rooms. An intern took my vital signs and gave me a fairly complete physical exam. He then took a detailed history from my point of view on what had happened since the ruptured disk. He was a nice guy, not much older than I was.

"I have some good news," he said. "And by the sound of it, you could use some. You'll be the patient of a visiting professor from England. I hear this guy is a real whiz kid, supposed to be one of the top three in the world in his specialty."

"Thanks," I said. I was impressed and relieved to have some big shots involved.

After he left to give the information to my attending physician (even the name indicated there was a team involved), I began to feel better emotionally. The whole place had an air of confidence and prestige.

My new doctor came in accompanied by four interns. With a thick British accent, he introduced himself.

"I'm Dr. Brian Hedgewood. Pleased to meet you."

He extended his hand, and I shook it. He had delicate hands and a small, wiry frame. He was also rather stuffy and stiff, but there was no mistaking that this guy was good, and he knew it. It was all over him. He had an air that said, "I'm going to fix you even though no one else can."

"I've spoken with both of your previous doctors. After carefully reviewing your case, I am confident that we can help you."

It seemed to me he reveled in the challenge. The interns were looking at him as if he could do miracles. As he talked about what he planned, I really thought this man could do it. His confidence was exciting. Once again, I had faith that my doctors were going to fix me.

With infected bone, it was standard procedure to cut out as much infected material as possible, then create drains so the body could discharge anything that was left. Couple this procedure with a good antibiotic regimen, and the body would do the rest. Why I thought Dr. Hedgewood could do this procedure better than my former doctor, I'm not sure. But I did.

Because the pain was already increasing, Dr. Hedgewood wanted me admitted the next day. He rushed through all the preliminary steps and sent me home with more pain medication.

The next morning, I hurt like hell but was excited about my prospects with my new "team." I took a pain pill, and we headed for the hospital. After going through the admission procedures, Karen and I were shown to my room—a private room again, because of the infection.

By now, the pain medication had worn off. I was exhausted and hurting. I immediately requested some medication from the nurse, who said she didn't know if the doctor had prescribed any for me, but she would check. In a few minutes, she came back with a pill.

"Is this a strong pain killer? I'm really hurting."

"I'm sure it'll do the trick," she said.

I swallowed it and got into their hospital pajamas and robe. Feeling no relief after twenty minutes, I went searching for the nurse.

"That pill hasn't done me any good," I reported.

"It will. Give it time," she told me.

I went back to my room, unconvinced. After almost an hour, with still no relief, I tracked the nurse down again with the same plea.

"When your doctor comes through for rounds, he'll prescribe something stronger, but I can't give you any more for another two hours."

"I don't understand. This pill should be helping."

"Well," she admitted. "Maybe not. The one I gave you wasn't very strong."

"What? Why not?!"

"I thought your pain might just be the stress of checking into the hospital. It's not uncommon, you know."

Heat ran up my neck to my face. I was outraged, remembering all the times hospital staff had played their games at my expense. I barreled back to my room with the nurse following at my heels. When I arrived, I threw off my robe and tore off my pajama top, buttons flying everywhere.

"We're going home!" I told Karen.

I knew I still had some strong pain medication at home, and I was going to get it.

"Wait a minute, you can't just leave," the nurse said.

"Go to hell," I responded. I took off my pajama pants and started getting dressed.

Truthfully, I wanted to cry. It wasn't just this nurse and her stupid assumptions; it was the whole "being sick" drama. I was tired of others running my life, and I was tired of hurting and having to plead and bargain for medication that would make the pain bearable. I was tired of feeling humiliated and discounted by some of the staff with their "I know best" attitudes. I was done putting up with people like Nurse Richards, who had given me antibiotic shots that hurt for days. I was going to stand up for myself.

I was putting on my shoes when a resident came in.

"Hi, I'm Dr. Griffin. What's going on?"

With angry tears running down my cheeks, I told him. It wasn't just the nurse; I was scared and in pain. I began pouring out my heart, "It was supposed to be a simple fusion, and now I'm here for my seventh surgery in thirteen months with an infection that is supposed to be chronic."

As he stood beside me, it wasn't the words he heard, it was my cry for help. And then he did something I will never forget.

"Terry, I apologize. I'm truly sorry for this entire mix-up. If you'll wait for just a moment, I'll be right back with a shot that will stop the pain. Will you do that?"

I looked at him and my anger evaporated. I felt the compassion the man had for me. He understood what I was going through. He cared, he really cared. It was like being tossed a life ring when it felt like I didn't have the strength to stay afloat any longer.

"Yes, I'll wait . . . thanks."

Dr. Griffin returned in moments and gave me the promised shot. I don't know what it was, but within minutes the pain was no longer an issue. I got into a new pair of pajamas, crawled into bed, and went to sleep.

Later, the head nurse came in and also apologized for the young nurse. Then she took Karen and me on a tour of the orthopedic floor. It was still a hospital with all the hospital smells and trappings, but it so was much nicer than Smith Medical Center, home of my six previous surgeries.

There were significant differences. Most importantly, they had no preset visiting hours and allowed children on the floor. I was thrilled to know Kris could come visit any time.

The nurse explained that as much as possible they tried to make it like a home away from home. There was a patient refrigerator where I could keep my favorite foods, and they even allowed beer or wine on the floor. Many of the patients were there for long periods of time, sometimes six months or more, and the staff had special training in extended patient care.

After showing us around the orthopedic floor, she took us down to the cafeteria, then pointed out the food and dessert vending machines. As long as I was not confined to bed, I was allowed to go to the cafeteria or vending machines whenever I wanted, even in the middle of the night.

What a difference from the strict, regimented policies I had lived under before. When the tour was over, I was grateful to be where I was. It wasn't like home, but it would do while these new doctors fixed me.

Early that afternoon my "whiz kid" doctor came into my room with his team of interns, a nurse, and the chief resident of orthopedic surgery, none other than Dr. Griffin, who had given me the shot earlier. Needless to say, I liked him a bunch.

Dr. Hedgewood made a point of introducing himself to Karen and including her in the conversation. I really appreciated that and Karen did too. This guy had class, and he brought his air of confidence with him.

"We'll begin by doing a battery of tests starting tomorrow," he explained.

"As soon as we know the extent of the infection, we'll schedule surgery."

They were in a hurry to get on with the surgery to alleviate the pain from the fluid buildup. Because the infection had spread out, it wasn't as easy to aspirate the fluid with the syringe-and-needle trick like before. But they would continue to do it anyway to keep the fluid and pressure down as much as they could.

After the team left, I felt even more impressed. This was not just a doctor placing me in a hospital then dropping in once a day to see how things were going. It was an integrated team of doctors, nurses, and staff working together, dedicated to getting me healthy.

In the back of my mind I still had all the negative information about bone infection I'd heard over the past year. But these guys had never once mentioned any negatives. They weren't saying it was going to be a cakewalk, but failure wasn't part of their plan, in any shape or form. They never sat me down and guaranteed success; they just focused on what they were going to do to help my body get rid of the infection. And the tests over the next few days would give them the information they needed to develop their surgical strategy.

"We'll need good X-rays to develop a comprehensive surgical plan before we open you up again, Terry," he told me that day. "We don't want to be surprised. Once I know what we're dealing with, I'll confer with the other specialists, and we'll decide on a course of action. Then I'll get together with you and Karen to explain what we're planning to do and why."

After he left I was so happy, I was all smiles. It was as if the entire medical center was amassing its resources to support me. My previous doctors had done good jobs, but best of all, they had referred me to the University Medical Center, where specialists from all the allopathic disciplines worked in close contact in the same building. And now some of the world's finest were working on me.

With all the new freedoms at University Medical Center,

such as seeing Kris and Karen whenever I wanted, I knew the environment couldn't be better to enhance my chances of getting well.

By the time Karen left for the night, we had talked ourselves into believing we had a new "savior," a team of caring individuals who would develop a plan, and with this plan they would fix me.

CHAPTER 5

YOU CAN'T EXPECT TO COME OUT
OF THIS ONE WHOLE

D r. Hedgewood's biggest concern was to get a clear picture of the extent of my infection. Until they got accurate X-rays of the bone and tissue involved, they would
not operate. Though he had expected this to take only a day
or two, it took much longer.

Several times I went to Radiology (the X-ray department)
where the doctors attempted to inject a special dye into the
hole in my back that drained the infection. They used the same
type of big eyedropper used at Smith Medical Center and did
the same procedure of inserting its tip into the drainage site
and squeezing the bulb to allow the dye to flow into the infected area. Here though, University Medical Center had a TV
monitor they could watch before taking the X-ray. Twice they
injected the dye but decided not to take pictures because the
dye was blocked before reaching deeper areas of the infected
tissue. They considered exploratory surgery but first would
need better pictures even to do that.

Meanwhile, my pain steadily worsened. Fluids created by
the infection were building up inside me and pressing nerves

against bone. The doctors increased my medication until I was taking morphine several times a day.

For ten days, I went through an assortment of tests and was examined by countless specialists. I was stuck and poked, looked at and looked into more that I thought possible. At first it was okay with me; all the tests and examinations would assist my team of doctors in coming up with a game plan. But as days passed with no results, I grew impatient.

Because this was a teaching hospital, a gallery of interns and residents (both male and female) always accompanied the big guns, observing the examinations. Often, my most private parts were on display; it was humiliating.

On the eleventh day of my stay, I returned to Radiology for the third time. Although I could walk, I had to use a wheelchair—standard procedure. Pushing me along, Dr. Griffin filled me in as we took the elevator to the second floor.

"We've come up with a different procedure in hopes of getting better pictures. I'm going to attempt to insert a small tube called a catheter into the hole in your back," he told me. "Then I'll close the hole and insert the dye with a big syringe. This should prevent the dye from squirting back out. I'm hoping it'll do the trick."

When we arrived, the technician asked me to lie on the table on my stomach.

As they got ready, I silently prayed, "Please, God, let's get some good X-rays this time."

Dr. Griffin flipped on the monitor and fired up the equipment. Turning my head, I could see on the screen the small tube being inserted into my back. As Dr. Griffin pushed on the syringe, dye spread into the immediate area then stopped, just like the times before.

"I know that's not all of it," he said, "It's more involved than that." As he talked to the radiologist, I sensed they were going to give up again.

"Dr. Griffin, why don't you just push on the syringe harder until it breaks through?"

"I've thought of that, Terry, but I'm concerned it might push the dye into normal tissue."

"But we have to get good pictures, right?"

"That's all we're waiting for."

"So let's go for it. It seems like it's worth the risk to me." *Anything to get this show on the road*, I thought.

"I don't know . . ."

Finally, with my encouragement, he began to push harder. I could feel the pressure building. Then suddenly, the dye broke through whatever had been blocking it. As Dr. Griffin emptied the syringe, immense pressure forced my nerves against bones. A wave of excruciating pain hit me. I gasped, burying my face in the pillow. Clenching my teeth, I did the only thing I knew to do with the pain—bull my way through it.

"Hang in there, Terry," Dr. Griffin said.

"We got it! We finally got it."

Then he dashed to the door and grabbed a nurse. "Quick, go to 4-South and get eight milligrams of morphine. Tell them it's for Terry McBride, and do it STAT!" he said, turning back to the room.

"Okay, Terry," the radiologist said, "take a breath and hold still." A moment later, he said, "Got a good set of pictures from your back. Now you'll need to roll over on your side so I can get another set from that view."

With Dr. Griffin helping me, I turned, and the searing white pain made me want to scream. I didn't know pain like that was possible.

Dr. Griffin leaned close and brushed the hair out of my face. "Hang on, Terry. This is what we've needed. I've got pain meds coming," he said. I nodded, gasping for air.

As he stepped behind the glass into the protected area, I heard the technician whisper, "My God, it's everywhere!"

In a fog of pain, his words barely registered. He finished taking the X-rays, and a nurse rushed in with my shot. Sitting close to me, Dr. Griffin found a vein and slowly released the morphine into my system. Had he simply administered the shot into muscle, it would have taken fifteen to twenty minutes to have an effect. By injecting it into the vein, relief began immediately.

He was visibly shaken. Face ashen, his hands trembled slightly as he held the needle. As the pain began to subside, my rapid breathing slowed, and my clenched hands began to relax.

Dr. Griffin took a cloth and wiped the sweat off my forehead. "I feel terrible about the pain, Terry. I didn't realize it was going to happen, but we got great pictures. We got really great pictures."

All I could do was nod my head in acknowledgment.

He motioned to a nurse. "We're going to need a gurney." Turning back to me he smiled. "As a special bonus for your bravery, Terry, I've ordered transportation for you!"

I smiled back weakly. What he and I both knew was that if I tried to stand, my knees would buckle. When the gurney arrived, they transferred me and wheeled me back to my room on the fourth floor. As I came off the elevator, I was pleasantly surprised to find two nurses there to meet me. One was Liz, the head nurse, who always managed to find a little extra time for me. Although not much was said on the way to my room, I felt their support and concern. I knew they really cared.

When they helped me into bed, the jostling stirred up the pain again, making me wince and suck in breath. Liz sat down and took my hand in hers. Under normal circumstances, a small gesture like this might seem trivial, but at that moment, it brought tears to my eyes.

Liz leaned close to me and said, "Terry, while you were down in Radiology, some friends came to see you. We asked them to wait here in the room."

I looked to my side and saw Ted and Brenda, friends I knew through school. Man, was I in bad shape to miss that!

"Hi, Terry," they said.

"Hi. It's good to see you!" I said. They had known about the first six surgeries but had never visited me in the hospital until now. It was a nice surprise, even though I knew I was in no condition for a lengthy visit.

Liz excused herself, and as we chatted, the full effects of the morphine kicked in, and I felt much better, just a little tired from the ordeal. They wanted to know why I had been in so much pain. When I told them what had happened with the X-rays, Ted's eyes welled up with tears.

"How can you stand it?" he asked.

"How do you hold up and keep your attitude so positive?"

I was going to brush off his questions, but I wanted to explain, for myself if for no other reason. I took a long drink of water to clear my head.

"What option do I have, really? Think of it this way, Ted. Imagine you're leaving a department store, wearing a brand-new suit. And you're moving down the street feeling good when *Bam!* you slip and fall into a mud puddle. Your new suit is a mess! Now at that point, you've got two choices, right? You can either sit there and wallow in self-pity, or you can get up and make the best of a bad situation."

Ted nodded at me, his eyes still sad.

"Besides," I said, "now they have good X-rays."

Soon they saw I was fading and said their good-byes. Tired, I closed my eyes, and awareness of the room retreated. I was back on the X-ray table, remembering the experience. What had the X-ray technician said? It slowly came back to me: "My God, it's everywhere!" What did he mean by "everywhere"? *I'll have to ask Dr. Griffin the next time I see him,* I thought as I drifted off to sleep.

≈ ≈ ≈ ≈

As word spread about finally getting good X-rays, many staff members came in beaming with congratulations. Yet it seemed that within a few hours, the lightness in their congratulations ceased. I felt a subtle uneasiness in their attitudes, a wariness I couldn't put my finger on, but it was there—I could feel it. I wondered what caused the shift. Could it have been something in the report from Radiology?

Later that afternoon, Dr. Hedgewood came in with Dr. Griffin and a group of interns. "Great job, Terry. The X-rays are high quality, just what we need. Now we can develop a surgical plan.

"My preliminary review of the films shows that the infection is far more extensive than we thought." Touching my arm, he paused, shaking his head. "It's the worst case of osteomyelitis of the spine I've ever seen."

I noticed the interns looking at each other.

"I'm going to confer with the General Surgery Department on this, and in a few days, we'll do the big one."

As the group left, I looked at Dr. Griffin and blew out a breath I didn't know I was holding. I sensed something in Dr. Hedgewood's attitude that made me uneasy. His stuffy presence had subtly changed to become more gentle, more caring, and I didn't understand why.

Dr. Griffin sat down beside my bed, his face knit in concern. "In my opinion, Dr. Hedgewood is one of the best in the world. You couldn't ask for a better doctor to head up the surgical team that'll decide what to do."

I was touched by his efforts to comfort and assure me but an alarm was sounding in the back of my mind by his reference to a surgical "team." Even with the group of experts at Dr. Hedgewood's disposal, I always thought he would be the only doctor to perform the surgery. Now there was a *team* of surgeons? Why?

The next day as I waited for news about what was being decided, I could feel the tension building inside of me. There was so much I didn't understand, it was impossible to concentrate on anything. I was about to crawl out of my skin when Dr. Griffin finally came in.

"I've got news of a sort," he said. "Dr. Hedgewood and some department heads and chief residents have a meeting scheduled for five o'clock today, and they'll come see you after they've worked out a plan."

"Thanks."

"Gotta run, see you later."

As the hours passed by slowly, I began to feel something new to me: a deep sense of dread. Something had changed. Why all the brass in a big conference? I wished I had asked more questions. But as a twenty-four-year-old novice to illness, somehow I never knew what to ask. It was easy to slide into complacency and assume the doctors would take care of me, make me well. It wasn't something I thought I needed to focus on. Now, confusion growing by leaps and bounds, I wished I understood more.

At three o'clock, an orderly came into my room. "Hey there, I'm Jack," he said. Taking my arm, he checked my ID bracelet against his chart. "Terry McBride in the flesh."

"That's me," I said, accustomed to this routine. "What's up?"

"Oh, I'm here to prep you for surgery. Says here you're scheduled for tomorrow morning."

This was a drill I was familiar with. I started to roll over so he could shave my back.

"No need to roll over. We're going to do a front and back N-to-N prep, and we'll do the front first."

I knew prep was hospital jargon for shave, but I had never heard of an "N-to-N prep."

"What's an N-to-N?" I asked.

"Knees to nipples, and I got orders to shave your front and back," he said with a nervous laugh, "and everything in between."

I felt as though I'd been kicked in the stomach. For a moment I couldn't catch my breath.

Misunderstanding, the orderly smiled and said, "Don't worry, I've got a safety razor."

But I didn't laugh. With a shaky voice I asked, "Why do you have to shave so much?"

"Don't know. Those are my orders."

Fifteen minutes later, I was as hairless as a newborn baby

from upper-chest to just above my knees. Before, they'd only shaved the area around where they planned to cut. As the afternoon dragged on, I was haunted by the extensive prep, the comments by the X-ray technician, and the subtle shift in the attitude of the staff after the X-ray results were known.

≈ ≈ ≈ ≈

Karen and Kris arrived while I was having dinner, and other family members drifted in and out during the evening. This was the "big surgery" we had known was coming. Everyone was positive that these great physicians had the skill to finally rid my body of the infection.

Concerned about where the doctors were, I called for a nurse.

Liz came bopping in. "What's up?"

"Have you heard anything from the doctors?" I asked.

"I think they're still in their meeting."

"Why is it taking so long?"

"I don't know, Terry. I'm sure they'll come in as soon as they're done."

Shortly after Liz left, family members said their good-byes. One by one, they left until it was just Karen, Kris and me. We were talking about my concerns and the staff's recent, subtle shift in attitude when the door to my room opened. Dr. Hedgewood entered, trailed by five other doctors and Liz, the head nurse. Among the group, I only recognized him, Dr. Griffin, and Liz. He greeted Karen and introduced those with him: the Chief of the General Surgery Department, the Chief of the Infectious Disease Department, and the head residents of those departments.

From my experience, good news was usually carried by one person, and bad news was brought by a committee. As I waited for the introductions to be over, I felt my palms grow sweaty. It was now a little past seven at night, and here was a group of staff physicians who usually went home around five leaving interns and residents to run the hospital. I knew they had been meeting for hours discussing the best course of action. And now I wasn't sure I wanted to hear what they had decided. The mass of humanity standing in my room was daunting.

Dr. Hedgewood began. "As I mentioned this afternoon, the X-rays are excellent and, for the first time, we know the extent of the infected area. But, it is much worse than we had imagined."

The gentleness I had noticed earlier was still evident, and his voice seemed even softer.

"The infection is no longer just in your spine and the surrounding tissue. It has spread." He paused for a moment, shaking his head. "It's now throughout your pelvic area and has moved into your abdomen. It also involves both of your buttocks and your upper thighs. It appears to have followed your sciatic nerves down into your legs. We're also concerned that there might be a hole in your colon."

Now I knew what I had been feeling all day. He was putting words to all my fears. Stunned, I glanced toward Liz. She was looking at Karen and Kris, a big tear running down her cheek. As I looked at the five other doctors, some of them had tears in their eyes too. As Dr. Hedgewood continued, my temples started to pound.

"I know this is hard to grasp all at once, Terry, and I need to impress on you how serious this is, how important it is that we take aggressive measures to eradicate the infection now before it becomes even more life-threatening."

I heard a small gasp from Karen. And everything seemed to gear down to slow motion as Dr. Hedgewood stepped over to her and put his hand on her shoulder, then gently patted Kris as she snuggled into her mother's arms. With huge eyes, Kris looked from the doctor to me, then back to the doctor. I remember the look on her face when she got it; there was something very wrong with her daddy. When she started to whimper, my heart broke. As brave as I knew Karen would try to be, tears were welling up in her eyes as she rocked Kris.

Dr. Hedgewood continued to fuss over Kris as if to postpone giving us his conclusion. And even as I felt fear taking over my senses, I felt for him too. He was having a tough time continuing. I'd always seen him as stiff and standoffish, and now he seemed sort of lost. I wanted to say something to support *him*. I wanted to sound confident and brave, but I felt on the edge of control, afraid if I opened my mouth, I'd lose it. So I just lay there speechless, waiting for him to get to the point.

I realized Dr. Hedgewood was trying to convince me that because the infection was so extensive and now life-threatening, the procedure he was about to explain was the only option they had. It was like a mechanic telling you how broken your car is before he tells you how much it will cost to fix it. As this caring man talked, I knew it was going to cost me to get fixed.

Finally, he approached my bed and sat down on a stool. He pulled the stool up close, looked into my eyes, and it was just me and him—and I *felt* him.

He touched my arm as he began to speak, "Tomorrow, we're going to do a very radical and extensive procedure. First, we'll insert a catheter in your back, just like they did to get the X-rays, except this time, we'll inject a blue dye that will follow the various sinus tracks and essentially color all of the infected material. We'll do this while you're under anesthesia, so there won't be any pain—I *promise* there won't be any pain.

"Next, the general surgeons have to clean out your abdomen and pelvic areas. Their incision will start just above your penis and move up around your navel toward your sternum. They'll open up that whole area and literally cut out all the infected tissue down to the spine. Then I will scrape and chisel off the part of your spine that's infected. When that's done, we'll turn you over and the orthopedic team will open you up from your back. We will start just above your rectum and go up to about mid-back and again open that area up so we can cut out all the infected tissue there. Then I will scrape and chisel off the infected part of the spine from the back." He took a deep breath.

I couldn't believe what he was saying. I looked at Karen, silent tears tracking down her face. He went on.

"Then a team will start from the incision in your lower back and open your left buttock and thigh to clean out the infection along your sciatic nerve. Then, if necessary, they will open your right buttock and thigh as well. Finally, the team will go in between your scrotum and rectum to excise that area because the infection has completely engulfed your sacrum and tailbone. We need to get all the dead and infected bone and tissue out of there."

In spite of his attempt to keep me present with touch and his eyes, a great void opened up in me. I felt as if I was spiraling down into an abyss. My God, they were going to open me up and clean me out like a dead deer. I had never imagined anything as hideous as this.

I knew that all of those doctors had come so I could ask questions, but I had none. I was too shocked, numb, devastated. I felt empty. Then a feeling came over me the likes of which I'd never known before. It permeated my mind and body. When I realized what it was, I lost control; I knew terror.

My body began to visibly shake. With Kris in her arm, Karen came over and took my hand. Liz came around the bed and took the other. Dr. Hedgewood got up from the stool and motioned Karen to sit. He stepped back and continued.

"Terry, the entire team knows this is very drastic. And we know how devastating this must seem to you, but we all agree that it offers the best chance, maybe the only chance of finally eliminating the infection."

He stopped and cleared his throat. When he started speaking again, his voice was strained. "We also believe that the chances are great that you will suffer some nerve damage. Understand, we are dealing with a life-threatening infection." He paused as if to gain some strength. "We're fairly certain," he continued, "that through this procedure, you will lose the use of your left leg."

He began to explain about the sciatic nerve and how this result couldn't be avoided when I held up my hand to stop him.

Overwhelmed, I said, "If it's got to be done, let's do it." I couldn't take any more; I wanted the conversation over before it got worse.

He looked at me, and I knew he understood. "I know, Terry, but if it's as bad as we think it is, there is also a good chance you will lose the use of your right leg, and you will probably lose control of your bowels and bladder. And, there is a great possibility you will end up sexually impotent."

With a trembling voice I asked, "What's that?"

After a pause, one of the residents replied, "Everything will be there," nodding at my privates, "it just won't work."

With that I was gone. My temples screamed, the roar of blood in my ears drowning out everything. Dr. Hedgewood's face became a bright pinpoint; the other doctors standing around him receded into shadows.

He leaned close to me and said, "Terry, do you understand?"

Understand? What, is he crazy? I thought. *How can I wrap my mind around what he's saying? I'm twenty-four and he's telling me this operation will rob me of the use of one leg, probably both, and there is a good chance it will leave me sexually impotent and without control of my bowels and bladder.*

Understand? Hell, no! I don't even want to understand. I don't want to hear that this E. coli bacteria is eating me alive. I don't want to believe that my life could be over. I want to unzip myself from this body and get out!

The room was deathly silent except for Kris's soft crying. How I held myself together I don't know. Most of these men were married with children at home who also counted on them. With years of medical training and skill, it must have been a terrible feeling to present such a nightmare solution when one had committed oneself to helping others. Yet they had all come to face me and support me, to answer questions, possibly to justify their decisions, to explain their beliefs.

I don't know what they expected of me, but I was lost. There was nothing I could do. I couldn't think, and I didn't have any questions.

After several more minutes, Dr. Hedgewood broke the awkward silence. "Your team of surgeons are the best available. We'll be as careful as possible. But," he added, "with all the scar tissue already in that area and the extent of the infection, we simply won't be able to avoid damaging major nerves.

"We really don't know what will occur," he said. "What we do know, Terry, is you cannot expect to come out of this one whole."

CHAPTER 6

THE HELL I CAN'T!

Affter the doctors left, Karen and I were too stunned to talk. Kris was getting sleepy, and I wanted them near me.

I moved to the edge of my bed and patted the empty space. "I need you close, honey." For awhile, the three of us curled up together with Kris in the middle. As she drifted off to sleep, I stroked her hair and tried to think how blessed I was to have a healthy, happy daughter and a loving, caring wife like Karen. But I couldn't get there. I didn't feel blessed. I didn't feel grateful. I didn't feel anything.

Later, Liz, the head nurse, came into my room. She just stood there for a few moments looking at the three of us. Then she whispered to me, "You should get some rest. Tomorrow's a big day, and you need to be ready."

Karen and I held each other a little longer. Then we bundled up Kris, and I walked them to the elevator. As the elevator doors closed, I thought, *she's a strong woman.* Though she was just over five feet tall and a hundred pounds soaking wet, she was still a fighter. I couldn't ask for a better mother for my child.

Liz followed me back to my room with a sleeping pill and a shot of morphine. With the pain a constant throbbing, I was receiving morphine every four hours. After she gave me the shot, she asked if I wanted a back rub. I declined, and she sat on the edge of the bed, holding my hand. After a few moments of silence, she said, "I'm sorry," squeezed my hand, gave me a smile, then left.

Suddenly, I was alone with my thoughts and my fear. I was too tense to sleep; even the rain lightly tapping against the window did not calm me. As I lay there, I remembered a story I had once heard about a little girl. It reminded me of how I felt now.

She always wanted to say things, but no one seemed to understand. She always wanted to explain things, but no one seemed to care. So she would draw. Sometimes what she drew wasn't much of anything. Other times she wanted to carve her drawing in stone or write it in the sky.

When she would lie in the grass and look up at the sky, it would be only her and the sky. The sky was big and blue and full of everything, and she too was full. She was full of wonderful things inside of her that needed saying.

It was after one of those times that she drew the picture.

It was a beautiful picture. She would keep it under her pillow and let no one see it. She would look at it every night and think about it, and when it was dark and her eyes were closed, she could still see it. This picture was about her hopes and her dreams; it was about who she would be, and she loved it.

When she started school, she brought it with her. Not to show anyone, just to have it with her like a friend.

And it was funny about school. She sat at a square brown desk, like all the other square brown desks, and she thought her desk should be red. Her room was a square brown room, like all the other square brown rooms, and it was tight and close and stiff.

Oh, how she hated to hold the pencil and chalk, with her arms stiff and her feet flat on the floor, with the teacher watching and watching. Then she had to write numbers and they meant nothing to her. They were even worse than the letters that could be something if you knew how to put them together. The numbers were tight and square, and she hated the whole thing.

One day the teacher came and spoke to her and told her to wear dresses like all the other little girls. She said she didn't like dresses, and the teacher said, "That doesn't matter."

After that, she drew. And she drew all yellow; for it was the way she felt about morning. It was beautiful and full of promise.

The teacher came and spoke to her again; she smiled and said, "What's this? Why don't you draw something like Jan is drawing? Hers is much more useful." But to the little girl, Jan's drawing was just silly.

Shortly after that, her mother bought her more dresses, and she began to draw dolls and play house, just like little girls were supposed to. And then one day she just stopped drawing, and she threw the old picture away.

Later when she lay in the grass and looked up at the sky, it was still big and blue and full of everything, but she wasn't any more. She was square and brown inside. Her hands were tight and stiff, and she was like everyone else.

And all those wonderful things inside of her that needed saying, well she decided they just didn't need saying any more.

I felt like that. Tight and stiff, square and brown inside. I felt as if something had died within me, as if I had no dreams, no great vision for myself now. Slowly over time, even though I resisted, I had given myself over to what others thought, what others held to be true about me and my life. And in that giving up, I didn't even know who I was any more.

Oh, I had plans. I was about to start my senior year of college. I was majoring in business, but I didn't know what I wanted to specialize in. My college counselors had pointed me toward areas with job mobility. I had taken tests where I filled in the boxes of multiple-choice questions and later got a computer printout telling me what I should do with my life.

It wasn't that one day I had just caved in to the subtle pressures of conformity. It was a step-by-step process where I had been taught to seek outside of myself for the answers I longed to know.

I had allowed my teachers to tell me if I was smart or gifted in my studies. I had allowed my coaches to tell me about my athletic ability. I had allowed my music instructors to tell me whether or not I could hope to be a professional musician. I even let them tell me if I could sing. It wasn't that these people were negative. From their point of view, they were realistic. They had studied in their respective fields, and they encouraged and acknowledged me when I agreed with their opinions about me. And they made fun of me and put me down when I didn't.

As I lay there in bed, I thought about what I had said when Dr. Hedgewood told me I would lose the use of my left leg. I told him it was okay! I had given them permission to take away the use of one of my legs. What the hell was going on? What had happened to me that I would so easily give up the use of my body? What had happened to the part of me that had dreams, that knew I could have it all?

I buried my face in my pillow and wept. I cried not just because of the fear of living in a body that wouldn't work, but for all of my lost dreams. I cried from a sense of desperation, for I realized I was giving up *me* to become who I should be. By doing so, I had no idea what to do now that the system I had put my trust in was failing me.

I didn't sleep much that night. A nurse came in several times with a pain shot, but I declined each offer. Somehow, the pain wasn't as bad as it had been.

Around five in the morning, the department head of Infectious Disease came in and sat down. He was a kind-looking man in his early seventies, and he had a gentle demeanor. I had a bad night, and as we talked, I felt comforted. I'm not sure why; we really didn't talk about the coming surgery, but I felt better.

When the conversation lulled, he said, "I noticed on your chart that you haven't taken any pain medication since ten last night. Any reason?"

"It just doesn't hurt as much."

"That's odd."

"I have this feeling the infection's broken through to my bowel, so the pressure's relieved. Don't ask me to explain, it's just something I sense."

"Well, I'll pass that on." Standing, he said, "Thanks for sharing your time with me, Terry. I enjoyed our talk."

An hour later, Dr. Griffin came in. "We heard about the change in your pain. So the doctors have decided to postpone the surgery for a few days."

"Really, why?" I asked, not knowing if I was relieved or not, thinking about repeating another hellish night of anticipation.

"Remember they originally wanted to wait until one special general surgeon was back from vacation?"

"I remember."

"Then they decided to go ahead because of the severe pain you were in. Well, now that the pain's no longer a factor, they'd prefer to wait for his return. We're going to discharge you this morning." He asked me what medications I'd need and left to get them.

Karen came in shortly after Dr. Griffin left.

"You're not going to believe this," I told her. "They're discharging me this morning."

Her face lit up then clouded over as quickly. "Have they given up on you," she asked with a quivering voice.

"No, it's nothing like that," I assured her, explaining everything that Dr. Griffin had said.

"We better call the family and tell them not to come," Karen said.

"Good idea." I packed my bag, and we were out of there after breakfast.

≈ ≈ ≈ ≈

The five days spent at home were a nightmare. I walked the rooms at night, my stomach in knots, searching for something to stop the fear that again and again escalated into terror. Even taking the tranquilizers and painkillers, it was a bad, time, and one thought kept nagging at me. What did it mean if the infection had caused a hole in my colon?

Once readmitted, I was told the surgery was scheduled for the next morning. A few hours later, I was given another full N-to-N prep. As I was being shaved, Dr. Griffin came in.

"Hi, Terry, good to see you again," he said. "As soon as you're done there, I'm going to inject the blue dye so it'll have a chance to seep in and color all the infected area during the night."

My eyes grew big, thinking of harrowing pain.

He smiled. "I know what you're thinking. Look." He showed me a syringe. "It's morphine."

When the orderly finished the prep and left, Dr. Griffin gave me the shot of morphine, then he inserted the catheter into the hole in my back and began pushing on the big syringe filled with the dye. This time there was no blockage, and all the dye went in easily. There was also no pain. I only felt pressure in my bowels as he emptied the syringe. When he finished, I got up to use the bathroom while Dr. Griffin cleaned up the instrument tray.

When I sat down on the toilet, a gush of blue dye came out. I opened the bathroom door and called to Dr. Griffin. "You better see this."

He came in and looked into the toilet. "Well, there's the blue dye!" He shook his head. "I'll be right back."

Fifteen minutes later he returned accompanied by Dr. Yelton, the head of the General Surgery Department. I remembered him from the night the committee came to see me. He was in his mid-60s with graying hair, and he didn't seem too friendly.

Dr. Yelton said, "This has to mean the infection has damaged your colon and has made a hole in it. We need to close it immediately so the bacteria in your colon won't get into your abdomen or the other places associated with the infection. This can be very serious. Ever heard of peritonitis?"

"No."

"It's an infection in the lining of the abdominal walls, and it's very dangerous. You don't need this on top of what you're dealing with. We have you scheduled for surgery first thing tomorrow morning.

"If all goes well," he continued, "We'll close the hole in your colon tomorrow, and after you've recovered for a week or so from this minor repair, we'll do the major debridement."

When I came out of the anesthetic the next morning, there was a huge bandage covering the front of my left side just below the belt line. This was my first abdominal surgery, and it was much different than the ones on my back; it had a different kind of pain: not as excruciating as cut bone, but it hurt like hell.

A few hours later, Dr. Yelton came in with his resident and interns. *Another committee*, I thought.

"I'm so sorry, Terry, we couldn't find any specific hole in your colon. The infection has deteriorated your colon so much, it now looks like a sieve. We had to perform a colostomy to prevent further contamination from your bowels."

"A what?" I asked.

"A colostomy. That's where the lower colon is bypassed, and your bowels are diverted to your side. You'll wear a plastic bag that your bowels will empty into."

My head was spinning from this new setback. "Okay," I said, "This is temporary, right?"

Dr. Yelton looked at me for a moment. "I can't say for sure when we can reverse it. A lot depends on your infection. But we'll do everything we can for you."

Later, when a nurse changed the dressings, I saw two holes in my abdomen that looked like a double-barreled shotgun. It was the two ends of my cut colon sewn to my abdomen. As I watched her, I thought, *My God, what is happening to me?*

The next day, they removed my catheter. But I was still having trouble urinating. Finally, thinking gravity might be the answer, I asked an orderly to help me stand so I could pee into a bottle. When it still wouldn't come, I strained to push it out. All of a sudden my abdomen began to spasm, and I was engulfed with pain, so intense I couldn't speak.

As I buckled over, the orderly was afraid I would fall and held on to me. I was panting too hard to be able to tell him to let go, and I needed to lie down to take some pressure off the incision. So I struggled to break his grip, but he misunderstood and wouldn't let go. Finally, with a rush of adrenaline, I pushed him away so hard he flew across the room. As I fell on the bed gasping for breath, a nurse came in and helped the orderly up.

"Sorry," I said to the orderly between gasps of breath, "No idea that . . . was going to happen." I lay on my side holding my abdomen, the incision throbbing with spasms. "Pain's so bad, spasms in my stomach."

"That's all right," the orderly said. "I just didn't understand what was going on."

A few minutes after they left, I felt a wetness spreading over my stomach. I pulled back the covers and saw blood pouring out from under the dressing. Scared, I grabbed a towel, pressed it hard over the bandage, and yelled for help. I thought I was bleeding to death!

One of the nurses and a resident ran in. When he took off the bandages, blood was everywhere. He sent the nurse out for supplies.

"Shit!" I said. It was more blood than I had ever seen.

"Don't worry, this isn't that serious."

His carefree attitude did a lot to calm me down. He applied a pressure bandage and stood there with his gloved hand on the dressing, putting his weight on it.

"God, that hurts," I told him.

"I know, but this is the only way to stop the blood flow."

After nearly half an hour, the surgical site stopped bleeding, but it had swelled monstrously. Within a few hours, Dr. Yelton was back by my side.

"We need to take you back in to surgery to drain the swelling. What you have is called a hematoma, a big bubble of blood. While we're in there, we'll cauterize any bleeders we find."

I didn't like the way he was talking down to me. I felt like he was scolding me as if I was a bad little boy. He reminded me of how Nurse Richards treated me. I wanted to punch him, but I was so beat up emotionally, I just stared at the ceiling.

"Terry, listen, you need to quit pushing yourself, like standing up to go to the bathroom only days after a major surgery. You're in the middle of something that is life-threatening. And the damage to your lower colon is very severe. I don't know if it will ever heal enough for your bowels to be reconnected. You're a very sick boy, and you need to accept that." He turned around and stomped out of the room.

I began to shake with rage. *They* gave me the infection. *They* were destroying my body. And now the son of a bitch made *me* wrong for doing something I didn't even know I wasn't supposed to do.

≈ ≈ ≈ ≈

The next few days in the hospital were the worst I could have imagined. For months I had been preparing for the final surgery that would make me well. And now, just days after I was told that I could never expect to have a body that worked, I was recovering from a surgery that left me with a colostomy. My life was absolutely out of control. Now I went to the bathroom in a plastic bag, and my surgeon doubted that the lower bowel would ever heal enough for the colostomy to be reversed.

In a few short days, I had moved from being confident about my doctors' abilities to get me well to being absolutely at the mercy of this disease. Now that they knew the extent of my problems, the entire medical team changed position about my ability to recover. My doctors didn't believe I would ever again be completely healthy. Now I was like so many other people on my floor who had limitations and were learning as best they could to live with them.

It was a horrible time; I especially hated the colostomy. It was dirty and smelled bad. Even with the nurses helping me, I got my own body waste all over my hands and side whenever I changed the bag and did the required morning irrigation.

After this fifteen-day hospital stay, they wanted me to take a month or so to recover fully from the abdominal surgeries and regain my strength before they operated again. *They're sending me home to get used to going to the bathroom in a plastic bag*, I thought darkly.

At home, I had to spend the first hour of every day irrigating my colostomy. "Irrigation" was too mild—it was hell! I filled my bowels with water through a tube I inserted into the hole in my side. Then I had to hold the water in for about forty minutes while the peristaltic action of my colon worked to push the water out. It hurt, it was humiliating, it was dirty, and I hated it. I *really* hated it.

I had to do this each day so my bowels would empty completely in the morning. Otherwise at some unexpected time during the day, I might have a bowel movement in my shirt. And even with the plastic bag in place, I didn't want that to happen.

During that month, I had a lot of time to think, especially that first hour of the day closed in the bathroom. And every day I got a little angrier. Again and again I remembered those times I had been encouraged to give up my dreams, my priorities, and to conform. Oh sure, I saw myself as a fighter, but in reality I was right on track doing what others thought I should do. My life was going to hell.

The advice wasn't always as blatant as "face reality," "don't try to be something you're not," or "don't be too big for your britches." But the subtle pressures were there, and the anger growing within me wasn't just about my current problems. At first with this health challenge, it was just "oh well, things sometimes are more difficult than we anticipate." Then it was "sometimes you don't get to have it the way you want." Then it became like those people in the infection support group: "Sometimes we have to learn to live with what we do not want."

The boxes I was feeling pushed into appeared a little at a time, and I knew they started by my listening to what others had to say about me. I began to realize that one great obstacle that would keep me from getting what I wanted was conforming to what others thought about themselves and what they thought about me. I also started realizing that others couldn't see something for me that they couldn't see for themselves.

My mind kept coming back to "there are only two choices." I could conform to the world around me, giving up my personal priorities, living my life the way others advised. Or, I could be free, absolutely free to create my life any way I saw fit. There was no middle ground for me. I was either free or I wasn't. And to this day I believe that anything other than absolute freedom leads to depression.

One morning in the bathroom, with both of my hands on the side of my abdomen to prevent water from escaping from my bowels, I made a decision. I would no longer let others determine if my desires were valid or attainable. I knew what I wanted. I wanted to be well again.

I came from good stock. My people were Montana people, and they were fighters. Dad was killed in the Second World War; my mother was widowed two days after I was born. Yet as a single parent with two sons, she put herself through school and earned a Master's degree in education. My brother had been diagnosed with diabetes when he was five and wasn't supposed to live through his teens. All through my life, he was as healthy as anyone I knew.

I had many wonderful aunts and uncles. And the family member who taught me to be a man was my Uncle Larry. He was like a father to me. One of my mother's younger brothers, he and my dad were best friends. When Dad was killed in the war, Uncle Larry assumed the responsibility of teaching my brother and me and loving us as his own. He and Auntie Lil lived across the street from us when I was a little boy, and I grew up calling him "Uncle Dad." He was the one who taught me how to hunt, how to fish. He taught me about being a man. And more than anything, he taught me to stand on my own two feet.

In his heart, Uncle Larry was a Montana cowboy, and he loved a good fight—and I mean barroom brawls. I always thought he was born about a hundred years too late. He was a man's man and a big drinker. I didn't always like him, but I loved him with all my heart, and he loved me as if I was his own son.

One morning while involved with irrigating my colostomy, I sat thinking about my Uncle Larry. I was back on the porch sitting with him listening to his advice. I was eighteen, just out of high school, living with him in Lewiston, Idaho, working my first construction job. We were talking about what it meant to be a man. That's when he looked at me and stated in plain terms, "Son, now that you're a man, there may come a time in your life when you have to fight. Even if you aren't sure you can win, you *will* know you must fight."

I heard his voice as if he was in the bathroom with me, and I knew he wasn't just talking about fistfights. In his own way, he was a philosopher, but on that occasion he didn't elaborate on what he said. He just planted the seed of something he thought was important, as he had done so many times before, and let me figure out what it meant to me.

Remembering his statement started a shift in my overall attitude about myself and what was happening to me. My reality didn't alter immediately. I just noticed small changes in my awareness, small changes in my focus. But as the month wore on, I knew I was becoming different.

That month, I read my first personal growth book, *Psycho-Cybernetics*, written by the famous plastic surgeon, Maxwell Maltz. On page two I underlined:

"This self image becomes a golden key to living a better life because of two important discoveries: (1) All of your actions, feelings, behavior, even your abilities are always consistent with this self image, (2) The self image can be changed."

This idea was more than just fascinating; it held the possibility of being life-changing. I didn't understand how I could control the circumstances in my life, but I knew that I was through listening to what others thought about me.

I had been taught to put my trust in others, listen to their guidance, and follow it. And I had done that, just as I was supposed to, and through no fault of the experts, I had come to a place where they could no longer do it for me. Those I had put my trust in came to the limits of their own abilities, their own beliefs. And then they told me I needed to face the reality they believed in. As I thought about this, I decided next time my answer was going to be "NO!"

I had been pushed far enough. From now on, I would find my own way. I would no longer listen to those who spoke about my limitations. I was going to make up my own rules. Nobody or nothing was ever, again going to tell Terry McBride what he could or could not do. I wasn't sure how I could beat this thing;

I wasn't sure *if* I could beat it. But I did know I was going to fight.

Thirty-five days after the colostomy surgery, I checked into the hospital determined not to seek from others the answers to what would happen to me. I didn't have a calm, sure knowledge of my ability, and my attitude was more belligerent than courageous. But when I thought of others telling me to face reality, I imagined telling them to get out of my way before I crushed them like a bug!

Though I didn't have the courage to hang it on the wall, I kept a poster hidden among my clothes. I took it out and looked at it periodically to remind myself of my new attitude. It was a picture of a big, ugly, hairy guy in a loincloth with a large club over his shoulder and a scowl on his face. The caption beneath the picture read: "Yea, though I walk through the valley of the shadow of death, I shall fear no evil—because I'm the toughest son of a bitch in this valley!"

I was pissed, and I was committed to getting out of the hole I was in. I wanted my health back, I wanted a body that worked, I wanted to get rid of the colostomy, and I would not be denied.

After a day of tests and examinations, the same orderly came in to shave me for the big surgery the next morning. This time as he lathered me up and shaved me front and back, I no longer felt confused. I was not in the same place I had been the first time he prepped me. I did have fear, and I was angry. But there was no terror. For that I was grateful.

After friends and family left that evening and I prepared for sleep, I remembered what the doctors had told me about this coming surgery: "You cannot expect to come out of this one whole."

From deep within me came my response, "The hell I can't!"

CHAPTER 7

IT GETS WORSE

I awoke early the next morning feeling little of the resolve of the night before. I stared out the window into darkness, dreading the two hours that remained before they would come to take me into surgery and glad that it would finally be over.

What condition would I be left in after they cut my body from end to end? What would losing the use of my left leg be like? What other damage might occur? Would I be able to walk, would I be able to make love to my wife?

I was battling to force these despairing thoughts from my mind when the door opened and Karen and Kris came in. With a huge smile on her face, Kris said, "Hi, Daddy!" as she scrambled up on my bed, then curled her soft two-year-old arms around my neck. She smelled like heaven.

My eyes turned to Karen as she sat down beside me. "Hi, honey," she whispered, smiling bravely.

I took her hand. "You okay?" I asked.

"Oh . . . ," her voice trailed off. She shook her head, tears welling in her eyes. I pulled her to me, moving over so she could lie down. Cradled between us, Kris was soon sleeping peacefully. I cherished each second we lay together, clinging to the comfort of our warm intimacy, wishing that I could stop time. I had so much to live for . . . so much to get well for!

My thoughts turned to the feeling I had experienced the night before. I wanted it back. It wasn't a feeling of peace or joy or positive expectancy. It was a sense of readiness, of being alert, a feeling full of anger. I was preparing for the biggest fight of my life. I knew I was going to get my butt kicked, and I wanted to be ready for it. I remembered what Uncle Larry had said, "You may not know if you can win, but you will know when you have to fight!"

As I lay there holding the two most important people in my life, I knew I was ready to do battle for myself and for my family. I promised myself I would get up again and again, no matter how many times I was knocked down, and I was no longer going to buy into anyone else's model for how my life would work. I had always wanted to go into battle for a just cause; now that cause would be me! Finally, I gave myself permission to tell everyone I didn't agree with to go to hell.

I heard a soft knock at the door, and Mary came in. She had been a nurse on that floor for twelve years and had the heart of an angel.

"Sorry, Terry, we have to get you ready now."

Karen moved over to the chair. Kris stayed close by my side, watching every move.

"You know the ropes, Terry." Mary said, motioning for my arm.

"Yeah, I know," stretching my arm out, thankful for a tranquilizer shot to steady my nerves.

I stroked Kris's head as Mary inserted an IV into each arm so they'd be ready for the operating room. When it was time to go, Mary got an orderly to help move my bed.

"Okay, sweetie," Mary said to Kris, "you get to ride with your daddy all the way down the elevator. Think you'd like that?"

Kris smiled up at her and nodded.

I could have kissed Mary for her wonderful kindness, which helped to bolster my resolve. As she and the orderly rolled my bed out of the room, Karen walked beside me, holding my hand.

At the waiting room just outside the surgical center, my mother, stepdad, and Karen's parents were already there. "Now, I'm impressed," I grinned. "Five a.m. is a little early for you guys."

My mother squeezed my hand. "We're going to be here every minute, honey, until you're safe and sound and back in your room."

After a few minutes of sharing, Mary spoke softly, "It's time to go, Terry."

Karen kissed me, wetting my cheeks with her tears. "I'll be praying for you, honey, and I'll be right by your side when you wake up. I know you'll come through this like the fighter you are."

I hugged and kissed Kris, then said, "See you later," as I handed her to her mother.

"Are you going to be all right, Daddy?"

I nodded and said, "I'll be just fine."

The moment we went through the doors into the restricted area, my bravado faded like a sinking stone in water. I wasn't sure I'd be fine, and again was glad they had given me a tranquilizer.

As I fought back tears, Mary stayed by my side, holding my hand until they transferred me to the operating bed. "I'll check on Karen and Kris throughout the day," she said, "so don't you worry about them."

When they wheeled me into the operating theatre, I squeezed my eyes shut, trying to control my fear. Then I heard a doctor say, "Terry, I'm putting something in your IV to help you relax."

Almost instantly, a soothing calm washed over me. I opened my eyes to see Dr. Hedgewood approaching.

"Hi, Terry."

His words seemed to come from far away. "Hey, doc."

"We're going to put you under now," he said.

Through sleepy eyes I said, "Please, be careful," then slipped away.

≈ ≈ ≈ ≈

This was to be the most radical surgical procedure ever attempted by my surgeons for an infection of the spine. Several teams of doctors were involved in the actual surgery, with many more observing. In an effort to find and remove all the infected areas, the plan was to first open me from the sternum to the pubic bone, then turn me over and open me from midback to tailbone. Next, they would open my left buttock, following the sciatic nerve into my left thigh. If necessary, they would go into my right buttock. Finally, they would go between my scrotum and rectum.

One of the residents later confided grimly, "During surgery, we could have shaken hands through your body."

I also was told later my family had endured their own form of suffering that day, watching the action from the cloistered waiting room. Hour after hour, they saw nurses rushing in and out of the surgical area to order and retrieve blood. One time, they saw a nurse burst out and almost run to the desk where she ordered more blood from the blood bank.

After six hours, tension was building in the waiting room, and there was still no end in sight. Finally, a surgical nurse came out to tell them there was nothing to report yet, that they were still operating. "He's handling the procedure well" was the only assurance she could offer.

The hours dragged slowly into afternoon, into evening, and blood was still being taken in. Over the fourteen-hour ordeal, my family saw the surgical support teams, which were assisting the doctors, replaced three times.

At nine p.m., Dr. Hedgewood finally came out after fourteen straight hours in surgery. He was visibly shaking. "We couldn't stop the bleeding," he said. "He took twenty-two units of blood, and we couldn't stop the bleeding."

Staring at his bandaged hands, my mother asked, "Why are your fingers bandaged?"

Dr. Hedgewood steadied his trembling body against the wall as he looked at his hands. "I had to cut so much bone from his spine, the instruments blistered my fingers. Then the blisters broke, and my fingers bled." He stopped and took in a deep breath. "We weren't able to complete the surgery because we were losing him, but he's stable for now."

He explained that I had been under as long as they could push it. My blood had been completely replaced almost three times, and that in itself was dangerous. Combined with the extensive tissue and bone debridement, it made my condition very guarded.

"He's a very sick boy," he said. "We'll know more in the next few days."

In the recovery room that night, one nurse was assigned to be with me at all times, on the alert for signs of complications.

The next morning I was stable enough to be moved and was wheeled back to the orthopedic wing to a room directly across from the nurse's station.

The room was equipped with a "circle bed," a high-tech bed for patients who were too severely injured to be moved or rolled over. They told Karen that the special bed was necessary because any movement would put pressure on one or more of the incisions.

Two enormous wheels were attached at the ends of the bed. When it was time to be turned over, they sandwiched me between two mattresses, then the whole bed would slowly rotate 180 degrees like a spit on a barbecue. When the extra mattress was removed, I'd be lying on my other side.

Karen was with me almost constantly during those first precarious days. I was heavily sedated and went in and out of a coma as I fought for my life. When I temporarily gained consciousness the first day, I was delirious, not remembering where I was. A tube going down my throat into my trachea was taped to my mouth. Panicking, I ripped the tube out, then tore the IV from my arm. Fortunately, Karen was there to calm me, to reassure me that I was okay. For the next few days, for my safety, I was subjected to the added discomfort of being loosely tied down.

Even when awake, I was still delirious and had to have Karen hold my hand. Otherwise I just knew I would die. On the second evening, I was awake, holding Karen's hand, feeling woozy, half asleep. When the resident came in, Karen asked how I was doing.

"He's doing as well as can be expected," he said. "But it appears his kidneys are failing."

"Oh, no," Karen said, looking at me.

The words barely registered to me.

"Well, it's not that bad, really," the resident said. "In fact, we've been watching closely for it. You see, when they opened Terry from the front, they had to disturb his organs to get at the infected tissue and spine. It's not uncommon for the organs to be traumatized and to shut down for a while."

"Oh, I see," she said quietly.

"If there's no change in a day, we'll put him on a dialysis machine to clean his blood. After that, they'll probably kick back in."

The next morning, my kidneys did in fact "kick back in." Karen told me later it was a great relief to her; I was too out of it to celebrate this small victory.

≈ ≈ ≈ ≈

During that time, I had a memory of two "beings" coming to the end of my bed and telling me it was time to go. I grabbed the bed railing and said, "I won't go. I'm not done yet!" At some level I knew I was refusing to die.

On the third day, I woke up sure I was dying and had an urgent need to purge my soul. Clinging to Karen's hand for courage, I disclosed every evil I had ever done, sparing no details. When I was finished, there was a long silence, then she withdrew her hand. I looked over and what I saw made a shiver run down my body. Karen wasn't in the seat—it was my mother-in-law! *Oh, SHIT!* I thought. I had woken up holding my mother-in-law's hand, assuming it was Karen's!

I didn't know if I wanted to laugh or cry, but I did nothing; I was simply too weak. My mother-in-law pretended she hadn't heard a word. And to this day, she has never even hinted at knowing my deepest secrets. Now that's character!

≈ ≈ ≈ ≈

On the fourth day, I woke up early, my head feeling clearer, and I knew the real danger was over. I lay there wondering about the damage to my body. I would be the first one to find out what parts of me worked or didn't. My first concern was my legs. I gathered my courage and instructed my left leg to move. It came up off the bed a few inches, but I was too weak to accomplish more than that. This is great! I thought with relief. The real test would be putting my weight on the leg, but I had hope.

The fifth day after the operation, my condition improved enough for the doctors to go back in to finish the debridement. Although they had to open up my entire left buttock, they only needed to go into my right buttock a few inches.

The next day, I was moved into another room with a regular bed, and the day after that was allowed to get up. Earlier, my body had been so physically devastated from the surgery and blood loss, I hadn't been allowed to stand, let alone try to walk.

When I took the first steps, relief flooded through me. They were shaky steps, but I was physically able to walk.

"I knew you'd be okay," Karen said, as she walked alongside for support. I thought about my resolve to kick this thing, and I stood up a little straighter.

That same day, they took the catheter out. This was another hurdle. Several hours later, my bladder was full, and I felt the glorious sensation of control! A few days later, I woke up with an erection. "Thank God!" I said aloud. *Can't wait to tell Karen*, I thought with a smile.

Somehow, I had come through this incredible surgical procedure without any severe nerve damage. Oh, I was in a great deal of pain and had a lot of numbness (some that would stay with me for years). The doctors were even more tentative about whether my colon would ever heal enough to have my colostomy reversed. But I had won the first round. I had demonstrated to myself that through my own personal commitment, I could make a difference in how my life went.

I really wasn't sure whether or not my change in attitude had made *the* difference. But as Uncle Larry had taught me, "Son, if anything good happens within twenty miles of you, take credit for it." And that's what I tried to do.

However, my "I can make a difference" attitude was short-lived. The surgeons went back in two weeks later to redo the drains. After I was back in my room and awake, Dr. Hedgewood came in and sat down beside my bed, his usually erect British posture replaced with slumping shoulders.

"We found the infection still has a good hold," he said. "We can only hope that with the new drains and antibiotics, it won't spread."

My confidence crumpled, and depression set in.

After a total of thirty-seven days in the hospital and three surgical procedures, I was finally sent home to mend and learn to live with my disease.

CHAPTER 8

AND EVEN WORSE

Within a few days, severe pain returned, caused by new pockets of infection, and I was readmitted to the hospital. I hadn't even been home a week!

When I returned, Dr. Hedgewood was gone. His time as a visiting professor was up, and he had returned to England the previous week. I became a patient of Dr. Kalata, the head of the orthopedic department. He was a hard-nosed, arrogant doctor with an attitude. Dr. Hedgewood would be sorely missed.

After more high-level meetings with the general surgery and infectious disease specialists, they decided on another course. They told me they would cut out all the skin, muscle, and connective tissues down to my spine. Rather than close the wound, they would leave it open and put me in a body cast to restrict my movements so I wouldn't be able to bend. Leaving the wound open would let the tissues granulate, or heal, from the inside out and leave no place for the infection to take hold. Also, with access to my spine, it would allow them to try some new procedures with antibiotics that might have more of an effect. I was told I'd be in the cast for about six months, which would mean I would not be able to go to school the next quarter.

When I awoke from surgery, my body was in a cast from my armpits to just above my knees. The cast had an opening in the back where the tissue had been removed; bandages were covering that area. The cast also had an opening in the front left side for the colostomy bag and one between my legs for my genitals. It was designed so that my legs were spread apart, with a foot-long brace between the knees to give the cast strength.

The bandages on my back were changed twice daily. On the third day after surgery, I was curious about the operation and wound. When an intern came in to change the bandages, I asked, "Could you get a couple of mirrors so I could see what it looks like?"

"That would be kind of hard with you in the cast," he said. "And we don't really have the right kind of mirrors around."

I could tell the intern didn't want me to see the surgical site, which confused me because they had always accommodated me in the past. *What was the big deal?* I thought. Well, I'd find out.

Taking matters into my own hands, I had a friend bring in a small wall mirror and set it on the windowsill next to my bed. He also brought me a hand-held mirror, which I hid in my nightstand. I practiced pushing myself up on my side, which was no small task while in a body cast from nipples to knees. After I got it down, I waited for my chance.

The next day during one of the two dressing changes, when the intern moved to get new bandages, I pushed myself onto my side, took the hand-held mirror from under my pillow, and looked at my reflection in the windowsill mirror. What I saw shocked me so much I almost dropped the mirror. In the cutout space of the body cast, I saw a gaping wound, like a raw steak. There were two pieces of red, raw meat side by side, each about two inches wide and a foot long from my mid-back down to my buttocks where there was a hole big enough to put my fist in. Between these two strips of raw flesh was an almost transparent tissue covering what looked like a yellow bumpy thing.

When the doctor turned back and saw me, he just shook his head.

"What's that yellow thing?" I asked.

"That's your spine, Terry. Lie down."

When I lay back down, I was horrified. I felt like I was going to vomit. I broke out in a cold sweat. First they had mutilated my front with the two ends of my colon sewn onto my stomach, and now they had destroyed my back! How was I going to function with no meat, no tissue, no muscle over my spinal column?

"What in God's name have they done to me?" I cried.

"I thought they explained it all before the surgery," he said.

"You've got to be kidding! I didn't hear them say they were going to destroy my back!"

"I know it looks bad, but it will heal," he offered. "It's a good plan."

"Yeah, right," I quipped.

After the intern left, I lay there seething. Every time I envisioned my ruined back, I became more enraged until my body was shaking. These were supposed to be great surgeons, but now I felt like they were a bunch of butchers, and I was the side of beef they were butchering.

Some would say that the outrage and horror I felt was just a transfer of some inner anger about myself or some other bullshit like that. But unless one has seen his or her body being taken apart one piece at a time, explanations like that are just book-learned knowledge. And knowledge alone doesn't come close to feeling the visceral rage and horror of the experience itself.

I had felt lost before, knowing there was nothing I could do. Now I also felt like I was being destroyed physically. I lay there in a body cast unable to care for myself, with a plastic bag attached to my abdomen for my solid waste and a tube up my penis so I could urinate. And slowly my anger turned to deep despair.

Beaten down, I slipped completely into the belief that there was no way to be whole again. They had cut out and tossed away the muscles in my back. What would be next?

I went to sleep that night in a black depression. Around midnight, I awoke. My bowels were about to move, but the plastic bag to catch my body waste had come loose. I grabbed a small towel for wiping up spills and shoved it into the hole in the cast. Pressing it hard against the opening of my bowels with both hands, I held back my own body waste.

I got it in time, but if I let go with either hand, the waste would pour out into the cast. The door to my private room was closed, and the nurse call button was pinned up by my head where I couldn't reach it unless I let go of the towel. I tried to get it with my mouth, but the body cast wouldn't let me move that far. I was completely at the mercy of my diseased body, and there was nothing I could do about it.

For about thirty minutes, I called for help; my screams were getting louder and hoarser. *Where the hell were they?* I kept calling until I was beside myself with outrage and despair. My arms were getting tired holding the towel, and I hurt all over. Finally, the door opened and two night-shift nurses rushed in.

"Where were you . . . where *were* you?"

"Oh, Terry, we're so sorry! We were at the other end of the hall working with a lady in trouble. We didn't hear you."

"The bag's come off and I couldn't reach the call button." Suddenly, emotions flooding me, I began sobbing and couldn't stop. I had gone over the edge, and there was no way back. All my talk about fighting was lost. I didn't want to be here any more. It was too much. The terrible things that were being done to my body and the prospects of living with what was going to be left were no longer tolerable. I wanted to die.

"Terry, it's going to be okay," one nurse said, trying to calm me.

She put her hands on the towel so I could release mine, while the other nurse found the bag. They got it back on me without letting too much of the waste leak out. But it didn't matter to me any more. It was over. I had given up and I knew it.

The next day, the staff could tell I was in serious trouble. I met each question with grunts and closed eyes. I ignored their encouragement. I took all the pain medication I could and checked out, drifting in and out of a drug-induced sleep.

Two days later, the surgeons went back in to do another cleaning out. During this surgery they found that the infection was again spreading. This news was the last nail in the coffin of any remaining hope I had.

Time and time again when I asked my doctors what they thought, I was told that sooner or later there would be permanent damage. They said up until now I had been lucky. Although they were no longer specific about what damage would occur, they were consistent in their belief that I could not expect to come out of this whole.

In the four-and-a-half months since coming to the University Medical Center, I had seven major surgical procedures. I was a mess both physically and mentally. And they told me this was the way it was going to be for the rest of my life! I wanted out of the pain and trauma that was being done to my body. I simply couldn't take the mental strain any more.

Some of the finest minds in medicine believed that the infection in my spine was not curable and that it was highly likely I would become disabled. Although I learned about the following letters much later, they confirm the attitudes and conversations of my doctors. In response to a letter from the insurance company, my doctor wrote:

"This has been a particularly trying case to manage because of the severity of the problem and the many ramifications of the infectious process. However, it is pertinent to say that at this juncture, it is highly likely that Mr. McBride will be left with significant permanent disability."

In a second letter written some months later, my doctor wrote:

"This is a chronic osteomyelitis that is really not curable. I would anticipate, unless Mr. McBride is extremely fortunate, that new abscess formation and symptoms will probably reoccur and require subsequent hospitalization and drainage."

From my doctor's own lips, I knew the raping and pillaging of my flesh and mind would be never-ending, ever-present, and I couldn't take it any more. As far as I was concerned, it was over. I wanted out. For weeks all I thought about was dying. Then came the night that my "daughters" saved my life.

At this time, I had learned how to stand in my body cast, and a couple of times a day I got up to brush my teeth and pee. The doctors told me they didn't want me to do that, but I didn't care what they wanted. They could all go to hell.

The cast went to my knees with my legs spread apart by the brace between them that supported the cast. I was standing by my sink that night brushing my teeth when Karen and Kris came in. As always, Kris lit up when she saw me. This was the first time she had seen me standing in the cast. Before I knew what was happening, she ran to me, grabbed the brace between my legs and swung, ready as always to play with her daddy. The momentum pulled me forward, and as I started to fall, Karen rushed up and helped me regain my balance. For a second, fear jolted through me as I saw myself crashing into the sink, bouncing onto the floor.

"Kris! What the . . . ." I stopped the scolding on my tongue. Hobbling to the bed, I flopped on it. I wasn't happy and it was obvious. Even though I hadn't seen her for several days, I brooded, lost in my own troubles. It wasn't fun being around me any more, and they only stayed for thirty minutes.

As they were leaving, I noticed Kris was crying.

"What's wrong with Kris?" I asked.

Karen looked me right in the eyes and said, "Your daughter misses you more than you know. She's been sitting on your bed trying to play with you for half an hour, and all you've done is complain that the nurses were ten minutes late with your pain shot."

As they walked out the door, Kris turned and through her tears said, "'Night, Daddy."

After they left, I kept seeing Kris's tear-streaked face, and my heart broke over my thoughtlessness. My whole life was going to hell in a hand basket. When I thought things couldn't get any worse, they did. But what could I do? I was being taken apart physically and mentally one piece at a time. And every day it got worse. Now it was affecting those I loved the most, and my depression deepened.

Even with the sleeping pill that night, I couldn't get to sleep. I kept coming back to Kris. If it had just been Karen, I might have checked out and let her find someone else to share her life with. But if I left now, either in form or by sinking deeper into the depression that had a grip on me, I would leave Kris, and I would not get to be the kind of father I had always wanted for myself. And she would never really have a dad. At least that's how I thought about it, and that thinking made me feel even worse.

Hours later I finally fell into a restless sleep. In the middle of the night I had a life-changing dream.

During that year, Karen and I had been trying to complete our family so the two children would be close in age. She had two miscarriages. Her doctors said it had nothing to do with her; it was just nature's way of making sure only healthy fetuses grew to full term. So we kept trying.

In the dream I was with Kris. She was just there, loving me, and I knew the reason she had been crying when she left wasn't because she was hurt by my actions and inattention. She was crying because her daddy was giving up and thinking about leaving her. Words weren't exchanged; it was more of a knowing.

Then Kris seemed to call to someone, and beside her appeared another being. I had the impression this radiant presence was another little girl. Kris stood there so very proud to be holding this little one's hand.

The other little girl wasn't sad. I'm not even sure she was loving; she was defiant. She looked right at me as if to tell me that I was not leaving. There was no anger in her expression. She just knew the way it was going to be for her, and I was expected to play along. They stood there holding hands in solidarity, sending the message that I did not have a choice; I was staying. I believed there was still room for me to have my say in this life of mine, but from their reality, I was staying.

It was a vivid dream, a realization, and I was certain I had met my future daughter. When I awoke, I knew I was not going to die. I wasn't even supposed to think about doing that, at least not now. As Uncle Larry would have said, "These two little ones have read to you from 'the Book'."

I didn't jump out of my depression all at once, but as the days wore on, I kept thinking, *What the hell!* The infection had taken its best shot at beating me, and I still didn't have any permanent limitations. I had big holes in my front and my back, but those could heal, and I could still fight. In the long run, this thing could beat me, but I had the choice of whether or not I would go out like a whipped puppy or go down fighting. If I couldn't or wouldn't do that for myself, I should at least do it for Kris and that little person who wasn't here yet.

My physical and mental conditions were much worse than they'd been when I first decided to fight. Then the fight, the challenge was only in theory, based on what the doctor's had said and what I thought that meant. It was like a John Wayne movie where it's easy to talk tough and strong. But now I had been beaten and kicked. I was in the middle of this battle, bloody and surrounded by disease, and I could see no way out. I had no way of foreseeing how bad it would get, and I never dreamed it would be this devastating to my body and my mind. There was no question I was down, but damn it, I didn't have to stay down.

About two weeks after my dream, I made up my mind. Physically and mentally, it was time to stand up again, get back in the game, and kick some ass. That's how I felt about it. It wasn't pretty, it wasn't loving, and it wasn't full of understanding or peace. It was about power, self-determination, and commitment. I had two little girls depending on me, and I was going to be bigger and tougher than anything that could happen to me!

In my cast, I struggled up and got over to my closet. I took out my poster of the big, ugly, hairy guy in a loincloth and hung it in clear view on my wall. I stepped back and read the words aloud, accepting them as my own: "Yea, though I walk through the valley of the shadow of death, I shall fear no evil, for I am the toughest son of a bitch in this valley!"

CHAPTER 9

COMMITMENT BRINGS HELP

When I woke up the next morning and saw the poster, I smiled. I knew it could raise some eyebrows, but I wanted it there to remind me of the commitment I had made. I knew I had to start focusing again on what I was going to do to combat this terrible thing that stood between where I was now and where I wanted to be.

I didn't expect that I would suddenly have a bright, shiny new attitude. After all, I was still living in hell with a body that seemed broken beyond repair. But I had support in many forms to help my new focus in taking charge of my life.

Around the time my doctors began to say they couldn't fix me, admitting they had reached the limits of their science—the limits of their beliefs about healing—people began bringing me books and articles dealing with the part I could play in regaining my health.

I didn't have much interest in the materials at the time. After all, I was just trying to survive and had been stuck in my anger and self-pity. But now that things had settled down and

I would be in a body cast for months, I decided to explore this material. Some of it was about individuals who beat the odds. Some was about the methodologies that allow people to take charge of their lives. For the most part it was good, positive input. Not all of it touched me or seemed useful, but I was grateful and inspired by the new concepts I was being exposed to.

One sheet, which was sent in a get-well card, was to become my standard for how I wanted life to work for me. It was a quote, which read:

On Commitment
"The moment one definitely commits oneself, then Providence moves too. All sorts of things occur to help one that would never otherwise have occurred. A whole stream of events issues from the decision, raising in one's favor all manner of unforeseen incidents and meetings and material assistance which no one could have dreamed would have come their way."

Spending months in a private room gave me time to think, and I had an abundance of great material to think about. Over and over, one thing kept coming into my awareness. In the year following the fusion, even with all the surgeries and talk about complications, I had received very little written information about how to take control of my life, but as soon as I decided to fight, a wealth of material started showing up to support me in my fight.

Just like it said in the quote, the moment I committed, all sorts of things occurred to help me in that specific commitment. I began to believe that "Providence" was moving too. I wasn't even sure what "Providence" meant exactly, but I felt that I was not alone in my fight.

As days turned into weeks, I continued to read and absorb the material, but it wasn't as if I was always on purpose or on track with success blinders to help me stay focused. Hell, I'd never been really disciplined and rarely stayed on track for long. I was not what one would call a great success. If I thought to win this fight I'd need to work really, hard and always be focused, then I was lost to begin with.

Yes, some of the material I read inferred that lots of hard work and self-denial were required to win in the face of insurmountable obstacles, but I wasn't ready to buy into that. Besides, most theories I was studying said I could start right where I was now and simply do what I could do. Then as time went along, I would learn I could do more.

One major advantage I had in my studying was the constant reminder that one of the greatest disciplines in the world—modern allopathic medicine—had come to the limits of its reality about me, and those who believed in that discipline told me I couldn't win. Because of that, I was not going to accept any doctor's reality about me—or anybody else's. I did not care how much they had studied or what they were supposed to know. Nor was I going to let some new discipline, some new methodology become my guru or my truth. And that attitude spilled over into my exploration of miracles. I know that the word "miracle" has a different meaning for everyone, but that's what I needed—a *miracle*.

Earlier, in a conversation with one of the doctors, I finally squeezed out of him what he thought the odds were regarding my getting well. He said, "At least a million to one against you."

I thought for me to be that "one," it would take a miracle, and it would be up to me to make that miracle happen. At that point in my private war, it seemed clear: if it was going to be, it was up to me.

What I liked best in the books and articles was the idea that each of us has something within our own beings, a wonderful facet of ourselves, that is always moving us toward what we believe to be true.

I knew I had heard it all before. How much clearer does it get than "as ye believe so shall it be done unto you," or "as a man or woman thinks in their heart so are they," or "consciousness creates reality"?

But always before when I was exposed to the idea that we are the creators of our lives, I was too busy to listen. I was too busy buying into the model I currently believed in, and certainly too busy to explore either my beliefs about myself or my beliefs about how life worked. It was easier to listen to whoever the current experts were and try to do it their way.

But this time, as I was exposed to personal-growth and self-determination ideas, I heard what was being said. I brought it in and thought about it. That didn't mean I accepted the information as "the truth." But I looked at the concepts and thought about how the information being presented might assist me to get what I wanted.

In all the reading, what really got me excited was the evidence that any of us can start right where we are now and begin moving toward our dreams, our own personal priorities. Oh, there might be something or someone out there or even a part of me that would say "no, you can't" or try to tell me what I should be moving to. But that was just negative programming, old limiting beliefs, or someone in one way or another saying "face reality." And I didn't have to listen to that any more; I didn't have to believe that any more. I wasn't interested in facing anybody's reality, because I knew for me to get what I wanted out of my life, I would need to be able to *create* reality, not face it!

Taking charge of my life wasn't an easy-flowing experience. I didn't get it figured out all at once. The process of understanding my own personal power (and how I could use this power to get what I wanted) seemed full of inconsistencies and contradictions. And one of the most troublesome aspects of the personal-growth disciplines I studied was that most teachers wanted some allegiance to the methods they taught.

Too many teachers inferred that their way was the best way, and that only by accepting their methodology, their discipline, as the "true path" could I hope to gain freedom. But I had already tried that with the medical system. I had given up my power, my ability to choose freely, and accepted that some-one else or some discipline knew what was best for me and where my limitations were. Doing that did *not* allow me to get what I wanted. So now I was on guard. I made sure that what I was studying and accepting within myself all fit into my model of "the hell I can't."

While I was absorbing new concepts and trying to shift my beliefs, I realized that "the hell I can't" seemed to be a nega-tive way of stating "yes, I can." But I couldn't change my model at that time because truthfully, I really didn't know if I could win. I had never excelled before or been singled out as the best in anything. Besides, that wasn't where I was starting from. This was a fight. This was what Uncle Larry had talked about on the porch that night. It was just as he said it might be: I wasn't sure I could win, but I did know I had to fight. And I especially needed to fight against the establishment and the people "in the know" who wanted to put me in the boxes they believed in.

"The hell I can't" was the cornerstone of my fight. Later, if I needed to, I could try to shift it to something more positive. But for now, it was enough to be discovering the secrets of self-determination so I could fight better. And I had learned my lesson well; I was always on guard not to blindly believe in what I was studying.

CHAPTER 10

THERE IS POWER IN CHOICE

While I was in and out of the University Medical Center, I was in my senior year in college, working toward a Bachelor's degree in business administration. In the past, I had been highly creative in finding ways to get my course work done. Sometimes friends would bring my assignments to the hospital, where I used my free time to study.

Since the hospital was on the same campus as the school, there was one time when the hospital allowed me to leave for a few hours to take a midterm exam. I arranged to have a golf cart available and someone to take me to my class. I had no business being out of the hospital; I was still on morphine, but I went anyway! I didn't get a very good score on the test, but I had great fun. And I was very original in my answers.

As a finance and marketing major, I was learning how to understand business information and thereby be better at allocating the resources at hand to achieve a higher degree of business success.

That's the way I approached the personal-growth information I was reviewing. I wanted to achieve specific results, and I was studying the resources or assets I could use to make those results happen.

One such resource came from an unexpected corner. I found a ready sounding board in Mary, my nurse ally. She was working evenings now, and one night shortly before Mary's shift was ending, she came in to see if I needed anything. Just then, the backs of my thighs under the cast were itching terribly.

"I can't reach my thighs, and they're driving me crazy from itching. Is there anything you can do?"

She thought for a moment. "I'll be right back," she said. "Don't go anywhere."

We both laughed and before the smile was gone from my face, she was back with a coat hanger.

"The answer to your prayers. Watch."

I did, as she pulled the hanger from the top and bottom to make a long, narrow round end perfect for sliding between the cast and my thigh.

"This should do it," she said, as she sat down on the side of the bed. I pulled myself up on one side a bit, and she slid the hanger under the cast and gently rubbed in and out scratching my thighs.

"This is heaven, Mary! You can't imagine how frustrating it is not being able to scratch an itch."

The next night before she left, she came in with the hanger without asking. Soon it was a nightly ritual and something I looked forward to all day.

Each night for the ten minutes or so it took her we would chat. Soon we developed a rhythm born from routine. She began to ask me about what I was reading, and I found she was very interested in the information I was studying.

During the day, I would read from a book or article and think about what I'd share with her. When I'd talk about ideas with her, they would come alive.

She'd usually start with, "So what did you learn today?"

"You know, out of all the information I'm reading, I especially like the ideas in self-image psychology that state I have a success-striving part of me that will automatically move me to get what it's programmed to get."

"Interesting. Why does that appeal to you?"

"Because they say I can choose the program. I can change my self-image, my consciousness, my beliefs about myself, and if I do that I can change the results I'm having in my life."

I went on to explain that the books and articles I was reading addressed success in money, relationships, health, and so much more. In their own way, each spoke to me about freedom. I could be free of old habits and old patterns, and change the way I did things.

"I see," she said as she did her magic with the hanger.

"Yeah, it's as if I have an autopilot inside of me that's always moving me to the destination it's programmed to achieve."

Some called this autopilot the subconscious mind, some the creative consciousness. Others called it the subjective or the supraconscious mind. Some even referred to it as the law of cause and effect.

Although many disagreed on what the autopilot was and how it achieved these results, they all seemed to agree on how it worked.

"Listen to this." I had earmarked a page I wanted to read to her. 'Once the autopilot is programmed, it will move with mechanical regularity to achieve that program. And, like any autopilot, as it gathers data, it will make adjustments as it literally zigzags its way to the goal or outcome it was programmed to seek.'"

"This is powerful stuff you're studying, Terry. I'll be interested to hear what you come up with tomorrow." As she turned to leave she said, "Now you have a good night."

After she left, I thought about our conversation and how much I was learning. Until that time, my life seemed like it had been a huge jigsaw puzzle with untold pieces that gave me no clue as to what the finished picture was going to be. The concepts of self-image psychology inspired and led me to believe I could create the end result—the picture my life was going to be—and then my autopilot would begin to arrange the pieces to create the picture I chose. There was a freedom inherent in self-image psychology that ignited something within me that I can only describe as joy.

As I thought about this, I realized that as I had accepted the responsibilities of having a family, I began to see that I was using my bravado and loner attitude to hide the fact that I had been changing to fit some programmed patterns and beliefs. My life had really become about not biting off more than I could chew, not risking too much in case I lost. I could hear an inner voice saying, "Don't try to be someone you're not. Be careful what you ask for, be careful what you pray for."

In those ideas of being careful, I had lost my dreams, my excitement, my freedom. Yes, I had hopes and aspirations, but they weren't my *dreams*. They were wants that were tempered with various facets of facing reality.

But these new ideas were based on the concept that all things are possible if I believe they are. And I could choose my belief. Time and time again, I was reminded that I could stand up for myself and choose again. One book said, "The great methodologies pertaining to healing have within them the possibility that finally one can be done with the problem."

Even Alcoholics Anonymous, the foundation for many of the twelve-step programs, and one of the finest methodologies about healing and creation on the planet, begins with the idea of complete recovery. The forward to the first edition of the AA book published in 1939 starts with:

> "We of Alcoholics Anonymous are more than one hundred men and women who have recovered from a seemingly hopeless state of mind and body. To show other alcoholics precisely how we have recovered is the main purpose of this book."

I had experienced that hopelessness in mind and body. To me it was the terror I felt when they said I could not expect to come out of this illness whole. It was the helplessness I felt as I witnessed my own body being destroyed one piece at a time.

The material I was studying said I could choose my destination, the outcomes I wanted, and begin right where I was to make them come true. It didn't matter that I was sick; it didn't matter that the odds against my getting well were a million to one. Time and time again I was reminded that I could do it. I could recover from this hopeless state. And from a place deep within, I began to look forward to my future.

I still had down times, but it seemed that studying the principles of success kept the negatives and the problems of my everyday experience within tolerable limits. I was finally learning about how powerful I was and how the choices I made could make a difference in the quality of my life.

Just as my commitment to fight had set in motion the unforeseen events and material assistance that gave me information about my own power, the other choices I could make would also bring support. As the Commitment quote said, "The moment one definitely commits oneself, then Providence moves too. All sorts of things occur to help one that would never otherwise have occurred." I was studying the tools of choice that would allow me to commit to anything I wanted, and Providence would move to support and help me in that commitment, whatever it was.

First I could use goal setting, not as a way of beating myself up for what I didn't have or wasn't getting, but simply as a way of choosing what outcome I was focusing on. I could go after my heart's desire.

I learned to write out my priorities concerning what I wanted and to review them before my day got into high gear. If I didn't have them written so I could review them, then I found I could get so busy with other stuff that by the end of the day, I would realize I hadn't been focused on going toward what I wanted. My written goals acted like blinders that kept me moving forward toward what I wanted rather than being distracted by all the other possibilities available to me.

I still wasn't sure if I really could get well. I wasn't even sure what real health was about any more. But the study of taking charge of my life (and writing out what I wanted and what it would be like to have it) started to move me away from just fighting the disease and pointed me to the possibility of creating health.

But just studying the tools of choice (and once in a while feeling a sense of power and wonder about taking charge of my life) did not make the evidence that I was extremely sick disappear. Sometimes I would review my goals or read exciting stories about real people who achieved success in the face of insurmountable obstacles and feel a great surge of hope. Then I'd be taken to an exam room where a group of doctors and nurses would look up my backside with an instrument they jokingly referred to as the silver stallion. All the while I'd hear them make comments about how it was unlikely that I would ever be able to heal, and my newfound hope would be severely challenged.

Over and over I heard my doctors tell each other or even tell me that I was lucky I hadn't had any severe nerve damage *yet*. And the "yet" was always in the back of my mind, tucked away with information like the doctor's letter that read, "It is highly likely that Mr. McBride will be left with significant permanent disability." But I knew that if I didn't study choice, if I didn't come back to what I wanted, then I surely couldn't expect to come out of this whole.

As I continued absorbing the material, I realized that the second major aspect of choice as I understood it was my choice of action. I discussed this with Mary.

"Most of the stories or books about taking control of my life say I need to make a list of things I need to do, or actions, to accomplish my goal."

"Tell me more."

"Well, the theory around having a written plan is the same as creating a road map to get me to a place I've never been before. I can make a list and divide up what needs to be done into bite-sized pieces that allow me to believe I can do it."

"That sounds like a good thing to do."

It did to me, too. When I studied the concept of taking specific action steps, I paid close attention because I sure didn't know what to do. So as I studied, my to-do list became more and more complex. Even so, it was exciting to be exposed to how to do it, how to get what I wanted.

We chatted a few minutes more until Mary was finished. After she left, I thought about our conversation. The planning aspect of choice reminded me of the first time I attempted to climb Mt. Rainier in Washington State, prior to hurting my back. As Jim, my instructor and climbing partner, and I approached a small ice wall that we were going to climb, I became overwhelmed by the immensity of it, even though it was only around two hundred feet high. Jim saw my apprehension and asked me to mentally pick out a route where we could leapfrog up the wall in twenty-foot increments. He had studied the wall as we approached it and pointed out some possibilities he thought we could try. As he made coffee, I laid out my plan of attack starting with his suggested route.

When I was done, I showed him the route and explained how we could do it if he took the lead in the most difficult parts.

"Okay. Now, are there any individual parts you couldn't climb with my help?" he asked.

"No."

"Good. Remember, we aren't going to climb the whole wall. We're just going to climb that little part, then that little part, and that little part. When we're all done with the little parts, we'll be at the top."

That's the way we climbed the whole mountain. In its totality, it looked huge and insurmountable. But when the climb was broken down into individual pieces, it became simply a matter of following the plan and putting one foot in front of the other.

And that's the way it was with my health challenge. In its totality, the infection in my spine and the resulting complications appeared impossible to overcome. But when I was focused on the positive outcome I wanted and continued my study of success principles, I began to think I could find a way. If I could make a plan with little steps, why couldn't I accomplish what others had done? They had faced real challenges and had chosen to beat the odds, and they had succeeded. If they could do it, why couldn't I?

I tried to convince myself that it was simply a matter of finding the right game plan and then sticking to it until I got what I wanted. One of my favorite sayings about winning supposedly came from Sir Winston Churchill who said, "Never give up. Never, give up."

I made that another of my mottoes. I would develop written and specific goals, and I would never, give up.

The third major concept of choice was that I could choose my own mental environment. I already had a voice in my head that flowed with constant chatter. This area of choice, sometimes called affirmations or self-talk, was about choosing what the internal voice would say.

When Mary came in the next day, I was eager to share. "Mary, I'm learning about how I can control my thoughts. They call it self-talk, and they say it's one of the main ingredients in the reprogramming or reconditioning of my self-image."

I pulled out Dr. Maltz' book. Mary was used to me having quotes ready to read to her. "Just like it says here, 'All of our actions, behaviors, even our abilities are always consistent with our self-image.' Pretty good, huh? We act like the kind of person we think we are."

Mary thought for a moment. "You know, that makes a lot of sense."

Over and over, I read about the incredible power of thought and how my thoughts influenced my results. Some authors referred to controlling our thoughts as mind power, and at first I didn't like that term because I associated it with negative practices like voodoo or witchcraft. But as I continued to study, I found most were simply referring to my ability to choose my thoughts so they would support the outcomes I wanted.

Affirmations helped me choose what I was thinking about. I could consciously choose my thoughts or choose to be exposed to situations or information that inspired me about my ability to win. I could watch movies or read books that inspired me. I could listen to good music or talk with positive people. There were many ways I could take control of my internal voice so it was supportive and consistent with my staying focused.

It was through my exploration of affirmations that I began to realize how powerful the negative influences had been in creating my state of hopelessness and quiet desperation. I couldn't count the times that others had told me to quit being a dreamer and face reality, or how many times I had asked my doctors what they thought my chances were, knowing their opinions were not how I wanted it to be.

Through the study of affirmations, I learned how I could control my mental environment. And part of that control could be to eliminate the negative input of others. I could stop listening to and asking for opinions that didn't support me in believing I could do what I wanted. I could also write out positive statements that spoke to my ability, and reminded me that I was studying and learning how to use choice to create the reality I longed for.

Sometimes these practices didn't make much of a difference; other times I was absolutely set on fire with positive expectations. Even lying in my hospital bed surrounded by evidence of my disease, I could focus my attention and intention on the innate power I had within me to create. Through that focus, sometimes I felt powerful and could feel that it was really possible for things to work out the way I wanted.

The fourth major tool I explored in the area of creating

belief was the use of my creative imagination through what is sometimes called visualization.

That night when Mary came in, I was eager to bounce these ideas around because the material said that creative visualization was a powerful tool in changing the self-image.

"I've been reading about visualization, that my mind can't tell the difference between a real experience and a vividly imagined one. That means if I can imagine something in enough detail, my mind will take that imagined experience and record it as memory. Isn't that a great idea?"

"Yes, it is," she said as she relieved the itching under my cast with her trusty hanger. "I've read about it myself. I think there's a doctor somewhere using that idea to help cancer patients visualize away their cancer."

"You know, Mary, I'm not sure I can do this. Most of the material on visualization describes seeing the desired outcome in pictures, and I don't daydream in pictures. I've been trying it, but I don't think I'm doing it very well."

"Don't worry, with practice you'll get better," she said, rising. She patted my arm and smiled. "I know your motto is to never give up—you'll figure it out."

Mary's little encouragements bolstered my efforts to understand and use these new principles. I wanted to try to get underneath the specifics of how to use visualization, so I could understand how they could work for me. The more I read, the more I hoped that by integrating my choices, I really could create a new belief about my health and greatly improve my chances of getting what I wanted.

There were many variations on how to use these tools and what was right for me to be choosing. Yet to me, they all seemed to have the same central theme. I could conform to what others said about me and what I could expect my life to be like, or I could choose something else. I could choose a new destination, a new possibility, and develop an action plan to get there. I could choose new thoughts that would support me, and finally, I could use my imagination to build new beliefs.

It all made sense that my thoughts, actions, and feelings had some effect on the results I could achieve. But would the actions I could take and the thoughts and beliefs I could choose really be the key to creating the health I wanted when the consensus of opinion was that I needed a miracle?

It seemed to me that just changing my beliefs was only a part of what I would need to do to get well. I needed to beat million-to-one odds, and to me that would require more than just a positive attitude. As I studied, I began to think I might be leaving something out of the equation.

In the material I was reading, the references to miracles inferred that they were only possible because of "God power." The authors used different names for this power, but in the great discourses on human endeavors, miracles were attributed to the Divine, and I wasn't sure where I should look to understand this or who I should believe about how this "God" stuff worked. So I decided I'd have a long talk with my Uncle Larry about it when I got out of the hospital.

I was finally going home in a few days. The skin graft over my spine had healed, the body cast was removed, and I would be released after only three months instead of the anticipated six. Even though I was terribly weak and would need to build up my strength, I was thrilled to get back home, not only because I had missed my family and a normal life, but because I'd be able to get back to school.

During the first days at home, I continued to think about God power and how to use it. I had a wonderful extended family of uncles, aunts and cousins. Many of them were very active in their respective religions or denominations. But in the past, when they had talked to me about God, I had the feeling they were just reciting their doctrine but were not willing or able to really explore religion and spirituality with an open mind of discovery.

I had been raised going to church and Sunday school. I had been baptized. I believed in God, and I considered myself a Christian. Karen and I went to church—not all the time—but it was part of what we did. However, I had never actively tried to make the "Divine" part of my everyday existence.

On the third day home, I went to see Uncle Larry. We sat out in his back yard in North Seattle drinking beer and tomato juice.

"Red beer—the best health drink in the world," he said.

I laughed. How good it was just to sit outside feeling the sun and the breeze on my skin.

After small talk about Karen and Kris, I said, "Uncle Larry, I'm chewing on a tough question, and I need your help. Do you think I should start reading the Bible?"

He looked at me with that twinkle he would get in his eye and started to rub his chin. He always did that when he was thinking something through. Finally he smiled and said, "You ought to ask your Uncle Creathe about that one. He's a deacon or something like that, and he knows all about that stuff. Or ask Murray. He's a Catholic, or his wife Pat is, and Catholics, they know everything." Then he sat there smiling at me.

"Yeah, I know," I said. "I've talked with them all through the years about religion, but I think they'll just recite their own beliefs, and I need more than that. I've been reading about different kinds of beliefs."

He looked up at the sky for a moment, then turned to me. "Well, son, I don't read the Bible. Oh, I've read some of it in past times, but I don't read it now. I believe in God, and I think Jesus was one great teacher. And I think I'll be going to heaven when my time's done. But then I think we're all going to heaven, and I don't think the idea is right that only a select few really got it down the 'true way.' So I don't think you'd be in trouble with God if you didn't read the Bible."

"I'm not worried about getting in trouble with God. I'm worried about getting well."

There was a long silence. He rubbed his chin again then asked, "Do your doctors believe they're going to be able to fix you?"

"No, they think I'll end up in a wheelchair." I paused for a minute and said, "I think it will take a miracle for me to get well."

Almost before I was done, he blurted out in his best cowboy talk, "You need a miracle? Then if I was you, I'd read the Bible!" and we laughed.

"But really, Uncle, why should I read it?"

He paused for a moment then smiled and said, "If you're laying in your hospital bed some night praying and God does show up, you know how authors are, the first question He'll ask you is 'Have you read my book?' "

I laughed so hard I thought I was going to fall off my chair. He had a wonderful way of teaching me by making a very serious subject light and fun.

Then he continued, "Using the force of God or Spirit to help you create something is much like anything else. In carpentry, if you want to learn how to build something, you need to study carpentry and how it works. In the idea of bringing God into the equation of your getting well, you should probably study God and how that stuff works. Now, I believe there are plenty of people out there who will tell you that their way is the only way. But I'm not sure there's only one right way, especially if that way condemns everybody else." He paused and I waited.

"You know, son, religion, or whatever you'd call the study of God, has one interesting habit you might want to think about. In almost every other study, there's a striving for new and better ways to understand a problem or a solution. Look how carpentry has changed. But in religious matters, some folks think the way it was thousands of years ago is still the only way it can be. And when the leaders of some of these different faiths were afraid they might lose their control, they made it up so if somebody didn't agree with them, there was supposed to be an evil force behind that disagreement. They used to burn people at the stake who disagreed with them. They don't do that any more, but some might get real upset if you suggest there may be a different way than what they believe, especially about working with God so you can get well."

"Then what should I do?"

"You have to figure all that out for yourself, son. Try to keep an open mind and try not to make others wrong just because they think different. And if they make you wrong for not agreeing with them, don't let that discourage you from what you're looking for. And ask God for help."

Our conversation made sense to me, and from that day on I read the Bible. I started with the Old Testament, but I didn't like that set of books. I thought the God of the Old Testament had an attitude problem. It seemed He was always punishing, always judging, always making people prove themselves worthy. It said that He turned one lady into a pillar of salt for looking over her shoulder and not following directions. And I had done a lot worse than not following directions. So I moved on to the New Testament, which I liked because the scriptural teachings were different. They seemed to be about life principles and how to use them to be joyful and have abundance.

I wasn't reading scripture from a devotional point of view. I didn't want to be holy; I wanted to get well. I was reading scripture trying to figure out how miracles happened because the scriptures were one of the few places where miracles were recorded. And most of the healings in the New Testament were accompanied by comments regarding belief or faith. When some got healed, it was said their faith had made them whole. Others were told to go and "Know it will be done according to your belief." I saw many similarities between the great spiritual teachings and the ideas that consciousness creates reality and the power of belief.

In their own way, the materials I was studying spoke about power. Some were about the power of goals and goal-directed action; others were about the power of self-talk, consciousness, or belief. Some spoke to the power of imagination and others to the power of God.

As I saw it, my task was to integrate these magnificent

concepts so I could regain my health. There was a power that was available to everybody—all the material agreed on that. I just wasn't quite sure how to tie it all together so I could use that power to get what I wanted—my health back. But through it all, I began to understand: power is centered around choice.

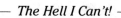

Chapter 11

From "The Hell I Can't!" to "Hell, I Don't Know"

As fall turned to winter, life once again took on a routine. Karen was finally well into the pregnancy we had wanted, and I continued my studies about having choice in what my life could be like.

Although I was a long way from being full of joy and positive expectancy all the time, the process of studying about choice inspired me. At times I could feel that my study and what I chose to focus on was making a difference. I was learning that there was a "power for good" in the Universe and a possibility that I could use that power to get well.

In different ways and situations, I was reminded that my beliefs and my perception of myself could create my reality; that a facet of me, my consciousness, or whatever it was called, could determine what my life would be like.

I read that there was evidence that the human body is constantly rebuilding itself based on a blueprint, an internal program that created this body I lived in. Some authors stated that through my own choice, I could make changes in that blueprint. There was evidence, especially in the area of physical healing, that my beliefs played a significant role in what healing took place.

I wasn't seeking a magic pill that would heal me in a split second—although I'd gladly accept it if that happened. I believed healing was a process that sometimes took time, and I believed in the medical procedures being done to me. Even the colostomy had its purpose. As a bypass, it was allowing the lower end of my colon to have a chance to heal. And that's the way I chose to think about it. My job was to figure out how to participate, how to facilitate or create that healing so I would no longer need the colostomy.

I had been taught to believe in the debridements and the surgical drains. Throughout my life, I had been taught to believe in antibiotics and other medicines. Now I was studying and searching for the part I was supposed to play to have a chance at being whole again. For I also believed that if I was going to have my dream, if I was going to live without limitation, then I would have to play a significant role to create that. And I wanted the healing I desired to be determined by something within me or something I would do. Otherwise I wasn't in control, and I wanted to be in control. I wanted the quality of my life to be up to me.

I read articles about magic cures or special ingredients that had facilitated incredible healing. I even tried some of them. I'm not talking about snake oil cures; I'm referring to natural cures used in many cultures that seemed to work for some. But they didn't work for me.

Yet within the framework of my disease, I did have some small wins. I was supposed to be in the body cast for six months because they didn't want me to move. But the tissue filled in much more quickly than was thought possible. Three months after that surgery, they took skin from my thigh and grafted it over the long trough-like hole. I felt I had played a role in the early healing because I was using the tools of choice and directing my body to heal. The doctors were amazed, and in my medical records the resident wrote, "The granulation tissue closed quite remarkably." And I had done that, or at least I gave myself some of the credit.

Every day I was aware of what thoughts I was thinking, the self-talk that went on within me. And I tried not only to be positive outwardly, but also to think in a positive way.

When I was in the body cast, I took time every day to daydream and to pretend that the tissue was filling in quickly and easily. During many of the dressing changes, the resident would encourage me and confirm that it was healing much faster than anticipated. Of course, I had asked him to tell me things like that. I had told him what I was trying to do, and I wanted his help so I would begin to believe that what I was doing was making a difference.

But that win was short-lived. Only a month and a half after being discharged with a huge part of my back missing, the old familiar pain returned, and I was readmitted for another surgery. They found that the infection was still widespread. This time there were no grand plans to rid me of the E. coli infection. From now on, it would be damage-control procedures using drains to keep me comfortable. Though they didn't come right out and say it, I knew that the doctors had given up.

So they had taken out a large chunk of my back in the hopes of healing me, and I was still in the same place I had been before—filled with the infection. Once again my "I can" attitude got lost in anger and resentment.

≈ ≈ ≈ ≈

When I was first seeking, and studying in the human potential field, almost everything inspired me. I was like a kid in a candy store. Each new story, each new book held the possibility of the answer I so desperately wanted to find.

But after awhile, the quick-fix stories no longer interested me. *Okay, it can be done, so what?* I thought. Many had beaten the odds. Many had achieved what others said was impossible. Many had declared a new reality and then achieved it. But how was it done? How could I do it? These questions drew me to the disciplines and methodologies that addressed how to create reality by choice.

Almost every night, I took time for personal exploration. I explored positive thought, affirmative prayer, and mind control. I studied disciplines on breath, relaxation, and stress reduction. I practiced choice by using goals, plans, affirmations, and visualization. I created "good" cells in my body that would destroy the "bad" cells. I worked on blood flow and circulation with biofeedback methods.

I read the Bible most every night and even started underlining the material that I thought was good. Then I would hold it up in the air and say, "This is great stuff. Fix me!" But the drainage surgeries continued.

As the months wore on, I began to notice that I was getting more and more confused about how the ideas I was studying should be used. Many of the authors disagreed with each other on which methods were most effective. And even if they agreed on the methods or techniques, many times they disagreed on how to use them. Everyone seemed to be saying they had the only answer. It was like the grocery store advertisements where all stores claim to have the lowest overall prices.

After awhile, it was almost a joke. Many times when I went to see people, I could figure out what they were going to tell me to do by the certificates hanging on their walls or by the credentials they listed at the front of their books or training.

Those who taught about self-image said healing came by changing the image of self. Those into nutrition spoke about diet and food supplements as the way to health. Past- life people wanted me to do past-life regressions to uncover the hidden clues to why I had this illness. Astrologers wanted to know where and when I was born. Numerologists wanted the full spelling of my name and important dates. Drug and alcohol counselors wanted to talk about the drug and alcohol use in my family. Reflexologists wanted to get ahold of my feet.

Some of the religious folks wanted to know if I had been "born again." Although it seemed that many had their own private beliefs about reality and how it worked, very few were open to having their beliefs explored or questioned.

The more I immersed myself in personal-growth material, the more I began to notice that the joy and enthusiasm I had felt at the beginning of my journey to freedom was getting lost in all the things I needed to do and pay attention to.

At first I was focusing on the end result I wanted. It was as if my destination was center stage in the play of my life. Then as I read and studied, the stage became cluttered with all I had learned. What I wanted had become lost and mired down in all the rules of how to get it. I moved from being results-oriented and feeling the joy and anticipation about those results to focusing on the methods of getting there, and I always had more to do, more to know, something else to study.

In the beginning, I had felt united with others who were on the path of self-discovery. But as time passed, I felt divided from other seekers because of the convictions we had acquired along the way. In the beginning, it seemed we were all asking the same questions, but as we each found answers, we became separated by our convictions when our individual answers disagreed. And who was I, as a relatively new student of this material to disagree with those who may have had more training?

Each discipline started with the possibility that I was capable of creating a new life based on my own priorities. That's what "as ye believe, so shall it be done unto you" represents. All held the possibility of health, the possibility of joy, the possibility of being happy and satisfied with who I was, what I was doing, and what I had. But, and it was a big but, moving the possibilities in my life into probability, moving from what *might* happen to me to what *was* happening to me seemed terribly confusing.

The problem I was facing was that every discipline said I would have to do enough of something, but what was that magical something, or the list of things I had to do enough of, before I could get what I wanted?

One of the challenges for me was being right in the middle of one of the "list book" cycles. About every ten years, someone writes a glorious book that has a list as part of its title. After it becomes a best seller, a flurry of new list books arrives in bookstores. I had received or purchased many of them: The One True, The Two Most Important, The Three Hidden, The Four Magic, The Five Secrets, The Six Principles, The Seven Strategies, The Eight Essentials, The Nine Keys, The Ten Steps, The Eleven Points, The Twelve This or That. There were a lot of "list of twelve" books, I guess because twelve is big in most of the scriptures. And sometimes the lists were The ABCs of, The Bare Bones of, The Nuts and Bolts of, The Wisdom of, The Rules of. These list books seemed endless.

I had read my share of these books. And I thought many of them were good, a few of them even made sense to me. Most of them seemed to have scientific proof and testimonials that the lists they "sold" were in fact the things to focus on. Some even had ancient scripture references that their method was some mystical secret that had just been rediscovered.

My problem came from having so many different lists. Yes, there was some agreement on the specifics that needed to be done and some similarities among lists. But even if I grouped the ones that agreed with each other, that left a lot of different lists.

I was overwhelmed. How was I to know which I should use? Some books said that the tremendous power I had within me would be available when I had sublime confidence in it. Others said for mental peace and radiant health, I must forgive enough. One quote stated: "You must forgive everyone who has ever hurt you if you want perfect health and happiness." And I had never met anyone who had forgiven everyone who had ever hurt them.

Some even said that the miracle of health is not received by the direct search for health. They inferred that I must seek first the wholeness, the goodness of life itself, and then within that I would find the possibility of health, no matter what the odds were against me. Some suggested that I needed to accept the fact that I was already perfectly healthy now, even though I was immersed in sickness.

I even found disagreement in the teachings about prayer. Should I pray for the specifics I wanted like health, a strong back, prosperity, love and joy? Or should I trust in a bigger plan and turn my life and what happens to me over to God or some higher power?

And then there were the "disease" books. Although similar to list books, with these the authors would use the first half of the book to convince readers they are suffering from some disease, then in the second half they would suggest that they had the answers to fix the disease. And their answers seemed to be simply variations on the lists.

These kinds of books also tended to run in cycles. Most of them had a checklist that asked readers such questions as, "Did this ever happen to you?" And if the answer was yes, the reader was to put a check mark under that item. My opinion was that many of the authors had already made up their minds that their readers were suffering from the disease they had the fix for, so they designed the first part of their books to get the reader to agree. Then when the reader had the right amount of check marks under a specific label or type of experience from their past, then they were to accept that label as part of their identity.

That just seemed silly to me. Why would I want to limit my definition of who I was now and what my life would be like in the future just because of my past? That's what my doctors were doing—using my past to predict my future.

And yet these books began to affect my thinking and erode my resolve because these authors had credentials and studies to back up their claims of disease, and I began to wonder if maybe they were right.

I did not want to believe them. I did not want to learn to

live with my disease and deal with it better. I wanted to be whole again, and I began to realize that in my quest, I was seeking more than just the wholeness of my body.

I wanted to be able to come to my life with a simple joy about life itself. I wanted to be able to move through my days and nights with a calm confidence that my dreams were going to come true: dreams like being a good father, finding a job that I really enjoyed doing with people who were fun and inspiring to work with, helping my children grow up strong and healthy, and getting rid of the colostomy instead of going to the bathroom in a bag attached to my side. I was trying harder than I had ever tried in my life to learn how to take control and make these dreams come true. But it wasn't happening.

It was as if I was at the bottom of a huge hole, and I was trying to build a ladder that would allow me to climb out and create the kind of life I wanted. I had the pieces for the ladder, but I didn't understand how to put the pieces together in a way that would allow me to believe that I could make the difference that had to be made for me to produce the miracle I needed.

I had a great deal of love and support from my family and friends, but by then I didn't think anybody thought I would make it out clean. I could see it in their faces. I could hear it in their language as they talked to me. I could feel it when they hugged me good-bye. Even Karen had been worn down by the roller-coaster emotions of being by my side through surgery after surgery. More and more, I felt alone in the hope that I could find a way out and create perfect health.

I was easily overwhelmed with the immensity of my problems. At first the things I studied helped me, giving me hope that there might be a light at the end of this tunnel of darkness and despair. But as I learned and studied more, the huge list of rules I acquired just added to being overwhelmed. I began to feel that perhaps the healing I wanted was up to someone or something other than me and that my resistance to my colostomy, the infection, and the surgeries just made my life worse.

I had two daughters now, and they were so special. I was present at Sheri's birth only because my doctor had allowed me to leave the hospital for a day. When I saw her being born, I knew she was the one Kris had called to in my dream that night so many months before when Kris thought I was going to leave. As I held Sheri for the first time, there was no room for sickness in my life. There was only the joy of finally holding that little one who along with Kris had saved me from drowning in my own self-pity. She was perfect, she was beautiful, and I knew she had come into my life to fulfill a promise.

Over the next few weeks as I played with and loved my precious daughters, I began to think that perhaps I should stop focusing on the things I wanted and begin enjoying the things I already had. Having read that the healing I was seeking might not include the healing of my body, and finding the disciplines I studied becoming more and more complex, I thought it might be easier to learn how to go with the flow rather than always focusing on changing the course of the river.

However, there was more at stake in that choice than just the health I wanted. At stake was my happiness and the satisfaction I would feel about my life based on how I wanted it to be. Was I the creator of the movie I called my life, or was I in bondage to the limiting beliefs I had been taught? As I studied more and more, "the hell I can't!" slowly eroded to "hell, I don't know anymore."

CHAPTER 12

WHO DO YOU THINK YOU ARE?

The confusion and uncertainty I felt about how I was going to take charge of my life and become the master of my own destiny began to take up more and more of my time and affect my attitude. When I read or studied, even if I did start to get excited about the material, my doubts and "yes, but's" put a damper on the fire and determination I knew I would need if I was really going to stay on track to get well.

Even so, I still had more small wins. In new surgeries, I lost less blood and suffered less pain afterwards. I could control my bodily functions so the colostomy worked when I wanted it to work, and most of the time after a surgery, I didn't need a catheter to relieve my bladder. I had trained those parts of my body to do what I wanted them to do.

But the big wins continued to elude me, and I began to think that the miracle I was looking for was outside of my control. It was as if something other than me would be the one to choose whether or not I would really get well.

I knew things were coming to a head, something had to give, and I was afraid that the "something" would be my determination and commitment to regain my health.

≈ ≈ ≈ ≈

At the beginning of my stays at the University of Washington Medical Center, I met Reverend Gene Robinson. He had stopped in one day and asked if he could pray for me.

"Hi, I'm Gene Robinson. I'm an outreach minister for one of the big churches in downtown Seattle. Part of my job is to visit patients in different hospitals and ask them if they want help in the form of prayer."

Gene had a ready smile on a pleasant face. He was on the short side and soft looking, like a man who was unfamiliar with exercise. I liked him instantly. "Hi, I'm Terry," I said. "Thanks for stopping in."

"You're welcome, son. My church has an ongoing nation-wide prayer group that regularly prays for people in the hos-pitals where I visit. Would you like to be put on the list?"

"Absolutely!" I eagerly accepted his offer and without much more talk he said he would see me again and left.

What he couldn't have known that day was that he could have come into my room wearing a scary mask and asked if I wanted him to do magic for my health and I would have said, "Yes!" For I really believed there was something "unlimited" we can all call on for help; I just wasn't positive that there was only one way to call on it. So when he offered to do his brand of spiritual work, I naturally accepted.

At first I was a little wary that Rev. Gene might try to con-vert me to his point of view, but he didn't, at least not right away. And through my association with him, I was being prayed for by groups all around the country.

From those early days on, Gene came to visit me fairly of-ten. We would discuss various scripture texts and what they might mean, and for the most part he was very understanding and tolerant when my opinions about religion differed from his. Gene was genuinely there to help me explore spiritual concepts, and he consistently reminded me that people were praying for my recovery. He encouraged me to keep "seeking God," as he called it.

When I was in for my fourteenth surgery, Gene came in early one morning. Now hospitals are very busy places for the staff and patients early in the day, and Gene was aware of this. That's why his visits were always in the afternoons. As soon as he came through the door, I knew something was up. And it wasn't just the time of day; there was something unusual about him. He had a glow around him. He came over to my bed and said, "We've got to talk."

"Sure, Gene. What's up?"

"Just a moment. I have to close the door."

That too was unusual. I was in a private room, and he had never wanted to close the door before.

With the door shut, he pulled up a chair right to my bed and just sat there for a few moments, as if gathering something from within himself. I lay there looking at him wondering what the glow was about.

"Terry, last night God came to me in a vision!"

Oh that's it, he's seen God, I thought. I'd never met anyone who had seen God, but if I had to guess, I would think they'd glow just as he was. I'm not sure I understood it, but I could certainly feel that something very special had happened to him.

He went on, "I've been actively seeking the Lord since my mid-teens when I was born again. And in all my years of prayer and meditation, I've never had a vision of God until last night!"

"That's great!" I said, wondering a little why he had chosen to share such an amazing thing with me.

"Yes it is, you see, God came to me in this vision and told me what His plan is for you, Terry! I can't tell you how inspired I feel. God has delivered a sacred message to me to share with you! How many people ever have their prayers so directly answered? It's a miracle!"

I wasn't sure what to do or say. But quite honestly I didn't trust in "God's plan" for me or anyone. When I was a little boy

I asked others why my father had been killed in the war when other boys' fathers made it home safely. Often I was told that it was part of God's plan. And I never understood how a loving God could take the father and husband from a young family and leave them to fend for themselves.

When I was in my early teens, a friend drowned in a neighbor's swimming pool. At the funeral, the minister told us that God had taken this young boy back to Him to teach us a lesson. I remember thinking, *What kind of God would take a human life just to teach other humans a lesson?*

Then when I was in high school, one Friday evening a drunk driver killed three of my friends on the way to our high school football game. The entire school turned out for the memorial service. There were three different ministers from three different churches, and all of them suggested that these deaths were part of God's plan, and even if we didn't understand it, we had to trust in God's divine wisdom.

Gene's eyes filled with tears as he leaned forward, "God is going to use you to teach people with limitations that they can be whole in spirit even if they are broken in body. Terry, God's plan for you is to spend your life in a wheelchair. And because of your incredible spirit, you will rise above your physical limitations and become an example to all those with disabilities, so they too can rise above their physical limitations in spirit and lead a full life with God."

A part of me was so mesmerized by his glow that I could barely grasp his words.

"Hold on a minute, Gene." I closed my eyes and took a few slow breaths, getting control of my mind. "Would you repeat what you just said."

"I know you don't want to hear this, Terry, but God's plan for you is that you are going to spend the rest of your life in a wheelchair. This is . . ."

"Wait," I said in the middle of his sentence.

Again, I closed my eyes to think. I did not want to make this gentle man wrong. We had spent too much quality time together talking about God and honestly seeking the wisdom of the great spiritual teachings to begin playing right-and-wrong games now.

Maybe I should have been more appreciative of his having a vision, because looking at him I could tell that he really was moved by his experience. But when he broke the silence and said, "I'm talking about God's plan for you," I simply replied, "I won't do it."

I don't think he was shocked. He probably figured I was not going to accept this without a fight. He had spent too much time with me exploring how I might get well, and he knew how upset I was with my doctors' limited thinking to believe I would just roll over and give up what I was so adamantly going after.

He looked at me with great sincerity and said, "Terry, I'm talking about God's Will for you . . . not yours."

"I'm not going to spend my life in a wheelchair, Gene," I said hotly. "I am free to choose health and to choose the kind of life I want. Remember how many times you've told me that God wants us all to be healthy and happy?"

"That was before my vision!"

He wasn't going to hear me; he was on a sacred mission. We argued for about ten minutes, each of us getting entrenched more and more in our own positions.

"I don't want to believe you, Gene. I know you've had some kind of experience with God, but I don't want to believe that God wants sickness and disease for certain people.

"You cannot be the judge of what God wants. Your personal desires are unimportant. We all must accept that we serve God better if we accept His will." He was adamant that his way, his reality, was better than my personal desires.

"I will *not* believe this," I said fiercely.

He pulled back a bit, his face flushing. "Are you blind?"

"I can see just fine!"

"No! Your ego is running your life. It's your head talking, not your heart."

"Bullshit!"

His face turned red and in his best shaming voice he went on, "Don't you think if God wanted to heal you, would be well by now?"

I stopped cold, my stomach in knots. We were going nowhere. I took a deep breath and said, "Look, Gene, I'm okay with you having a different belief, a different vision for what my life should be. But why do you have to make me wrong just because I want to believe it's still possible for me to be healthy and have the full use of my body?" But my question went unheard.

"Don't be a fool. You need to rise above your petty ego-centered desires. You told me yourself that the doctors say what you have is not curable, and you will be left with major disability." Gene got up and began to pace.

I tried to quote scripture that supported my right to choose freely what my life would be like, but he knew scripture much better than I did. He was a Bible scholar. As the argument continued, my temples began to pound, and I could feel my anger building inside my gut. And my anger came out in some unkind words. At one point, I told him to go to hell. Another time I told him he could kiss my ass. I wasn't proud of those outbursts, but why did he have to make me wrong just because I wouldn't believe as he did?

Finally, Gene sat down and quietly said, "Terry, how can I convince you that you are wrong?"

In desperation I said, "Let me read you something," and I got my Bible. It was the King James Version of the New Testament. I went to Philippians, Chapter 2: verses 5-6 and read: "Let this mind be in you which was also in Christ Jesus, who being in the form of God, thought it not robbery to be equal with God." It was one of the quotes in the Bible that I believed held the promise about being able to do "greater works." I hung onto that quote when there seemed to be no light at the end of the tunnel.

I no more than finished speaking when he said, "That's blasphemy! How dare you compare yourself to Jesus!"

"Wait, that's not what I meant . . . ."

He stood holding his head down like a bull ready to charge and said in a hiss, "You better think about this because it's probably the most important decision you will ever make." Then he stormed out.

Stunned, I lay there in silence feeling my body pulsate with adrenaline. The entire argument was absolutely dreadful. As I calmed down, I began to wonder whether or not he would continue praying for me. I guess from his point of view, I was praying for the wrong thing. He wanted me to pray for understanding and acceptance in a wheelchair. But I wanted my heath back.

As the argument went along, I knew he was getting more and more upset with me, and when the swear words came out of my mouth he was offended. But I never expected him to get *that* angry. And why did he get so mad when I had just quoted from the Bible itself? All I wanted him to do was explain that quote to me.

After awhile, I began the routines of my day: irrigating my colostomy, taking care of the drains in my back, and generally cleaning up. I thought a lot about what he had said. I wanted to be at peace about how my life was unfolding. I was tired of always trying to be in control of what was happening to me and how I was creating my reality. But I was not going to give up my desire for the health I wanted and turn my life over to someone else's plan for me. Yet as I looked again at the poster I had brought in and put on my wall, I wasn't as sure as I had been that I had the right to fight this.

For the next few days, I was even more confused than before, spending long hours watching mindless TV to keep the deep turmoil at bay. Then just before lunch three days after the blowup with Gene, another unpleasant incident hit me over the head. The door to my room opened and in walked an older lady. She was dressed in hospital pajamas, robe, slippers, and had the dead giveaway—hospital hair. I knew before she said a word exactly what was going on.

Surely she had been sent by the staff to get me to do something. They'd used me in the past for the same kind of thing. If they wanted people to have a better attitude, they would send me in and I would give them a pump-up talk about being positive and working with the staff. I was sure this lady had been sent to do the same for me.

Before I could say anything, she came over to my bed, introduced herself and said, "I've had a colostomy for over ten years, and mine doesn't bother me a bit."

I knew what she was trying to do. I had a really lousy attitude about my colostomy, and the staff knew it. She had been sent into my room to try to get me to face reality and be more accepting. But I didn't want any part of what she could give me.

If I had been in a better mood, I might have said something kind like, "Thank you for sharing." But I was *not* in a good mood.

"I don't want to listen to you," I said, "and I don't want to talk about my colostomy. I'm not going to have my colostomy for much longer, and that's all there is to it. So would you please leave?"

"The doctors told me you were going to be tough. I know what you're going through. I hated my colostomy too when I first got it. But when I finally accepted that I would have it for the rest of my life, I learned I could live with it."

"I don't care what you've done, and I don't care what you have learned to live with. I'm not going to have mine that much longer." I'm not sure I really believed that, but I knew I was not going to talk with her about accepting my current situation as permanent. "Now, I'm asking you politely, would you please leave?"

No, she was there on a mission to help me face reality. Or maybe she just wanted someone to tell her she was right in resigning herself to living with hers.

"Now, Terry, there's no reason to be rude. I'm just trying to help you realize . . ."

Without letting her finish, I raised my voice and said, "Lady,

I'm naked underneath these covers, and unless you're out of here by the time I count three, I'm going to stand up and throw your ass into the hall."

"Well, I never!" she said and left in a huff.

Once she was gone I wondered, *Do I have a sign on my forehead that says "kick me, I'm down"?* I mean, it was tough enough to be beat up physically, but to have two people within days come in and tell me that the things I wanted to do with my life were inappropriate, and that I needed to accept the reality they believed in, was almost too much to take.

And that wasn't the end of it. The lady told the staff what had happened. And about an hour later, Dr. Reinhart, one of the residents in Orthopedic Surgery, came in.

"Get dressed, Terry, I want you to see another doctor."

Now I was used to this kind of thing because I was in a teaching hospital. It seemed that there was always some new person or new addition to the staff who needed to get acquainted with my case. They would poke at me for awhile and stick things in me until the new batch of interns and residents knew what was going on.

I got up and put on my pajamas, robe, and slippers and then combed my hair. We walked down the hall together chatting. I was surprised when he led me to the elevator because we usually stayed on the orthopedic floor.

Dr. Reinhart and I had become friends over the months he was on rotation in orthopedics because I always had cookies and cake in my room. When he or the other interns and residents had time, they'd stop in and chat for awhile and grab a few munchies.

As the elevator went down one floor, we made small talk. When we got off and started down the corridor, I looked up and saw a big sign, Psychiatric Ward, and I skidded to a stop.

Dr. Reinhart laughed. "What's wrong?"

"I'm not going down there. I've seen movies about what they do to patients in psych wards, and I'm not going."

He continued to chuckle. "I'm not bringing you down here

to stay. It's just for a visit."

"What kind of visit?" I said, looking around.

"You're going to meet with Dr. Walter Avery. He's a psychiatrist who's been involved with your case since you first came to the hospital."

I felt like a bug under a microscope. "How do you mean?"

"When patients have had more than four or five major surgeries, the staff believes it starts to affect their minds too. So after a specific number of surgeries, a psychiatrist is always brought in as part of the overall physician team."

Another damned belief system, I thought. "Okay," I said as I tentatively followed Dr. Reinhart down the hall. We went into a pleasant office where he introduced me to Dr. Avery.

As I sat down I noticed my medical records on his large desk. His office was neat, if not sparse, something like how he struck me. I noticed about a half dozen certificates hanging in perfect order on one wall.

"It's good to finally meet you, Terry. I've spoken to your family at different times when you were in surgery. You have a nice wife and daughter. Kris, I believe her name is, yes?"

"Yes."

"I haven't met your new daughter yet, but I bet she's just as pretty."

It was apparent that Dr. Avery knew an awful lot about me, and I didn't like that. As we talked, I realized he was trying to create a "safe space" by asking easy questions and getting me to relax. It didn't work very well.

"How are you doing these days?" he asked.

"Fine. Wow, you sure do have a lot of credentials," I said, changing the subject. I had learned that people really do not want to know how it feels to have one's body cut open and assaulted as mine had been. But he wasn't easily drawn off. As he kept at it, I found myself beginning to talk, then finally unloading. The more I explained my situation, the angrier I became.

"If you count the fusion and the operations at the other

hospital," I said, "I've had fourteen major surgical procedures on my body in less than two years. That wouldn't be so bad if they didn't say it would go on indefinitely.

"I feel like I've been raped and pillaged, opened from the front and the back and the bottom. I always have tubes running in and out of me, and I hate having to go to the bathroom in a plastic bag on my stomach. I can't begin to tell you how many nights I've spent alone scared to death that tomorrow would be the day when I would lose the use of my body."

Yes, I was an angry young man, and it felt good to have someone in authority listen to me.

"Even if there is a judging God in the Universe," I said, "what have I done to deserve fourteen major surgical procedures? I could understand maybe two or three, but not this many!"

I went on in this vein for twenty minutes or so venting my anger. Finally, I was emotionally spent. It had already been a bad few days with Gene's awful vision and then that lady telling me how her colostomy didn't bother her. And I told Dr. Avery about those two meetings also. I let him know exactly where I was and what was going on.

I think I was assuming he was going to encourage me to continue to believe in what I wanted. Boy, was I wrong!

He listened attentively while I spoke. When I was done, he said, "Terry, it's time you take off your rose-colored glasses."

As soon as he said that, a little voice inside of me screamed, "Get out!" But I had learned early on not to make doctors mad or they would get even. I didn't want to make him an adversary, so I stayed.

"I'm not looking through rose-colored glasses. I believe there's a power in the Universe that we can learn to use. I've been reading a lot of great books that often mention the power of belief and faith, and how with faith all things are possible."

"Terry, you're not listening to me."

"They say the body is a natural healing mechanism and that through the use of my mind, I can begin to direct that healing. What's wrong with that?"

"It's unrealistic."

"No, it isn't. I made my body granulate the tissue in that big trough in the middle of my back a lot faster, and I got out of my body cast in just three months instead of the six they projected."

"I doubt that you influenced your body that much. Now calm down."

I was getting annoyed by his repeated attempts to direct the conversation and where he wanted the conversation to go. "I think these small wins I've experienced are through my own effort, and I think it's possible for me to get back to perfect health."

While I was trying to convince Dr. Avery, I realized I was also trying to convince myself. Even though I was speaking forcefully, deep down I wasn't sure I really believed there was something I could do to create the health I wanted.

"Terry, you're living in a dream world. Attitude does make a difference, but you cannot determine if your body will heal completely."

I wanted to tell him to shut up and listen. "Dr. Avery, I do not want to believe the way you do."

"I know you've been depressed for months. In your medical records, the staff has written that they believe you're abusing your pain medications. Is it true that you never refuse an opportunity to take them?"

I ignored the question and glared at him, feeling trapped.

"Dr. Reinhart has also told me that he's concerned for you, and he thinks you're in real trouble. He says you lie in bed lethargic for long stretches or just watch TV."

"What would you do if you had to deal with a destroyed body?" I threw back at him.

"Terry, your anger isn't going to help you." He opened my medical records and continued, "I want to read you something." Then he read the letter from my doctors to the insurance company, which said it was highly likely I would have severe permanent disability.

"You see," he continued, "you've told me all these positive things about changing your life, but even if those things did work, which is highly unlikely, you're not demonstrating that you're disciplined enough to do them."

He wasn't fighting fair. It wasn't as if he was calling me names, but I felt he was questioning my character.

"I'd like you to begin to work with me so you can develop a better attitude. It seems that you think to be a real man, you have to be able to stand on your own two legs. This may have developed from having a father who was a war hero. I suspect that one of your greatest fears is having nerve damage that would leave you partially paralyzed and force you to use a wheelchair.

"I can understand how this fear might lead you to unrealistic hopes about recovery, but if you'll come work with me, I can assist you to face whatever may happen with dignity."

I looked him straight in the eyes. "I don't want to learn how to live in a wheelchair with dignity. I want to learn how to get well, and I only want to focus on that."

He leaned back in his chair and put his hands on the back of his head. He looked at the ceiling, thinking. Then he sat up. "Let's talk about your colostomy. I understand it keeps you from going out in public sometimes because you think it's dirty and smells."

Each time he pulled up some intimate detail about me, I felt violated.

"What are you getting at?"

"It's another way your present attitude isn't working for you. I've talked with your surgeons, and they don't think your colon will ever heal enough for them to be able to reverse the colostomy. They predict that you'll probably have it the rest of your life. Don't you think it's time to come to terms with this?"

"No, I'm *not* going to have it the rest of my life."

He pointed to the papers on his desk. "Have you read your medical records? Don't you think if your body was going to get rid of this infection, it would have already done so?"

"I'm not my medical records."

"Terry, who do you think you are? Just look at your past. You have had this infection for . . ."

I interrupted. "I am not my past."

"Terry, you're only human, and the body has limitations."

"I'm not *'only human.'* There is a part of me that is *not* sick. There is a part of me that's whole, a part of me that knows things can be different. Why am I wrong for wanting to believe I can be well?"

My question went right over his head. I don't even think he was listening to me. When he repeated his point of view and implied that I was wrong for not agreeing with him, I finally said in frustration, "Kiss my ass!"

"Look at your anger! You know, I wasn't going to tell you this, but I think you need to hear it. I believe your biggest fear is that with all these surgeries in your pelvic area, you're afraid they're going to cut the nerves that will leave you sexually impotent. And you have an opinion that to be a whole man you need to be able to make love to your wife the normal way. If you come work with me, I can help you . . ."

I stood up so abruptly the chair almost tipped over. Holding my hand out in front of me as if to block any more hurtful words, I said, "I will not listen to this kind of bullshit."

He backed off a little. "Terry, just sit down."

"No, I will not sit down. And I will not listen to this kind of negative stuff about me and what I am capable of. I am going to get well. I don't care what the odds are, I am going to be healthy. I will accept nothing else."

Quietly he asked, "Who do you think you are?"

Right then I realized that I didn't have a clue who I was or how I was going to get well. But I knew I was not going to listen to him any more. So I turned and opened the door.

"Terry?"

I stopped. "What?"

"Son," he said softly, "You are in denial." And I could tell he meant it.

I looked right at him and said, "No, doctor, I am at choice," and I left his office.

≈ ≈ ≈ ≈

I went back to my room and lay down in my bed feeling absolutely devastated. I didn't know if I was shaking from rage or disbelief. As I calmed myself down, I couldn't help but think about what had gone on these last few days. Over the months and after all my surgeries, I had noticed that many of the people who in the beginning had said, "You can do it, you can do it," had begun to think that maybe I wouldn't get well. They didn't speak about it openly; they didn't hit me in the face with it like Gene did with his vision. But the inference was always there. Maybe I was resisting, and through my resistance, I was making the condition persist.

But never had I been openly confronted by somebody who knew as much about me as Dr. Avery did. I thought about him. He must be a dedicated healer. After all, he had studied allopathic medicine to become a medical doctor and then went on to study psychiatric medicine so he could become a psychiatrist. When it came to people who were sick, he must know a lot about what they're doing and what they need to be doing.

When I replayed our conversation, I thought it wasn't that he was negative. He was a caring man who was dedicated to the healing profession. And he had an educated opinion about me and what I ought to be doing with my life. My mind kept going over and over the question that both Gene and Dr. Avery had asked me: "Who do you think you are?"

That night after all of my visitors had left and I was again lost in thought, Mary came in.

"How are you doing, Terry?" she asked.

"I feel like shit," I said flatly.

"I read the report from Dr. Avery in my records. I'm sorry the meeting didn't go well."

"I don't like him. He has to be right."

"You know I've been here a long time . . ."

"I know."

"And in my opinion, Dr. Avery is one of the most loving doctors in the hospital. I've seen him comforting Karen in the waiting room during your surgeries. One time, he played with Kris so Karen could take a few minutes to get something to eat. And I saw him hold your mother as she cried one evening."

"He said something like that."

Memories of our meeting flooded in again, and I felt even worse about what I had said to him.

"Dr. Avery dropped this off." Mary handed me an envelope with my name on it. "He asked me to give it to you after your visitors left this evening."

We talked a few more minutes then she asked if I wanted a back rub. I declined and she left saying, "Sleep well, Terry."

I looked at the envelope, hesitant to open it. No, I was more than hesitant, I was afraid. My whole world was crumbling around me. All I hoped for, all I dreamed about was in jeopardy, and I knew that what was in the envelope would support his position. I had insulted him by not agreeing with his opinion about me and what I could expect regarding my health. I knew he was not going to give up.

For an hour, I left the envelope on my nightstand, hoping it would disappear. But for some reason I thought I needed to at least honor his good intentions. He really did want to help me. I just didn't want to accept the direction his help would take me. Finally, I couldn't stand the tension any longer and opened the envelope. Inside was a fancy piece of parchment paper with a note attached.

The handwritten note said, "Terry, for the sake of your family and your own well- being, I suggest you read this over and over, Dr. Avery."

The page was outlined with an ornate scroll border that gave it a feeling of authority. It read as follows:

The Serenity Prayer

God, grant me the serenity to accept the things I cannot change, courage to change the things I can, and the wisdom to know the difference.

Living one day at a time, accepting hardships as the pathway to peace,

Taking as He did, the world as it is, not as I would have it.

Trusting that He will make all things right if I surrender to His will, that I may be reasonably happy in this life and supremely happy with Him, forever, in the next.

1926 Reinhold Neibuhr

I read it over and over as Dr. Avery had instructed, and I began to cry. Feeling lost, I cried myself to sleep.

CHAPTER 13

SUFFERING AS A WAY OF LIFE

When I woke the next morning, my heart felt sore, and my body was weary. I hadn't slept well; memories of yesterday's events had me tossing and turning all night.

I began my morning routine slowly, and before I had finished, Rev. Gene marched in. I was angry at him before he even said a word. I had my own priorities in the morning and he knew that. And it upset me that he now thought his priorities were more important than mine. I thought about telling him to leave but decided not to. He entered the room with a smile on his face and came over to my bed.

"I want you to read this," he said, thrusting his fancy Bible at me with the gold edging on the pages.

I was sure he wanted me to read the *one* place in the whole Bible that talks about God's Will versus our will, and I did not want to get into it with him again.

I crossed my arms and just looked at him.

"Come on, Terry, read this," again pushing his open Bible at me.

I looked at the pages in front of me and was surprised it was open to Philippians, the passage I had read to him when he had gotten so upset. And my heart leapt. *He has gone home and studied it,* I thought, *and now he can explain it to me.*

I scanned down to the part I was interested in, Chapter 2, verses 5 and 6, and read, "Let this mind be in you that was also in Christ Jesus, who though he was in the form of God, knew that equality with God was not a thing to be grasped."

I was stunned. I had read that passage over and over again to remind and encourage myself to stand equal in the creation of my life, with the power of Creation Itself. I reached over and picked up my Bible and thumbed back to that section, which read, "Let this mind be in you which was also in Christ Jesus, who being in the form of God, thought it not robbery to be equal with God." The two passages weren't just a little different, they had opposite meanings!

"I don't understand. How can these be so opposite?"

He stood there smiling and said, "Your Bible is wrong."

My mouth dropped open. I'd never heard of such a thing before. I grew up with the King James Version. He was reading out of the American Standard Version.

"Your Bible is wrong," he said again with a pompous attitude. "It's well known that the King James Version was not a proper translation, and the American Standard Version went back to original Greek texts to make the Bible accurate."

I feared this would happen that first day so many months ago when he walked in and asked if I wanted some prayer help. With all of his well-meaning attitude and talk, when it came right down to it, he was just one more of those people who thought they knew what was best for everybody else. No wonder he was smiling. Not only did he know best for me, but now he also got to top it off with my Bible being wrong.

I was infuriated. I felt like the S.O.B. had set me up. All these months he was just waiting to tell me his way was "the only way."

We had a bruising argument for a few minutes, and I finally said, "Get out of my room and never come back."

"Who do you think you are?" he bellowed and left.

Gene did not leave happy. And I knew I would be taken off the prayer circle lists he influenced because now I was praying for a healing that he didn't think I should have. But more importantly than his walking out upset, I was floored by the idea that my Bible, The New Testament, the story of some of the greatest teachings in the history of the world, couldn't be trusted. Or at least the one I was reading couldn't, because as he said, my Bible was wrong.

What if some of the other statements I was counting on were wrong? What if "all things are possible if only you believe" was wrong? What if "whatsoever you ask for in prayer, believing you have them, you shall have them" was wrong?

What a mess this personal-growth material was. First I was confronted with different disciplines, different teachers, and different methodologies that went hundreds of different directions concerning what one needed to do to heal a physical ailment. And now I was confronted with the idea that there were even differences in the Book that was supposed to hold "the truth" about humanity. Gene's version of the Bible said the complete opposite of mine about whether or not I could stand equal in the creation of my life with the power of Creation Itself.

Who should I trust? What book should I read? Where should I go to find the truth that would set me free? With my limited resources, how could I find the one discipline that would work?

I had been asking. I had been seeking. I had been knocking on doors all over the place trying to find a way to get well. And I was getting tired of asking. I wanted to be able to demand health. I wanted to be able to stand firmly in something that was not sick and demand that health be created. But even that thought brought up the same question Gene asked when he walked out the door for the last time: "Who do you think you are?"

As I opened my nightstand drawer to put away my Bible, I saw "The Serenity Prayer." As I read it again, I began to regret how I had acted toward this man of God. I had told him to go to hell. I wasn't even sure if I believed in hell, but I had condemned him. Maybe I was just mad at his smug attitude or the smile on his face. The smile could have been covering his embarrassment from our last meeting when he had questioned my character, but that didn't matter. He was a man of God and, from his experience, he had a real vision from God, and he thought he was doing God's work.

I had never known anyone who had a vision where they saw and spoke to God. I had read about that kind of thing happening, and when I finally met one of those blessed people, instead of listening and acknowledging the wonder and significance of the experience, I ridiculed it. I tried to make it unimportant and, in doing that, I made him wrong for who he was and what he believed. I did to him what I thought others were doing to me.

As I read "The Serenity Prayer" over and over, I began to know that I really was refusing to face what I believed to be true. I was in denial.

≈ ≈ ≈ ≈

When I was a little boy, I was taught that life was good. Oh sure, there were tragedies like my father being killed in the war. But I was taught that we were not supposed to let the struggles of life get us down. Even though my mother was often smothering, she taught my brother Gerry and me to keep looking to our dreams. But as I grew up, I found that most people didn't have the life they dreamed of. I saw that compromise came more and more into the picture.

There were thousands of books and articles about how I could take control of my life, but most of the people I knew had lives filled with struggle, challenges and obstacles. What right did I have to act like a child and expect my dreams to come true? Even with all the tools I could use, what right did I have to think that my life was like a huge garden where I could just pick what I wanted, as if my desires were ripe fruits on a tree ready for the taking?

As I lay there, I began to see that even though on the surface, I was taught to be positive, I was also taught that life was an ongoing series of lessons that involved sacrifice and suffering.

My father had been killed in the Second World War just after I was born. He was presented to me as a real war hero not because he dropped bombs and killed people, but because he had given his life so that others might live. I can't begin to count the times I was reminded that the Christian scriptures said there was no greater gift than being willing to give one's life for another.

Others in my family had been in that war, and they returned home safely after the enemy had been defeated. But they were not the heroes my dad was. And the only difference I could identify was that Dad died in the fight.

When I was growing up, my mother said that since he died just days before my birth she was sure that part of his spirit came to be with me. She said I would be big enough to live for him and fulfill his unaccomplished life's purpose. She said I would grow up to be just as wonderful as he was, and I would pick up where he left off. Even as a child, I remember wondering if I would have to die in a glorious worthwhile battle to really be a hero.

Time and time again I was exposed to the idea that suffering was the path to greatness. In my younger years, one of my favorite books was *The Old Man and the Sea*. It's a relatively short book about this old fisherman who isn't having much success catching fish. He works hard, he is kind to others, but success in his chosen craft eludes him. Nevertheless, he continues to stay focused and hopes for the best.

Then one day he catches a huge marlin, bigger than any fish he had ever seen. As he battles with this giant for four days and nights, he's pulled out to sea where he finally wins and kills the fish. But it's too big to get in his small boat, so he lashes it alongside and starts his long journey home.

Within hours after he starts back, sharks begin to feed on the dead carcass. Again for days and nights he fights with this new challenge until finally, just before he reaches home, the sharks take the last flesh off his prize, leaving only a skeleton of the great fish lashed to his boat.

As he makes his way through the streets of his village, he is tired and still facing survival without any fish to sell. He has lost the prize fish that he fought so valiantly for, but there is a sense that some greater good has been served. Surely as the village becomes aware of his struggle and how he dealt with it, they will have a new sense of his worth.

I remember tears filling my eyes as I read the final chapter of that book, silently hoping that someday I too could do something like the old man. It was as if his suffering made the world a better place, and I wanted to pick up my cross, my burden, and follow after him.

Even the great scriptures suggested that suffering was necessary to keep oneself on track. Manly P. Hall states in his book *The Mystical Christ*: "Mysticism has been called the path of pain, not because its way is one of suffering, but because most are brought to a recognition of realities by temporal or physical misfortunes. In the human experience, suffering nearly always resolves itself into a question. This uncertainty inspires a larger effort to discover the rules governing human activity."

A dear friend dying of Lou Gehrig's disease wrote to me, putting it this way: "Now hear this, dear one. I am not saying that suffering is necessary. What I am saying is, if we are gifted with suffering, it can evoke a depth and a truth and a peace and a beauty and a love *that is not knowable in any other setting*."

Again, suffering was the great teacher. And even as I fought to win, I would sing myself to sleep with "The Impossible

Dream," hoping secretly within myself that I would be selected for the glorious quest, where one man, scorned and covered with scars, would strive with his last ounce of courage to reach the unreachable star. And the world would be a better place because of my struggle and suffering.

Maybe that's why I was so angry with Gene and his vision of God's plan for me; maybe I was thinking the same kind of thing. Maybe that's why I was so unwilling to listen to Dr. Avery, the psychiatrist, when he said I was living in a dream world. I wanted to get well, I wanted to be happy and have the things that would make my life and my family's life easier. But within my own mind, I wasn't sure if that was what I should want. For within my beliefs, I thought suffering was an integral part of life. I was angry with them for making me look at that.

Being committed to only getting what I wanted and making my dreams come true seemed so petty and small in relation to "life's purpose." And this separation, this duality within myself was tearing me apart.

I was in denial. I wanted to deny that suffering had to be part of life. Yet, most of those I knew and respected as teachers learned through suffering. And many believed that their suffering, their ordeals were a major contributing factor in their growth. So, if I wanted to continue to grow, shouldn't I also want suffering and struggle to help me?

Accepting suffering as a way of life did not take away the possibility of health, the possibility of a life filled with joy. It just meant that I was not the one to determine whether or not that's what my life would be like. I would be giving up the control of my life to someone or something other than myself. It took the possibility of miracles out of my control.

There was still a power in the Universe that could create reality, a power that could do miracles. But who was I to think that I controlled this power or could influence it to get what I wanted?

Gene had said God's plan for me was to live within my limitations and rise above them in spirit so others could learn to rise above their limitations. Shouldn't I accept the things I could not change?

As Dr. Avery had said, my fear of living within a body that wouldn't work was keeping me in denial. Because of this fear, I was unwilling to serve a greater purpose. How selfish it appeared to seek good health at the expense of a grander scheme. Perhaps Dr. Avery was right. I was obsessed, engulfed by my disease, and the disease did not appear to be coming to an end, at least not according to the experts I knew. Perhaps the healing I was seeking would not include the healing of my body.

I'd had doubts before, but now I was told that God's plan was different than my wants, that the spiritual truths in the Bible I read were wrong, and that the psychiatrist's opinion was that I was living in a dream world. Now I was plagued with even deeper doubts. How could I stay motivated and follow through with all the things I needed to do if regaining my health wasn't possible? If my positive choices were not making that big of a difference, why should I discipline myself and continue?

Maybe they were right. Maybe I would be a better person and maybe I would be more fulfilled if I accepted the hand I had been dealt. I remembered the lady who came into my room, stating that when she had accepted her colostomy, her life became easier with fewer struggles. And my life was now a constant struggle. Even in my studies of positive principles, there was always more to do, more to become, more to pay attention to. There wasn't a great deal of joy in my life other than Karen and my precious girls, and I was so distracted I was even neglecting them.

Maybe real peace, real joy would only come when I gave up the idea that I could have the things I dreamed of, the things I wanted, even if what I wanted was a life without physical challenges. I wanted to be a hero. I wanted that for myself and I wanted it for my family. I wanted my daughters to be proud of me and look up to me. But maybe the hero's journey was a journey through obstacles, challenges, and frustration; and real heroes understand when they need to stop fighting, surrender, and accept the things they cannot change.

At first my desire for complete health seemed like the right course. But now that the odds were a million to one against me, now that I had not attained the health I wanted after years of fighting, I was being told that my commitment to health was obsessive and evil.

Maybe I could make a bigger difference in the world by giving up what I wanted and learning to surrender. Maybe I could be a better example to my children if I learned to live with my disease and deal with it differently.

Maybe I needed to work with Dr. Avery and learn to live and dream within my human limitations without anger. Perhaps life was only about learning lessons and having opportunities for growth. After all, war, pestilence, sickness and death were supposed to be inevitable truths.

According to the experts, I had just been in the wrong place at the wrong time, and now my task was to put away my childish vision of joy, wonder and abundance. Now it was time to seek peace and acceptance. The first step was to accept that suffering was a way of life. Perhaps the prayer was right: "Suffering is the pathway to peace."

CHAPTER 14

THE PITFALLS OF PEACE
AND ACCEPTANCE

Over the next few months, the surgeries became more routine. I had no big, invasive procedures intended to rid me of the infection. It was as if these great doctors had tried their best and now had resigned themselves to the fact that I would have the infection for a long, time.

They were no longer willing to risk the nerve damage they knew would come if they kept being that aggressive in their cleaning-out procedures. The debridements and drain reopenings still involved risks, but overall my surgeons changed their course of treatment. They gave up on eradicating the infection and focused on keeping it from spreading. I was encouraged to get my life back to as normal as possible, knowing that the colostomy and drains were permanent and that I would continue having periodic surgeries to keep the drains open.

More and more when I went to the outpatient clinic for checkups, Dr. Kalata, the head of the department, didn't even come in to see how I was doing. Instead, he delegated my exams to the current orthopedic resident. This validated my thoughts and fears that it was time to find peace, accept my life as it was, and let go of my focus on trying to make things different.

One day when I was packing to check back into the hospital for yet another surgery, I noticed that I couldn't find my "tough guy" poster. I sat down to think about where it might be and then remembered. Several months earlier when I was packing to go home from the hospital, I had taken it from my wall and put it in the trash.

As I remembered that moment, I felt empty, realizing a part of me had given up. I was still outraged about my disease but no longer believed that there was much I could do. Even when I pleaded with the surgeons to continue trying to completely eliminate the infection through more radical approaches, they told me I was "knife happy."

I did not want to accept suffering and hardships as the pathway to peace, but my experience was not showing me much proof that there was another way. In the hospital, most patients made it; they lived, but they weren't having one glorious healing after another. It really did seem as if life was a struggle until we reached an acceptance of the limits of healing, an acceptance of the limits of the human body, and then learned to live within those limitations.

During this time, I had been noticing a shift in my focus. More and more I found myself wondering how I might find peace in spite of my problems. I wanted to get well, but the constant struggle, the constant fight was just too much.

I longed for a way out of the battle I was in. And after all that had happened over the last few years, I began to believe there was little hope that my way out would be a big win where I would be as healthy as I was before.

I continued to read and study, but now I focused on material relating to peace and acceptance. And as always, the commitment principle was still at work. As my focus changed, the support and assistance I received also changed. I got more books and articles that supported my new focus on peace, acceptance, and going with the flow. I also noticed that the material I had been gathering about being in charge of my life—and the possibility of creating my life to be all I dreamed it could be—ended up on the bottom of my "to read" file.

It wasn't that I consciously wanted to disregard the positive "I can" material. I had just been led to other priorities and had chosen a new direction. A time or two, I received stuff that spoke to "you can do it," but I glanced through that material quickly and then tossed it in the wastebasket.

Going back and forth from one extreme to the other (from "the hell I can't" to "okay, I'll just give up") was even more depressing than the confusion I felt learning about choice. And the depression was because of the difference between the nonattachment ideas and what I really wanted my life to be like.

It became apparent to me that I had been studying two different models of life and how they should be played. On the surface they appeared to be consistent with each other: both addressed the possibility of a glorious life. But they disagreed about what the glorious life should contain.

On one hand, I was studying the principles of choice and self-determination, and to me that was about having belief and faith that my needs and priorities would be met because I could make my dreams come true. On the other hand, I was studying peace and faith within a spiritual framework where I was supposed to seek something beyond this physical experience, something other than my personal priorities and getting what I wanted.

If what I wanted came easily and quickly, then there wasn't an inference that what I wanted was wrong. But when what I wanted did not happen, when the results I desired were met with problem after problem, when the obstacles became too big for others to believe they could be overcome, then came the inference that I might be going after the wrong thing.

Most of the really sick people I had met in my hospital stays started out with an "I'm going to beat this illness" focus. But if they didn't beat it, if the things they knew to do did not work, then they began to shift their focus to living within the limits they ran into. This shift always seemed to be accompanied by a rationalization that had a higher purpose to it. I also noticed that giving up one focus to go to another was a function of how many times they had tried and failed.

If the seventh surgery had worked and I had ended up whole and healthy, I'm sure most people would have congratulated me for sticking with my vision for health. But now that the problem continued dragging on, I kept being confronted with the idea of God's Will versus my will, which was part of what I called the "Perhaps Models."

It was okay for me to believe in my dreams until I met with failure after failure. Then when the misses added up to some special number, the Perhaps Models came in:

- Perhaps God has a bigger plan for you than you just getting what you want.
- Perhaps the healing you are looking for may not include the healing of your body.
- Perhaps you shouldn't be so specific in what you ask for in prayer.
- Perhaps if it was easy, you might not appreciate what you have.
- Perhaps you can't know the light of the day unless you have experienced the darkness of the night.
- Perhaps this is some karmic debt you're paying or a choice you made before you came here.

In theory these Perhaps Models were not meant to be limiting. They were supposed to offer support. It wasn't that the ones who brought these ideas to me were negative. They had studied and found them useful for themselves. The problem I had with these models was that within most of these ideas, there remained the real possibility that I would *not* get the health I wanted. In fact, in most of the Perhaps Models, there was the distinct *probability* that I would not get the health I wanted.

In the beginning, my quest to regain my health was considered perfectly natural. But now that I had not gained that health and those in the know said I never would, continuing to seek that same health began to be associated with "sin." Not sin like killing or stealing, but the sin of being vain, the sin of pride, the sin of being too attached to the things in my life.

It wasn't always couched in religious terms. Sometimes the sin was the mistake of letting my ego run my life, the error of letting the needs of my small self determine my focus. Oh sure, I was just trying to get what I wanted with regard to my health, but it was still the idea that what I wanted my life to be like was different than what most of the experts said I should want.

When I told them I did not want to believe as they did, I was made wrong. And always in the "make wrong" was an inference that I would be a better person if I believed as they did. So it always came down to sin, or going against nature, or some other idea that I was not serving the greater good if I just went after what I wanted.

As I knew it, the power of choice was about staying focused. Part of the tools of choice, as Sir Winston Churchill put it, was to never, give up. Inherent in choice is the possibility of having it all, of making dreams come true. But in my exploration of my spiritual nature, I again seemed to be gently guided to let go of my cherished personal priorities.

If I did that, my consciousness still created the reality of my life; it was still done as I believed. But when I imagined giving up my desires and need to have things different, what I experienced being left with was only the ability to deal with my problems better. I could have faith in the face of insurmountable odds. I could have courage in the midst of disaster. I could learn some great truths through accepting my limitations. But I couldn't create miracles. Because in the materials

I read on peace and acceptance, miracles weren't up to me. So I was left with having to trust in a bigger plan than mine.

≈ ≈ ≈ ≈

My life had become one big battleground. It held no underlying peace or joy, for even when I was excited and confident, those experiences came from how the surgeries went, whether I was in a great deal of pain, how I did on a test at school, how I was relating to my wife and children. But these wins were short-lived because there were always more surgeries, another test to prepare for, and new challenges in my relationships or cash flow.

I wanted to have a life that worked my way. I wanted to be able to experience my life through my own senses based on my own priorities and have feedback that my dreams were coming true. I also wanted to experience peace and acceptance within the wonder of life itself.

Yes, I could let go and let God. I could turn the specifics of my life over to the Divine Wisdom out there or even the Divine Wisdom Within, and still there was the possibility of health. But then it wasn't up to me any longer. And if I acknowledged that my health challenge was too big for me to handle, then I opened the door for other aspects of my life to be out of my control.

Could I be the captain of my own ship, or was I just treading water in a vast ocean with a mind of its own? Could I be the writer, director and star of my own movie, or was I here to play a bit part in someone else's film?

My mind kept going around and around. If the health I wanted was not an option I could create, then I was not free. And it would only be a matter of time until this lack of freedom, this acceptance of limitation would be applied to another of my dreams, another of my priorities, and I believed this lack of freedom would ultimately lead to the "life of quiet desperation" that Henry David Thoreau talked about in his book.

I sensed that this conflict was ultimately about the separation between the goodness of my spiritual nature and the limitations of my human nature. For I had been exposed to the idea that human nature was weak and untrustworthy. The concepts that 1) we have a saboteur within our own consciousness that will always try to prevent us from having our dreams, and 2) that our ego will always try to separate us from God, do not create a confidence about trusting our human nature.

But there was a great deal of support for these kinds of ideas, reference to the small self, that aspect of human nature that would lead me astray. It wasn't always as blatant an evil force as the devil, but the part it played was the same.

Of course there was the risk of becoming too attached to the material aspects of my life which might lead me to focus on only getting things rather than getting enlightenment or getting saved, whatever that was called. But I wanted to be the one who got to choose. I wanted to have sovereignty over where and what I was committed to.

But if I were to let go and let God, if I were to seek peace and acceptance and go with the flow, which flow should I go with? Which perception of reality should I accept as the truth for me? Some spiritual writings said that life would always be full of discouragement and dissatisfaction. Others said I could not go after what I wanted and still reap the benefits of leading a fulfilled life.

So my questions were, could I lead a spiritual life of love and peace and joy and still be committed to having what I wanted? Could I keep my personal priorities, like having a back that was strong enough to pick up my daughters and wrestle with them and give them piggyback rides? Or to get peace and acceptance, would I have to resign myself to living in a broken body? Because to me "letting go and letting God" gave no guarantees.

Within peace and acceptance as I understood it, I could find no solid ground where I could stand in the midst of Divine Truth and declare that my dreams were going to come true. I could find no solid ground where I could serve my spiritual needs and hold onto my own personal priorities.

But I did find one fairly consistent idea throughout my studies: the peace and acceptance I should seek through my prayer and meditation did not mix with my dogged determination to get well.

CHAPTER 15

FROM SEEKER TO FINDER

During this time, Karen and I moved into her parents' basement so her mother could help with the children while Karen was at the hospital with me. They were wonderful people, and they had already helped us a great deal, but living with them added to my feeling of helplessness and despair. I wanted out of my desperation, my struggle, and no matter how much I hated the idea of giving up on what I wanted, there didn't seem to be any other way but to accept the hand I had been dealt and get on with making the best of a really terrible situation.

My attending physician, Dr. Kalata, was still the head of the orthopedic department. He had become more and more unavailable during routine checkups, and his unwillingness to be there for me reached critical mass one day.

It had been several months since my last hospital stay. One morning I awoke with severe pain going down the front of my right leg. Even though I didn't have an appointment, I went to the hospital's outpatient clinic as soon as they opened.

When I finally got in to see Dr. Kalata, he said with annoyance, "What do you want, Terry?"

"I'm in a lot of pain. It's shooting down the front of my right leg," I explained. "I thought it might be another pocket hitting a nerve."

After a brief examination he said, "It doesn't appear the pain is from the infection. I recommend you to go to your regular doctor."

"Are you sure?"

He gave me a stern look. "I have other patients waiting," and walked out.

I sat alone in the room for a moment feeling a balloon of anger swell and then just as quickly deflate into despair. *Why me?* I thought for the thousandth time.

Finally, I got myself up and traveled across town to my regular doctor.

After he examined me, he said, "I can't find anything that would cause the pain except for the infection."

"Well, can you give me something for the pain," I asked.

"I wish I could, Terry, but you know this whole thing is from the original accident you had on the job. And I can't treat you for that because it would violate the industrial insurance that's paying for the infection problems."

I didn't know what to say.

"I'm sorry, but you need to go back to the University Medical Center and get them to help you," he said.

When I returned to the University Medical Center, I waited for over an hour. When Dr. Kalata finally saw me, I explained what my regular doctor had said. Without examining me again he said the pain couldn't be from the infection and that my doctor was wrong.

Frantic with the need for help, I went back across town again, feeling more and more drained from the pain. My personal doctor again examined me, asked more probing questions, and came to the same conclusion. There was nothing he could do unless I wanted him to be the primary care physician for the Labor and Industry case.

By this time it was four o'clock, and I was reaching exhaustion, but I had nowhere to go except back to the University Medical Center. When I arrived at the clinic, I told the nurse everything my doctor had said.

"I'll tell Dr. Kalata you're here," she said and left. In a moment she returned. "I'm sorry, Terry, Dr. Kalata is leaving for the day and won't see you."

"But . . ."

"I'm sorry, the clinic is closing." She ushered me out the door, leaving me standing alone in the hall.

I stood there for a moment in shock, feeling totally deserted. Finally, with an aching body, I sat down on a bench in the hall and began to cry. I was twenty-five years old and felt like a little kid, completely lost and alone. It was a horrible experience and yet most people who have been sick for a long time have been there.

After about twenty minutes, Dr. Greenlee, one of the orthopedic surgeons, walked down the hall and saw me sitting there. Seeing my tears, he stopped and sat down next to me. "What's the matter, Terry?"

"Nobody cares any more. I've been in awful pain all day, and I've been trying to find someone who would help, but everyone said it was someone else's problem."

Between tears I explained the events of the day. Several times I broke down crying so hard I couldn't continue to talk.

Dr. Greenlee took my hand. "Terry, I've watched as the other doctors have changed their attitude about you, because no one wants to admit they can't help you. You remind them they aren't as good as they think they are." He paused for a moment, then looked me squarely in the eyes. "All that stops right here. From now on you are my patient, and you will never be alone again."

I wanted to hug him. In that moment, he didn't just toss me a lifeline, he attached it to his own belt. I had some great doctors during my illness, but when I look back on those events, Dr. Greenlee stands out as a bright star.

"I'll write you a prescription for pain medication to get you through the night."

"Thanks," I said, tears filling my eyes again.

"I want you to be back here at eight tomorrow morning to see me. And I guarantee I'll stay with it until we've found out what this new pain is about."

Over the next few days, I convinced Dr. Greenlee that the infection was moving over into my right hip area. It seemed that way because of the pain. My doctors had always been concerned that the hip joints would become involved, so he scheduled surgery to explore that area.

When Dr. Greenlee came in to see me after the surgery, he made sure I was coherent and then said, "I opened your hip area, and there was only pink, healthy flesh. Just imagine, there I was with a resident, a couple of interns, and the operating room staff looking on. When one of them asked why we were doing this, I pointed to your unconscious body and said, 'He told me to,'" then he laughed.

"Do you think I overly influenced you to operate?"

"Not at all," he smiled. "I'm glad your hip joint isn't involved, and we really did need to explore that area based on your symptoms."

From then on whenever the rotation of residents and interns changed, Dr. Greenlee would bring in the new group and tell that story. Then he would say, "This guy's been here longer than most of you, and he probably knows more about his situation than you ever will. But while you're on this rotation, don't forget you're the doctors and he's the patient."

Although it was a standing joke that I had influenced him as much as I did, he continued to listen to me and my opinions about what was going on within my own body. He believed that I should be involved in the treatment and decisions that were being made regarding my health.

A few days after the hip surgery, they went in again and found the pocket of infection in the front of the sacrum area and put in drains to open it up.

≈ ≈ ≈ ≈

During that hospital stay, I found the answer I had been so desperately looking for. One evening around ten o'clock, an orthopedic resident was in my room having some cookies I had on hand. A nurse rushed in and told him he was needed in surgery immediately. There had been a terrible auto accident, and a teenager in bad shape was on the way to surgery. With a wave the resident was gone.

The next evening I asked him about the emergency. He told me a seventeen-year-old boy had been in a head-on collision and had broken almost everything. A whole group of surgeons and specialists had worked on him throughout the night. But even though he was still alive, there was virtually no hope for him. He was just too busted up. And to make matters worse, he was the only child of a widow.

When the boy came out of intensive care, they put him down the hall in the room across from the nurse's station. A bed had been set up for his mother, and she was staying by his side. Walking around the floor that afternoon, I looked in his room and saw he was on a circle bed similar to the one I had been on after my thirteen-and-a-half hour surgery. It made me cringe to think what he and his mother must be going through.

I saw her throughout that day and the next. When I asked the staff how the boy was, they would shake their heads. One nurse even said she wasn't sure how he was still hanging on.

That night I had trouble sleeping, and around three in the morning, I was up walking the halls. The boy's mother was in the visitor's lounge having a cup of tea when I passed by. She looked lonely and scared, but I went on by without stopping.

When I got back to my room, I sat on my bed wishing I could do something to help her. There was not much reading material in that lounge, so I decided to take her something to read. I went through my drawers, gathered a few magazines, and as I lifted them out, I saw my Bible. I don't have the foggiest idea why I did it, but I put down the magazines, picked up my Bible, and went out to meet her.

I almost turned around and came back before I got there. What was I doing? I didn't even know this woman. And what was I going to say? But I felt she needed somebody. I knew what it was like to spend the night alone walking those hospital halls afraid the morning would bring tragedy and sorrow.

When I came into the lounge, she looked up. I felt as if she was glad to have someone around other than the staff.

"Hi, I'm Terry. I'm sorry to hear about your son."

She gave me a weary smile. "Hi."

"You know, some of the best doctors in the country are here."

"Yes, I've been told."

It was awkward not knowing what to say. I was sure they had told her some of what I had heard, that her son probably wouldn't make it. Finally I thrust my Bible in front of her and said, "In here it says all things are possible, and we should never give up hope."

She looked at the Bible, then me, and slowly reached out and took it. She set it in her lap and held onto it with both hands.

I stood there not knowing what to say next. "Well, I guess I better go to bed now. Good night."

As I walked out the door I heard her say, "Thank you."

Back in my room I thought of all the things I could have said and wished I had done more. Then I thought, *what am I doing?* I had told her not to give up hope, but that's exactly what I had done. And again I was overwhelmed with questions.

The next day, her son came out of his coma, and he did not appear to have any of the brain damage they thought he might have. Over the next few days, he continued to have what the staff called a miraculous recovery. Then five days after I had given her my Bible, the boy's mother came into my room.

Looking radiant, she stood there smiling at me for a few moments and then said, "You were right in telling me to not give up hope. And thank you for lending me your Bible. You had all the right passages marked. I can't thank you enough. I know my boy is going to get well and with God's help, he will have a full recovery." Then she handed me my Bible and kissed me on the cheek.

When she left I too was all smiles. I went to put my Bible in the nightstand and when I opened the drawer, sitting there on top was the prayer Dr. Avery, the psychiatrist, had sent me, the one about accepting the things we cannot change. I wondered what she might have felt if I had given her that poem to read instead, or if I had told her what the doctors had said, that there was very little hope her son would live, and if he did, it would be without the use of much of his body.

I also wondered if some of the doctors might have thought I had encouraged her to have false hope as the psychiatrist implied I had.

I felt glad for the boy and his mother, but lying in my bed that night, I wasn't glad for myself. Why had God answered her prayers and not mine or the others who had prayed for recovery and not received what they had prayed for? I felt as if my life was one big desperate fight. But my discouragement was not about the fight itself. It was about not being good enough to win the fight, not being supported by that "Divine Something" so I too could have a miraculous recovery. Why did so many prayers go unanswered?

I felt myself sinking into hopelessness. I knew these feelings came from the idea that something was constantly judging me and finding me lacking. It was as if I had been taught to believe in a God, believe in a Presence that was continually watching and judging me based on my failures, and disapproving of who I was and what I was focusing on. I had learned to believe in a Divine Presence that regarded me as "a miserable sinner," or at least someone not good enough to offer help to. And this belief was slowly paralyzing my mind and body and bringing an underlying sense of hopelessness to everything I was undertaking. It was as if my belief in my own unworthiness forced me to let go of my dreams, my aspirations, my personal desires.

That night after my visitors left, when I opened the nightstand to get my reading, I saw my Bible laying on top of the magazines—and I got angry. I wasn't just angry at the psychiatrist for telling me to face reality, and I wasn't just angry at Rev. Gene for his vision of God's plan for me to live in a wheelchair; I realized I was also angry with God. I was angry at the underlying teachings of many who said we were here to pay our dues, carry our cross, and bear the burdens of life in the hope of a better one hereafter. I was angry at the separation between my personal priorities, like being healthy, and the rightness of some Divine Plan. I was angry at the pestilence and plague visited on the human race in the name of personal growth and becoming worthy. And yet even in my anger, I felt I had nowhere to go except to the spiritual teachings because the truth that I was seeking, the power that I needed to be able to get in touch with was something beyond what was normally associated with the "human condition."

Suddenly in the midst of my anger, I had a tremendous awareness about how I was approaching these great spiritual teachings. I realized that I was a committed *seeker*. And I understood that as long as I was committed to seeking, I would not be able to find, because if I ever found the answer that I was looking for, I wouldn't be able to seek any more. And I realized my commitment was not to finding; my commitment had been to seeking!

In that immense realization, I made my first declaration to the Divine Presence that I call God. I picked up my Bible, looked up in the air, and said, "God, I demand to find the answer. This book says that if I ask, it shall be given, and I now demand that it be given. This book says that if I seek, I shall find, and I now demand that I shall find. This book says that if I knock on a door, it will be opened, and I now demand that door be opened."

I felt like I was being a little arrogant, but in truth, I was simply acting on the idea of commitment. Because I had been committed to being a seeker, the entire Universe, Providence Itself, moved in my life to fulfill my commitment to seek, rather than to find. And there was always a new book, a new methodology, a new ritual to support me in my seeking.

Now I was changing my commitment. I was openly declaring that I was no longer committed to seeking. I was now committed to finding, and if the principle of commitment held true, then the entire Universe, Providence Itself, would move in my life to assist me to find what I was looking for. And I could expect that all kinds of material assistance would come to me and guide me in my new direction.

I declared that the answer I would find would be short, concise, and directly related to my health challenge. I didn't want the answer in some parable that took pages to talk about and could be interpreted twenty different ways. I didn't want a story about a prodigal son who went away and spent all his dad's money, yet when he came home, his dad was glad to see him. I didn't want the answer I found to be ambiguous or about something that was not related to my specific health challenge. And with that, I randomly opened the Book.

On the two pages in front of me, there was only one short phrase underlined in red. That surprised me because by that time my Bible was not just thoroughly underlined, it was underlined so much that I started highlighting the really good underlines in yellow. Then there were so many things highlighted that I started writing notes in the margins and putting stars next to the passages I thought *really* important. I made cross-references to other scriptures that related to what I was reading. I even got gutsy and started crossing out some of the stuff I didn't like rereading all the time. So when I opened those two pages and there was only one short phrase underlined, my first thought was, *Wouldn't you know it, I've opened to a lousy section of the book.* But I read the underlined passage anyway. It said, "Thy faith hath made thee whole." Chills ran down my spine, and my breath caught in my throat.

After a moment, I backed up and read the story. It was about a woman who had been feeling poorly for a long time and had done everything she knew to get well. She'd spent all her money on doctors and cures, but none of them had worked. Then she heard about this great spiritual teacher who came into various communities around her home.

She had decided not to talk to this man directly. Instead, she planned to wait until he was not looking and then sneak up behind him and touch the hem of his garment. And she believed that's all she needed to do to be whole. As the story went, Jesus came into the area and, when he wasn't looking, she came up behind him and touched the hem of his garment and was healed instantly. Jesus stopped what he was doing and asked, "Who touched me?" But she was afraid and went back into the crowd.

One of Jesus' disciples said, "What do you mean, who touched you? Everybody is touching you." Then Jesus said, "No, somebody touched me and I felt the power flow, I felt something happen."

Finally the woman understood that she wasn't going to be able to hide in the crowd, and so she came up and told him what happened. She said she'd had this problem with bleeding for twelve years and that she'd done all this work but nothing ever happened; she'd received no benefit. But she believed if she just touched the hem of his garment, she'd be made whole, and in fact, when she had touched his garment, she was healed.

And he said to her, "Daughter, be of good comfort, thy faith has made thee whole. Go in peace."

I had read this story before, but the version I remembered was in the book of Matthew. The story I just read was in the book of Luke. I went back to Matthew and reread that story. It was exactly the same except it did not mention she was healed before Jesus turned around and said, "Who did that?" as in Luke's version.

In Matthew's version, when Jesus says, "Daughter, be of

good comfort, thy faith has made thee whole," the passage goes on and says, "The woman was made whole from that hour," inferring that she was healed only after Jesus spoke. In the book of Luke, it says she came behind him and touched the border of his garment and was immediately healed *before* Jesus did anything.

Luke's version of that story is the only healing in the New Testament where Jesus doesn't do something first. In all the rest of the miracles, he does something and then the healing takes place. It was as if the control of the power of the Universe was outside of the people who wanted to be healed. In the New Testament, the metaphor is that the power is in this person called Jesus and that if people wanted to be healed, they needed to do something, so Jesus would then speak His word and the miracle would occur. The subtlety of the power and healing ability within life being outside of the individual seemed to be in most of the disciplines and methodologies I had studied.

There was always something "out there," the right way or the right thing to do if I wanted to get healed. I had to take the right pills. I had to take the right antibiotics. I had to eat the right food. I had to have the right thoughts. I had to get the power that came from somewhere else to flow into me. There was always a right way to do meditation, a right way to do prayer.

It seemed as if I was taught that the power I'd been seeking was in the ritual itself, in the thing I was doing. I had to do enough of something to get the power behind creation to heal me. I had to let go enough. I had to be good enough. My wants had to be lofty enough. I had to be worthy. Then when I did these things enough, the power from out there, whether it was the power of God or the power of Creation or the power of vibration, whatever it was, would intervene on my behalf and I would be made well.

The problem was that there was no guarantee. I could do all the things I was supposed to do, but something other than me would decide if it was enough. It was not up to me to create reality. Yet in the story in Luke, it didn't say that this lady did any of that stuff. It didn't say that she forgave enough. It didn't say that she let go enough. It didn't say that she was willing enough. It didn't say that she had accepted the struggle in her life enough. It said she believed that if she touched the hem of His garment, she would be made whole. And when she did what she believed, the healing occurred.

I reread the scripture. The disciple said, "What do you mean who is it that touched you? Everybody is touching you." And Jesus said, "No, somebody touched me and I felt the healing occur." Why did she get healed and the others who touched Him didn't?

In reading that scripture, I understood that her belief was the catalyst in her healing. The power was available to all of the people, but she was the one who believed she was going to use it. And all of a sudden the great philosophy embodied in the Christian scriptures took on a whole new meaning.

It wasn't just the idea of self-image psychology or using the subconscious mind as a success mechanism. This was the great spiritual teaching that said once one was committed, once one had a belief system about reality, then Providence, that force of Creation Itself, would back up that belief. Consciousness *does* create reality. God always says "yes."

If I believed in sickness, in lack, and in problems, then the Infinite Power of Creation Itself would back up my belief, and I would get sickness, lack and problems. If I believed that I was involved in a great fight in which I could not win, then my life would become a great fight that I could not win. If I believed that life was about living on a dark planet where I needed to be problem-oriented and disease-focused, then that's what I would experience. And I would lock myself into problem after problem, disease after disease. And even within that perspective, the severity of my disease would only be there because of my belief about it. How many times had I witnessed people in the hospital with the same problem? And yet some got well and some did not. It seemed the outcomes always revolved around their beliefs!

Again I was reminded, "You have a choice." Truly it came down to the idea that Providence Itself, or the Divine Essence of Life, said, "You pick the game and I will play with you there."

In reading that Scripture, I understood that the underlying beliefs held deep in my consciousness would determine my reality.

I now had the piece that I had needed and wanted regarding freedom. Consciousness did create form. "As ye believe, so shall it be done unto you" was the way it worked. And I had the power to change my beliefs. The tools of choice were about creating belief. If I changed my belief I could also change how this Infinite Power would work in my life.

Sure, others might have different interpretations of how the power of Creation worked in one's life. And if I believed in those interpretations, then that's how it would work for me. But the various interpretations themselves did not have the power. It was belief in the interpretations that gave them their power.

As I lay there in bed, I knew it didn't matter how long I had been sick or how beat up my body was. I had an experience of the truth that set me free. I had found the answer at last. This human aspect of me called my belief system controlled the power of Creation Itself.

CHAPTER 16

WHAT IF . . .

T he next morning, I wasn't as convinced as I had been the night before. When I remembered playing with the concept that somehow my beliefs direct the power of God, I thought, Whoa, nobody thinks those kinds of thoughts unless they're nuts!

I had seen inferences pertaining to that idea countless times in the materials I had read. Authors presented ideas such as consciousness creates reality, or the Universe awaits your intention, or the law of cause and effect responds with mechanical regularity to the spontaneity of your thought, or all things are possible if only you believe. And to me, all of those ideas seemed to be based on the concept that the creative power of life said "yes" to one's beliefs. But to think that I controlled the power of God, now that was really out there. But what if it was true?

Wouldn't that and that alone be the only truth that would set us free?

If I believed in want, sickness and lack, then the power of Creation Itself would move in my life and assist me to have want, sickness and lack. But if I changed my beliefs to abundance, health and joy, then this same power would assist me to have abundance, health and joy.

The Commitment quote spoke directly to absolute support. It did not say when I only commit to certain things, then Providence moves too. It said that *whatever* I was committed to, I would find support from the nonphysical through a whole series of events, meetings and material assistance that I never even dreamed possible.

I had always thought the word Providence referred to the spiritual aspect of life and creation, the spiritual power behind life itself. I had read and reread material that spoke about how this power worked and the part I could play in directing or influencing this power. But what had always eluded me was how to use this power in the creation of something I wanted.

I'd get close to having a handle on it, and then I would run into obstacles, or rules, or fail enough times. Then the Perhaps Models would come in, and I would get confused.

I found it easier to think about these ideas when they were worded in vague terms such as Providence or the law of cause and effect, without a direct reference to God. But I needed a miracle. I needed something beyond what most believed was available to human beings through their own ability. I needed to tap the power that made all things possible (the power I called God) and be able to use that God power in a way that would create what I wanted. Because without some all-powerful Force backing me up, I would have to accept the inherently limiting belief that, after all, I was only human, with human frailties and human limitations.

Even so, I was uncomfortable with this new idea because I wanted to back up a little and be less absolute in what I was trying to understand. It was a real stretch for me to attempt to direct my own self-talk into saying, "I control the power of God." But isn't that what the story of the lady's healing was all about? Everybody was touching Jesus, and she was the only one to be healed. It seemed to me she was healed when she combined her belief that she would be healed with spiritual power.

She brought more than just a desire to be healed. She brought more than just a willingness to be healed. She believed that if she touched the hem of Jesus' garment, she would be healed. She did what she believed she needed to do, *she touched it*, and was healed. It was as if she had a "this is the way it is going to be" attitude. It was hard for me to grasp, but it was something she did that made the healing occur. It was just as Jesus said, "Your faith has made you whole." And that something, that faith she brought to her healing was what I wanted to be able to bring to mine.

What if it *was* that simple? What if belief was always the creator of our realities?

Accepting the fact that consciousness creates the reality we experience would explain how all the wonderful disciplines I studied could be right.

All of the models had miracles in them, proof that the principles they taught really did work, or they had scientific studies to back up their claims. There were scripture references that proved it, and most importantly, there was proof in form. Things really did work the way people believed for those who believed a certain way.

How could they all be right? How could all these teachers honestly presenting different models all be right, unless their beliefs were the key element in determining whether or not what they taught worked?

It reminded me of my friend Rev. Gene's vision. I had known Gene for almost a year. He and his prayer groups had been praying for me to regain my health at least twice a day for all that time. And he believed that God answered prayer. He cared about me and spent quality time with me. He was not a negative man, nor was he prone to telling me that he had all the answers. So what happened to change him and how he approached me? The only way I could figure it was with the idea that Providence always says "yes."

During the year he came to visit me, I was continually filling him in on what the doctors were telling me. And I think over that year, after witnessing all the failures in the surgical procedures and prayers gone unanswered, he brought in one of the Perhaps Models he believed in, like the one that goes, "Perhaps God has a bigger plan for you than you just getting what you want."

It seemed to me that in his mind he coupled his new limiting belief about me not getting well with a Perhaps Model, and Providence moved too; and he had a vision that got him off the hook. He no longer had the turmoil within himself wondering why his prayers were not answered. He had been shown the way, and now he could pray to support what he believed, which did not include me regaining my health.

I know this man had a vision that was very real and very significant to him. I'm sure he believed that this vision came from God, that it couldn't be anything he could have created on his own. But I think he just changed his mind, changed his perception of reality. And once he changed his commitment then Providence moved too, and he got the support he needed—his vision.

As I lay there thinking about this loving man who had dedicated himself to serving God and others, I realized how rude I had been to him. Even so, I wondered how many others he had influenced to accept the limitations he came to believe in.

In the game of results, there seemed to be a bar and when results were achieved above the level of the bar, I was supposed to give credit to God or Providence. However if the results were not so good, below the bar, then it was something I was or was not doing that got the blame. I had witnessed that kind of explanation in sports. No one on the losing team blamed God for his or her defeat, but the winners gave God the credit. I had no problem with that for them, but I wanted to be the one to determine whether or not I won this game of getting my health back.

If I needed a miracle to have a perfect body without any limitations, I wanted to be the one to decide whether or not I got one. This is why the Biblical text referring to having the same mind as Jesus and standing equal with God had always fascinated me. It was the co-creation part that was addressed in many writings. My question had always been: what share of the co-creation process did I control? How important was the part I played? I didn't know what standing equal to God meant, and I'm not sure I even cared about that, I just wanted to be able to get my health back. I believed I was co-creator with Spirit, and I wanted to be the one who got to choose what was being created.

In the middle of trying to figure all of this out, I started to laugh. I was lying there really sick and discouraged. The best opinions said that what I wanted wasn't going to happen, and I was thinking, "Well, I'll just figure out how to control the power of God." I marveled at my audacity to think even for a moment that I could learn to use, learn how to control the power of Creation and thereby create health in the midst of disease.

Who could I even talk to about this idea? I certainly couldn't see myself going to Dr. Avery, my helpful psychiatrist. And I couldn't imagine asking Rev. Gene to help me figure out how to control the power of the Universe so I could get what I wanted!

And what about simply trusting in God's wisdom? The idea of trying to manipulate the Universe to get what I wanted didn't seem to have much trust in it. What should I trust? Should I surrender to God's Will and be reasonably happy in this life and supremely happy with God in the next?

I wasn't worried about being happy in my *next* life; I wanted to be supremely happy in *this* life. I wanted to be healthy, I wanted to be a good father, I wanted to have a career that was fun and exciting, and I wanted my daughters to grow up happy, confident and full of joy. My concerns were worldly concerns. They were about what was right in front of me, finishing college and getting a good job. I wanted to trust that all things would work out, and it seemed easier to trust in something other than me that would take care of all my concerns. But if I did that, would I get well?

The idea of taking responsibility for all of the things I wanted to have, all the things that were happening in my life, including my health, seemed immense, and from my point of view unreasonable. Oh sure, I had cute little sayings around like "if it's to be, it's up to me," or "I am the master of my own destiny." But who really believed that kind of stuff? When push came to shove, when there was enough failure, the Perhaps Models always came in, and what was supposed to go was my dogged determination to get the health I wanted.

I wanted to trust, but what part of the divine plan, what part of my relationship with God should I trust? As I wrestled with these concepts and questions, what kept coming up was, what if God's plan is simply to support us in our beliefs? Even saying it to myself seemed so simplistic, so trite and ego-centered. Yet, what if that was the idea behind "it's your Father's good pleasure to give" or "whatsoever you ask for in prayer, believing that you shall have it, you shall have it" or "God always says 'yes' to your beliefs"?

Around and around I went trying to understand this incredible idea. I went back to some of the positive-thought material I had and reread the parts that addressed the power of mind, the creative force of consciousness, the power of belief. I ignored the teachings about limitations and acceptance. And as I restudied these positive, power-packed ideas (and took out the metaphysical weasel words that skirted the issue), what I was left with was, "I control the power of Creation."

With dawning understanding, I knew this was the Truth I had been looking for, this was the Truth I wanted to find. Because for me to be the one who could create the health I wanted, I needed to know that all things were possible if only I believed—*and,* I could control my beliefs. But to take something I can control like my beliefs and infer that Infinite Power was then compelled to act based on them was almost beyond reason.

≈ ≈ ≈ ≈

For weeks the ideas and thoughts that were in the forefront of my awareness all centered on this control issue. I couldn't get past them. If I tried to leave them and go to something else, my mind would tie all of it back to what if that really is the way it works? What if the power of Creation always backed up my beliefs? And what if I didn't have to change for this power to back me up? Wouldn't this mean my beliefs were already creating my reality?

I didn't care how my beliefs might have played a part in getting me to where I was. That was too complicated. Many of the books I had read addressed that issue, and I really didn't agree with any of their approaches; they just got too specific for me. Yes, my beliefs and attitudes had probably played a part in creating this health challenge I was in. But my focus was not on how I got where I was; my focus was how to get somewhere else. How could I use these ideas to get to where and what I wanted?

Again I tried to make this idea less confrontive by thinking, the Universe will support me in my priorities, or when I make a commitment, Providence moves too. But those kinds of statements seemed to water down what I really wanted, which was absolute control over my health. The statements that only spoke to my influence, my direction, my intention did not leave the outcome totally up to me. And I had danced with those kinds of ideas for years without getting the results I wanted.

It was a bold move, but there was no choice from my point of view. If I was going to regain my health, which required a miracle, then I had to be the one who directed or controlled how the power behind miracles was used in my life.

Finally, it was time to move on. It was like Uncle Larry said when I would get lost in the details of figuring something out. "Son, we're not building a piano here. Let's get on with it and figure it out as we go along."

So I consciously chose some new parameters to play with. From that point on, I was no longer the stuff that had happened to me. I wasn't the disease I was immersed in, and I was not going to identify myself with my disease. I was more than the accumulation of my beliefs, attitudes and opinions; I was more than my past. I was that "something" that was beyond anything I had ever done or not done. I was more than just what was going on in my now.

I was going to pretend, as some of the writings suggested, that I was a spiritual being having a human experience. And from that perspective, my beliefs, attitudes and opinions would create my human experience, but they would no longer be who I was. They would only be my current beliefs, attitudes and opinions, and they could be changed. After all: I controlled the power of God.

CHAPTER 17

THE OLD MODELS WOULDN'T WORK

To begin moving to the life I wanted, I had to create a frame of reference where what was going on in my daily life with all of my pain, fears, anger, and doubts was simply what was going on. It didn't mean anything unless I gave power to it.

I had to figure out a way to hold my experience of now without giving my current reality the kind of power that determined what the rest of my life was going to be like. Yes, I had negative stuff that I was creating or allowing to be created out of my own beliefs. But I was not going to be my stuff any more. Certainly I did not want my past to predict my future. But I also realized I did not want my now to predict it either.

I wanted to be able to hold my life in a way that would allow me to begin focusing on what I did want rather than being immersed in and focused on fighting against what I did not want.

Finally, I decided to view my life like a movie I had seen before, the kind of movie with a scary part in the middle where the hero or heroine doesn't appear to be able to achieve their dreams, a part where it looks like the challenges they are facing now are not going to be overcome.

After watching the movie all the way through the first time, it turns out they really do win, and everything turns out perfectly. They ride off into the sunset with the love of their lives by their sides, with the inference they will be happy forever after.

I was going to pretend that I was in the middle of my life, and it was like the movie I had seen where it looked like the situations I was in were going to prevent me from having it the way I wanted. But I knew that as the movie played out, I was in fact going to win. How could this be so? I control the power of Creation, and my new consciousness, my new beliefs could create it anyway I wanted it to be.

I wanted to create a place where I could feel and know that Providence was willing to support me in making my life up differently. Then I could turn my attention to creating the new movie of my life where I could play out not just having the health I wanted, but I could also have the kind of family life I wanted, and the financial success I wanted. I could make everything different, and the Universe would be called into action through my intention.

I was going to believe that the Universe always said "yes." I was going to choose to believe that I did not have to change for the power of Creation to back up my consciousness. It was now as it had always been, "as I believe so shall it be done unto me." And what had to go for that to be true was:

- The beliefs that spoke to separation and duality
- The beliefs that spoke to the judgmental aspects of Providence
- The belief that I was unworthy now

I still believed in the medical model and other realities, I was just going to begin to put the whole package together in such a way so I could choose the outcome. I would be the one who decided whether or not I could get well. And to do that, to believe that, I needed to make up life differently than how I had been taught.

I didn't want to challenge other beliefs, other ideologies about how God worked. And I wasn't interested in making any other belief wrong. I was simply no longer willing to believe the way I used to. And I was not going to expose myself to all the support there was for other ways to make it up. I wasn't going to read their books, go to their meetings, or associate with them, at least not on an intellectual basis. Of course, they had proof their way was the right way. That's what they believed.

It really was pretty simple. I was going to study and pay attention to the disciplines and methodologies, the thoughts and ideas that supported me to have the mind within myself that would allow me to do miracles. I was going to raise the bar all the way to the top of the chart. I was going to be the one who would decide whether I won or lost.

I decided I wasn't going to tell a lot of people what I was doing or what I was attempting to believe in. For I had noticed when I disagreed with others or stated opinions that were significantly different from their beliefs, many people became upset with me and wanted to tell me I was wrong. It was as if in making me wrong, they made themselves and their positions even more right. It seemed they could not accept that we as individuals are just making it up based on our beliefs, nor could they accept that my point of view might be just as valid as their point of view—because that somehow invalidated who they were.

I could understand how someone might be upset with me if when sharing what they had found to be true after years of study and practice, I simply stated, "That's certainly one way to make it up, but I don't make it up that way, and so of course, it's not that way for me." So I decided to keep my mouth shut and just go about making it up differently.

As I was getting clearer and clearer on changing how I made up my life, I remembered what I considered the second great declaration I had made in my battle to regain my health. The first had been "the hell I can't." The second came after weeks of being cut open, torn apart, and bombarded with hurt and fear. It was while I was in the body cast. It began to form the night when my colostomy bag had slipped, and help was a long time coming. I was engulfed with pain and deep sorrow, not just about the terrible things that were happening to my body and to me; it was a night of pain and sorrow for all the suffering within the human condition.

While lying there alone crying about the despair of life as one big problem, I heard myself say, "Nobody should have to hurt this much." It was both a cry for help and a declaration that there needed to be a new way to do life. But at the time, all that registered was the cry for help and the immense sorrow I was feeling about what we all have been taught.

As I thought about that night and my declaration that nobody should have to hurt this much, I knew it was time for me to eliminate my old ways of thinking and change my approach to life and the human experience in general.

I had a quote from Phineas P. Quimby that helped. In the mid-1800s, he had written extensively on the power of the mind to create reality, or at least that's what I thought he was writing about. The specific quote that assisted me in my desire to change how I approached my life was: "People are made up of Truth and Belief, and if one is deceived into a belief that they now have or are liable to have a disease, then the belief is catching and the disease follows." The "deceived into a belief" part intrigued me. It was as if his approach gave me permission to say "no" to some of the cherished concepts and beliefs I had been taught about life being hard.

There was an idea that somewhere way in the back of human heritage, some of our ancestors did something so terrible that the Divine Presence of the Universe, Providence Itself, kicked all of us out of the place where things were easy. The idea that I would have to work really, really hard to become something that I wasn't did not give me a sense of peace and confidence that the movie I was creating, the specifics I wanted in my life would end up to be everything I had dreamed of.

I thought that the old way of looking at life as suffering permeated many teachings expressed as, "We have to pay our dues before we deserve something," or "If we really had our acts together, we wouldn't need to be here in the first place," or "This is a dark planet." There is also the idea that life is about learning lessons and having opportunities for growth, and if you don't learn these lessons or don't take the opportunities and make the best of them, you go to a bad place forever or come back as a bug. For me, these ideas did not hold the promise that life was meant to be a joyous adventure where we get to make it up and have what we want.

The model of life I grew up with was not about consciously applying some basic principles and changing our beliefs, which would move the experience of being human to something filled with joy, wonder and abundance. Yet that's what I wanted and was looking for. And secretly underneath it all, I really did believe the health challenge I was facing was about more than me just getting well. It was fundamentally about the question, "Do we get to make our dreams come true?"

This stepping up and creating the reality I wanted was about my human priorities, my personal wants and needs, like having a strong back that allowed me to function and move like I used to, like getting rid of my colostomy, like having a body that was pain-free, like ending war on the planet, like respecting everyone as a unique incarnation of the Divine Presence.

I was beginning to understand that as a unique person, my wants and needs were valid, and I could say "no" to the idea that there was separation between me getting what I wanted and my purpose in life, or "higher calling."

I was not interested in an abstract idea of peace and joy while still being sick. I wanted out of where I was because living the majority of my time in a hospital being raped and pillaged did not bring peace, joy or positive expectancy. Instead, many times what was happening to me brought terror or the feeling of hopelessness that comes with the thought that life is one struggle after another, where we are never doing it "good enough." My terror and hopelessness came from being deceived into believing the lie of limitation and disease.

Many had tried to deceive me into believing in my limitations or my disease. The lady who came to visit me to tell me about her colostomy was like that. She wanted to convince me that I had the same limitations she believed in. Then when I wouldn't accept the way she did it as the way I would do it, she became upset. I wonder to this day if that visit with me was an attempt on her part to validate her position of accepting the limitations she had been deceived into believing.

Dr. Avery, the psychiatrist, even fell into this category. At the beginning, he didn't tell me to face reality. He waited until I had failed enough times, until I had met with enough resistance, and then his belief kicked in that I couldn't win based on the fact that I had not won up to that point. I remembered he kept asking me if I had read my medical records, if I had looked at my past. He was using what had happened to me in my past as a predictor of what my future would be. It's not that I wanted to make him wrong, but there was no way I wanted to believe like he did.

It was apparent to me that he thought I was my body and the things that had happened to me. He believed I was inherently limited, and he wanted me to come work with him so I could learn to live within the limits he believed in.

Many of the people I had met in the support group for those with chronic infections had the same approach to their lives. They were their diseases, and they spent their time talking about and exploring how they could learn to live with them, what great teachers their diseases were for them, how much they were learning because of them. And when I suggested they let them go away and do life differently, they were offended as if I was talking about getting rid of an old friend.

It was scary to throw out my human limitations and accept that I alone create my reality and the quality of my life. Because if I did that, there wouldn't be someone or something else to blame; the buck would stop with me. And whether or not I got well would depend solely on me. Was I willing to accept that much responsibility for my life? Was I willing to accept that much responsibility for my family and the quality of their lives? Wouldn't it be easier to pretend that everything was perfect right now, that there is divine order in all things just the way they are?

But the idea that everything is perfect now seemed to invalidate my desires, my priorities, and the things I wanted to be different.

Perhaps on some grand scale everything was perfect now, but I was not interested in some abstract idea that all things were perfect. I wanted to be healthy; I wanted to live in a world of peace without war. I wanted to be happy and joyous about what lay ahead of me and for the rest of humanity. I wanted to be able to make my dreams come true, and the only way to do that was to throw out the old model of who I was and how life was meant to work.

CHAPTER 18

APPLYING SPIRITUAL THOUGHT FORCE

N ow it was one thing to toss out what I no longer wanted to believe and focus on. But I knew that simply negating certain things would not give me the new model that would allow me to begin creating what I wanted.

As I thought about that, I remembered a quote from Dr. Ernest Holmes. He was writing about the basis behind what he called "metaphysics," the joining with that which is beyond the physical. He wrote: "Metaphysics is the conscious and practical application of spiritual thought force in the creation of solutions." The idea was that all of us can start right where we are and begin to use our abilities to move toward what we do want, rather than always moving away from what we do not want.

The immensity of applying what I knew to move *to* something, rather than *away from* something, had not registered when I had first encountered that quote. But as I thought about it, I realized the idea it encompassed was the basis for my argument with Dr. Avery and his approach. He wanted me to work with him so I could believe like he did and learn how to handle my disease better. I resisted him because I didn't want to believe in disease the way he did. *I did not want to focus my energy on dealing with what I did not want*, and I certainly wasn't interested in only learning how to deal with my infection better; I wanted it gone.

The quote by Dr. Holmes reminded me that I needed to focus on what I did want, what I was moving toward. For if I applied what he called "spiritual thought force" to deal with my disease, then the first thing I would need is my disease so I could deal with it. The same was true of my creating what I wanted. If I focused on what I wanted to say "no" to, then I would always have more and more to say "no" to. If I only used what I knew to heal something within me, then I would always have something within me that needed to be healed.

The foundation for all I had done up to this point was "the hell I can't." It was a declaration of battle, a commitment to fight. And what I created from that was a model of struggle and challenges to be overcome, the fight between winning and losing, the fight between health and disease.

I had declared early on I was a fighter, so of course, there always needed to be something to fight. I declared I was a survivor, so there was always more to survive. I hadn't gone as far as to identify myself as the disease I had, but I was certainly playing in that arena. I wanted to be a hero, and in my old model, I needed something to do battle with so I would be worthy of my hero status. And therefore, there was always more to do battle with. How simple and how profound; it was time to stop moving away from disease and start moving toward health.

I had been trying to incorporate the different ideas expressed by the teachers I respected into one sure-fire way that would work for me, and once in a while asserting, "I do not want to believe like that." But there were too many inconsistencies when I tried to bring the different ideas together. And although I had lots of have-to's and shoulds, I really wasn't sure what I believed any more.

If I was creating reality based on my beliefs, why not just make it up the way I wanted, rather than trying to select what I should believe based on what other people could prove? I could still read and study what others thought; I could still explore what others believed and found to be true. But I would do that from a mental framework of, "That's one way to make it up. Does this approach have anything within it that would assist me in making it up the way I want?"

If belief was the key ingredient in creating reality, why not choose what I was going to believe? Why not select the material I would surround myself with and thereby choose a belief that would allow me to

The approach I wanted to take was not about making other beliefs wrong, for I thought doing that would make what I was trying to believe trite and petty. I wanted to allow all beliefs to create reality. I was simply going to create a belief that supported the reality I wanted and allow others to do the same. Mine wouldn't be better than theirs; it would just be different. And I didn't have to make anyone else believe like me to validate what I held to be true. That validation would come through my life working the way I chose to believe it was working.

If I could make up a model of life and create health where there appeared to be only disease and human limitations, then that alone would validate the way I was making it up. Sure, it was all about me and creating the reality I wanted, but an important part of that self-centered model was to be all-inclusive; I wanted no right and wrong in it. I wanted to make life up in a way that allowed me to be happy and experience my daily existence as a joyous adventure where my dreams came true. And if others thought that too simple, I could allow them to make it up the way they wanted.

Yes, there might be times when I thought I would need to change others, such as my doctors' opinions about what type of surgery they would perform or whether or not I could be cured. But if I got to make it up, then I could do that too. And in having them do it the way I wanted, that would become the way they wanted to do it. All things were possible if I believed. My job was to create a belief that allowed all of what I wanted to come into form. As the old saying went, "The only limitations we have are those we place in our own minds."

First, I would need to create a new belief about how God, the power behind creation, related to me and what I wanted in my life. If I could only know the God I studied, if I could only experience the God I believed in, then I thought, *Why not just study and make up God the way I want? Why not create a relationship with Providence that will allow me to feel empowered and supported instead of judged and found wanting?*

The confrontation with Rev. Gene showed me there were different Bibles that claimed different truths. There were different ways to interpret what these great spiritual teachings meant. All I was going to do was choose which interpretation I was going to be exposed to. Sure, there would probably be people like Rev. Gene who had the arrogance to assume their way was the only true way. But I wasn't going to play with people like that any more.

I had already noticed the wide range of teachings regarding how prayer, or meditation, or God's power worked. There were a wide range of beliefs and rituals pertaining to how to receive Divine guidance, Divine intervention—that something that was associated with miracles or with the concept that with God all things are possible. I just needed to pay more attention to what I was studying and surrounding myself with so I could begin to find support for what I wanted to believe.

It was like Uncle Larry told me in the beginning of my searching, "In the idea of bringing God into the equation of your getting well, you should probably study God and how that stuff works. Now, I believe there are plenty of people out there who will tell you that their way is the only way. But I'm not sure there's only one right way, especially if that way condemns everybody else. But you have to figure that out for yourself, son. Try to keep an open mind and try not to make others wrong just because they think different. And if they make you wrong for not agreeing with them, don't let that discourage you from what you're looking for. And ask God for help."

I was going to be more specific in what I was looking for as far as believing that the Divine would support me in getting well. And I was going to ask for help.

Second, I would need to strengthen my belief that the concept behind the Commitment quote always worked, that what I was committed to was supported by Providence no matter what my commitment was. I had read about synchronicity and coincidence being the result of something that was done by the person involved in the event. I'm not sure any of the authors came right out and said, "We as individuals create those things that we refer to as synchronistic events." But why not? If the Commitment quote was right, then wouldn't my commitment be the cause behind the events and material assistance I received in support of that which I decided?

It wasn't that I had to make everything up from scratch. Most of the positive materials I had read suggested or inferred that we as individuals were powerful and had influence over how Providence moved in our lives. I just needed to tweak some of my thinking a little and toss out some of the other things that were clearly limiting. And I didn't have to figure it all out at once. All I had to do was begin right where I was, start believing in myself and begin focusing and moving toward what I wanted.

Third, I would need to discipline and remind myself to stay focused on creating and believing only what I wanted to create and believe. This was my part in following up my commitment with tangible real-world actions I would take. I had lots of lists from all the books and articles I had read. But I'm not sure I believed any of them held the key to what I needed to be doing.

It seemed that many disciplines held the possibility of creating miracles or having miracles happen. But I had never found one specific discipline or methodology that really grabbed me. I didn't think that one day I would wake up and find my bowels miraculously put back together and my body free from pain and infection. Oh, it was a possibility, but I didn't think that's what would happen on its own. I thought I would need to do something to create that reality.

This third area was about me following through and doing what I believed I needed to do. And it was this doing or action area that was the most confusing for me. There were so many different beliefs and theories about how to create health, and as I thought about them, I started to feel overwhelmed. But I wasn't alone any more in my commitment to moving to the health I wanted. I had company; I was receiving help and guidance, and Providence Itself was moving to assist me in figuring it all out. At least that's how I was making it up. All that was left was to start. I had a choice, and it was time to get on track making my choices count.

CHAPTER 19

THE FREEDOM OF CHOICE

In order for choice to be an inspiring process where I could get excited about the outcome, I had to have total freedom to choose what I wanted to create.

One of the huge stumbling blocks for me in the area of choice had been that there was always a list of the proper choices. And too many times, those correct choices did not relate directly to my heart's desire. So the motivation to accomplish those right choices wasn't there for me because I wasn't going after what I really wanted. It was that old model again where I was supposed to give up my human needs in search of my divinity.

But if I could completely accept the idea that the Universe only says "yes," that would allow me to begin to believe that my priorities were legitimate, that my life could be a joyous adventure where I could make my dreams come true. And if I really owned this, I figured it might give me the motivation I needed to keep me going if I ran into obstacles. Because the payoff for staying on track and using the principles of choice was now about having the life I had always wanted—a life where I enjoyed going to work, where money wasn't finally an issue any more, where time with my family was fun and play-ful.

The fundamental idea I had to come to grips with was the question, "Is what I am going after legitimate?" Can I stay fo-cused with my dogged determination to achieve what I want without questions and concerns around whether that's what I should be going after? Can I continue to be committed to what I want even if I run into obstacles, problems or failure?

If the Commitment quote was true and the Universe *did* support my consciousness, then the key—the most important thing for me—was to legitimize my priorities so I would no longer have any distractions or doubts about what I was fo-cusing on.

It seemed so simplistic, so self-centered to be starting with the idea that I get to have what I want. But if I did not have that kind of belief, that kind of assurance that what I was going after was okay, I knew I would spend needless time and en-ergy wrestling with whether or not that's what I should really want.

The first step in using the wonder of choice to make my dreams come true was not about applying the principles I was learning. It was not about applying the spiritual thought force or mystical intention, affirmations, or affirmative prayer to get what I wanted. The first step was to validate what I was going after. It was about making it okay to use not only my human abilities but also my spiritual abilities in making my specific personal objectives or desires a reality.

I had read about rules in the area of using spiritual power. One was that I could use spiritual power as long as I wasn't going after my ego-centered needs. Yet both Dr. Avery and Rev. Gene had said my need to be whole and pain-free was ego-centered. I had also read materials that inferred I could use spiritual power as long as it was for the good of everybody, that I couldn't put my own personal desires ahead of the good for the whole. Yet Rev. Gene had had a vision from God that the whole would be served better if I accepted my physical limitations, live in a wheelchair, and be an example to others so they too could be happy within the limitations they accepted.

It wasn't that I wanted to make that idea wrong for others, and it was okay with me if others wanted to teach how to live within limitations. I just did not want to be one of the ones who had limitations that had to be lived within. But if Rev. Gene was right about serving the greater good, should I want to be perfectly healthy?

There were others who said that I could use spiritual power as long as I was not trying to manipulate or change others. Yet I had a belief that in order to be perfectly healthy, I would need to change my doctors' beliefs and get them to go along with the more aggressive treatment I thought my body needed to rid itself of the infection. I even had thoughts that I would need to manipulate their thinking.

All of these separating beliefs and ideas had to be reconciled. No, they actually had to be eliminated so I could focus on moving toward what I wanted without any distractions regarding whether or not I was going after the right things. I had to be able to include my ego-centered priorities in the game of being the co-creator of my life. And for me that necessitated the freedom to be at choice in all things. I could have no separation between my human aspirations and my divine purpose.

≈ ≈ ≈ ≈

As I moved into the idea of being at choice in all things, I felt an added burden in my life. It was as if now that I was openly declaring, "If it is to be, it is up to me," I brought with that a heavy responsibility. Even with the idea that I was no longer alone, that Providence was really there to help me in all I desired, I still felt a weight, a hesitancy, wondering, now what do I do? And at the same time, I could sense underneath this heaviness an excitement about my life I had not known, or at least not experienced for a long time. I decided that rather than start right in on trying to figure out what to do, I would explore what the underlying excitement was about.

So I began to write out my thoughts on paper. This allowed me to let go of those thoughts and move on to new ones. I was not trying to figure out what to do next; that would come later. I tried not to get into judging whether the thoughts I had about this shift were right or wrong, I simply wrote out my thoughts with the intention of finding out what the excitement was underneath the feelings of doubt or fear that were causing me to be hesitant.

Many times I would get overly involved with what I was writing and lose the purpose of the exercise, which was to discover what the underlying excitement pertained to. But as I cleared my mind of these thoughts by getting them on paper, I got an amazing experience of the excitement. And for me it all centered around freedom.

At first I thought this sense of freedom revolved around what I was going after. I thought the excitement was a result of what I would achieve, the things I would have, the possibility of getting what I wanted. But as I continued to write out my ideas on how I felt about making my dreams come true, I found my enthusiasm was more than just a result of the different things I was going to have. My excitement seemed to be about my union with something good.

I kept asking myself, how can choosing a model, a new belief where the power of Creation just says "yes," how can playing with the concept of "I control the power of God" (which seemed at times like a big control issue) bring to me a sense of being closer to the Divine? And then it hit me: There is no separation.

For my whole life, I had been taught that I wasn't enough. Therefore, I believed my actions were never what they could have been, my thoughts were never lofty enough, my desires were never holy enough, I never performed up to my ability. On and on I fell short of some standard that I was judged against. And no matter what I did or accomplished, it seemed I came from being not enough now.

Underneath this shift I was making was the experience that I was wonderful just the way I was. It was more than the law of cause and effect responding to my commitment. It was more than using spiritual thought force to create reality. In realizing that I could make my dreams come true, I got that I was loved and supported by Providence Itself. The only reason that my prayers had not been answered revolved around my beliefs. It was not that the Divine saw me as unworthy, it was my belief that I was unworthy.

The separation and duality models that I had been deceived into believing, which had plagued me throughout my life, were no longer real. I still found myself thinking thoughts that could lead me to doubt my priorities, but they were just thoughts—thoughts that were given to me by people or writings I had trusted as my teachers. And those thoughts only had power if I gave it to them. All of a sudden, it became okay to choose openly and freely. And this freedom of choice was not just about me and my priorities; it rolled over to everyone else.

I can't begin to count how many people I had judged as wrong because they had chosen something around their health that I would not want to choose for myself. I had made the people wrong in the chronic infection support group because they were not as focused on getting rid of their infections as I wanted to be on getting rid of mine. I had even made my father wrong for dying in the war and leaving his family.

I wasn't convinced that those who died or left the hospital less than physically whole had chosen consciously to die or have physical limitations. But I made them wrong for not choosing something else. I made them wrong for not choosing what I wanted to choose for myself. I even made myself wrong for getting sick in the first place.

Now it was time to let go of all of that "make wrong" because I realized that most of the people I knew and many of the authors I studied did not know they even had a choice. At least they did not believe they had the choice to create reality rather than face it, and I could no longer make others wrong for not choosing differently just because they did not know they had that much power and authority.

The underlying sense of excitement I was feeling about my life was the realization that there was no right or wrong in what I or anyone else would choose to experience in life. Some might choose to go along with the way they had been taught, that death or disease was part of some divine plan or that they were powerless to change some of the things or conditions in their lives. Some might even try to convince others that the way they made it up was the only right way to make it up. And still others might believe that there was a judging and damning presence that created life's challenges, as if to test us or mold us into something we weren't. I simply wasn't going to believe that for myself any longer. I was going to feel that I was divinely created to rule and have dominion over the circumstances in my life. And with that choice came an experience of being truly loved.

In the past when I was motivated or inspired to use various principles or tools I knew to accomplish something or make changes within myself, the motivation came from a feeling that I was not enough now. As I explored this new approach and the feeling of excitement I had about myself, I noticed that I was creating a model where this "not enough now" belief was no longer legitimate.

The joy and enthusiasm I felt came from my awareness that I was enough! Sure, there were things I wanted different and changes I wanted to make in myself. But even with those, I was a magnificent expression of life. I was beginning to know the joy of being human, the wonder of life, the glory of form. And all of that was rolled into this new approach, this new model. It wasn't just about control and getting my way. It was also about believing in myself, loving myself, and respecting myself as a unique individual with valid wants and desires.

"Know the truth and the truth will set you free" now held new meaning for me. Part of the truth was about how the Universe backed me up in my beliefs, and part of the truth pertained to who I was.

After weeks of searching, I now understood that the underlying enthusiasm I felt was about being enough, being worthy, being magnificent. And from those feelings, I began to move into the process of creating reality, filled with wonder.

CHAPTER 20

CHOICE OF DESTINATION

This change of thinking that I was trying to make didn't come all at once in a flash of blinding light that represented Truth. Rather it was a process I consciously chose to focus on while my life went on pretty much the way it had been.

Well over fifty percent of my time I was still angry and immersed in my struggle. It showed up in all areas of my life. Many evenings Karen and I would end up fighting about the smallest things. I was still in denial, still abusing the pain medication, still lost in all that was right in my face that spoke to living within my human limitations. And there were also times when I could absolutely feel the truth of what I was hoping to create.

During the weeks when I was working on understanding the excitement and enthusiasm I was feeling underneath my hesitancy, I was also exploring how I was going to start in the game of moving to instead of moving away from.

I wanted to start with "I'm going to be perfectly healthy," but I couldn't get a grasp on what it meant. It was too all encompassing, too much like saying, "I'm going to make all my dreams come true." Yes, that was what I was hoping was true, it was the possibility included in my new model of life, but right after that idea came, "How the hell are you going to do it?" And I was at a loss to answer this question.

I went to pencil and paper in an attempt to get my confusion of thoughts organized so I could begin. And writing out my thoughts did give me a sense of organization. Again, these new ideas were like a jigsaw puzzle with all of the pieces on the table with no final picture to guide me. But as I wrote out my ideas on where to start and what to go for, I found I naturally began to group the things I thought I needed to do into a framework. It went something like "well, that might work," or "that might be a place to start." And the overall confusion began to be replaced with a hint of moving in the right direction. It was like getting a picture of the completed puzzle.

I still had all the pieces of what to do and where to begin all over the table, but I began to notice more confidence that I would be able to use the information I was studying to accomplish something. It wasn't a time filled with peace and delight. But what I was doing and what I was using my "woowoo" on allowed me to move into a greater awareness that I was going in the right direction. (Note: "woowoo" is a term I began to use for the various mental practices I was using.)

When I would get overwhelmed or lost, I would try to remember to stop focusing on what I needed to do, and remember—as well as experience—the "Providence moves too" part of my equation. I would consciously spend time feeling that I was worthy, I was loved, I was enough—the kind of experiences that were underneath the freedom of choice.

I was consciously choosing to remember that I was something more than the results I was getting or not getting. And then from that experience, I would move back into applying what I knew to create what I wanted.

At first I was not very successful at holding the feeling of "being," especially when I got too involved with what was next. But I worked at it. I worked at applying myself and using choice to focus on moving to solutions rather that just staying angry and upset about my problems.

During those times when I was confused and felt like I would never get all these new ideas into a workable model, the thought that gave me the most comfort was from the Commitment quote where it said: "A whole stream of events issue from the decision, raising in one's favor all manner of unforeseen incidents and meetings and material assistance which no one could have dreamed would have come their way." And that reminded me: "All you have to do is stay focused in your commitment to move toward what you want. Then Providence will assist you to get there."

≈ ≈ ≈ ≈

The biggest surprise for me during this time was the realization that I did not believe I would ever be perfectly healthy. I had spent so much time telling those who wanted me to accept my limitations to go to hell that when I found I had succumbed to believing the way they did, I was shocked. I'm sure the belief had been developing for some time, especially showing up in how adamant I was in making others wrong for insisting my disease was not curable.

And even though I had read that the first thing to get clear about in the creation of something new is to find what our beliefs are now, I found it very discouraging to know I didn't believe I could have what I was going after. This made it especially important for me to spend time in the experience of me as more than what was going on and more than my current beliefs. But even consciously spending time in the spiritual reality of me didn't get me out of my "so now what do I do?" confusion. Again I went to pen and paper to get my thoughts a bit clearer because I didn't know what else to do.

I had thoughts of just giving up and accepting my belief that perhaps it was time to focus on something I believed I could do. And I noticed I did not make giving up wrong, like I had when I was committed to the fight. Now that I was beginning to grasp that all decisions were legitimate, that all choices were okay from a spiritual framework, there didn't seem to be the same right/wrong energy around accepting the limitations I believed in.

It wasn't as if all of a sudden it was acceptable for me to live in a body that wouldn't work. It was more like I just didn't want to fight any more. I didn't want the constant struggle, and the only way out seemed to be to accept the belief that I was never going to get well.

Then I would argue with myself.

"Don't forget that all things are possible if you only believe."

"So what? You don't believe."

"But that doesn't mean I can't change my belief."

"Yeah, right!"

"I control the power of God."

"Okay, manifest a bar of gold on the table, and then we'll talk about getting well."

"I don't think I can do that."

"Yeah, and you also don't believe you're ever going to get well."

On and on, I would argue these opposing views inside my head. And as I did this, I spent more time feeling sorry for myself, and I quit being as consistent in writing down my thoughts and exploring what I was going to move toward. Finally, I didn't know where to turn except back to consciously spending time experiencing myself as more than just the dilemma I seemed to be in.

Then one day I simply thought, *"It's only a belief."* It wasn't a huge realization that set me on fire; it was just the simple truth I had been playing with for months. Beliefs create reality and beliefs can be changed.

Honestly, I'm not sure how much this realization helped me get over the shock of realizing that I did not think I would ever regain perfect health. But there wasn't a great deal of heavy drama about it. It was just a group of thoughts that added up to me believing I would be sick for a long, long time.

After a few weeks, I slowly got back to some type of conscious application of what I was trying to believe and incorporate in my life. And again I started writing out my thoughts as they pertained to using what I knew to create something different in my health.

One of the things I did was make a "dream list." I wasn't very motivated with this because I was wrestling with "How can I believe I can make my dreams come true, while not believing I can ever get back to perfect health?" So I agreed with myself to spend a few minutes every day making a list of what my dreams were. It wasn't a very organized endeavor. I just kept a pad of paper on my nightstand with a heading on top that said "Things I Want." My agreement with myself was every time I noticed the list, I was to add at least one thing to it.

This was my attempt to begin to focus on what I did want rather than just spending time angry about or focused on what I did not want. And to my surprise it worked.

There were lots of things I wanted that I could start on right now. I could be a better father, and I could be diligent in my college studies with positive expectations about getting a good job when I graduated.

As I consciously spent time thinking about what I was creating, I began to notice how much I disliked the time I was in the pits immersed in the good fight. And it became obvious, sometimes painfully obvious when I let my thoughts dwell on the struggle and "poor me."

It was okay for me to spend a little time in the "why me?" arena, but if I spent too much time there, I would build up a momentum of negative thoughts, and then it was much more difficult to get out of that mindset. So I set up what I called a "negative monitor." It was a game I played with myself. Whenever the negative monitor would "catch" me having negative thoughts, I would ask myself, *Do you really want to go there?* I gave myself permission to continue in the negative thoughts, but I asked within if that's what I wanted to do.

Sometimes I would cuss and say, "You're damn right I want to think like this. I have a right to think like this. I'm being screwed." And I also gave myself permission to change my focus and think about something else.

What I noticed was when I caught myself before the negative thoughts gained a momentum of their own, it was much easier to make a shift to thinking about something else. And there were still times when I would spend hours upset about my current situation.

One evening while writing on my dream list, I noticed there were several references to getting rid of the colostomy. And to my surprise as I thought about it, I also thought, *Why not?* What surprised me was I noticed that I didn't think, *Well that's impossible.* I was amazed that I was open to the possibility that I could get rid of the colostomy.

As I wrote out my ideas, it seemed so simple. Even though the doctors said my lower colon had probably been damaged beyond repair, I didn't believe it. It wasn't that I thought them wrong, I just didn't believe that it could be so. I had never had a part of my body that didn't heal. Oh sure, I had a knee that gave me some trouble from a high school injury. I couldn't pick up a big rock and throw it with all my might without hurting my shoulder. But even those areas where I needed to be careful had healed. They let me function normally with a body that worked.

Partially because I wanted to get rid of the colostomy and partially because I wanted to try to use the idea of moving *to* something on a big issue in my life, I decided to consciously apply the principles I was studying to getting rid of my colostomy.

I didn't think if I thought good thoughts and prayed a lot, some day I would wake up and my bowels would be sewn back together and put back inside where they belonged. That was possible, I mean all things were possible, I just didn't think that's what would happen. So I went to pen and paper in an attempt to get a clearer sense of how this was going to happen, how I was going to create this as a reality.

Now, I had read things like "give no concern about tomorrow, just give your thoughts to God and He will . . ." or "don't limit God by trying to figure out how to accomplish things. He knows beyond what you as mortals . . ." But from my point of view, none of those kinds of ideas related to "if it's to be, it's up to me." There was going to be a miracle in my life, and it was up to me. So what was it I had to do?

I tried to remember that I did not have to figure it out all at once and decided that every day I would spend some quality time with my thoughts with a focus on getting rid of the colostomy. I would spend a minimum of ten minutes a day writing, with the intention of finding what I thought I would need to do or what I thought needed to be done. The first big ah-hah I got was around what I was focusing on.

I had read many books on goal setting, time management, and resource allocation. And all of them made reference to setting positive goals and moving energy in a positive direction. But when I got that it was about the idea of moving *to* rather than moving *away from*, it made a huge impact on me in a practical way.

I had written down, "I am going to get rid of my colostomy," and many times when I started into the ten minutes I had allocated to work on this desire, I found I would get mad just reading my goal. I hated the colostomy. It was dirty, it smelled, and when I would start with "I am going to get rid of it," I was still focusing my energy on *dealing* with it. Sometimes I would spend the whole time being mad.

So I decided to play with how I might word what I wanted in such a way that it would be inspiring rather than setting me up to do battle. And then one evening I wrote it out this way: "Soon I am going to be able to go to the bathroom the way I used to go to the bathroom."

When I read what I had written, my eyes filled with tears. A wave of cleansing energy swept through my mind and body, leaving me with an undeniable experience of who I was. Lying in a sterile hospital room, still engulfed with disease, knowing I had limiting beliefs about my health, not knowing how I was going to do it, I was finally clear on *what* I was going to do. Soon I was going to be able to go to the bathroom like I used to go to the bathroom. It was one of the single biggest moments of my life!

The excitement I felt was around the idea of finally saying "yes" to something. I had spent so many years saying "no." No, I won't be sick; no, I won't be a lousy father; no, I won't be broke the rest of my life; no, I won't have a life that's problem after problem; no, I won't focus on dealing with my stuff. It was as if finally I had a sense that I could say "yes," and it was more than saying "yes" to the specifics I wanted. I could say "yes" to life, "yes" to the wonder of being me. It was a huge sensation, a huge realization. It was as if I was truly saying, "Yes, Providence is going to support me in all I want my life to be."

I had known it intellectually or at least had read it. I had reasoned it through; and now my life was no longer about struggle—I was free.

Choice of destination was not just about time management or stopping procrastination or all those other reasons I had gone to the tools of choice before. It was now about saying "yes" to my dreams, saying "yes" to the kind of life I wanted. And the whole experience proved to me that I could shift my energy.

It was more than the textbook explanation of focusing on the positive or thinking only positive thoughts. It was about managing my energy. It was a shift from thinking that if I do not do this right, I'll suffer the consequences of lack of focus, or all the other negatives associated with not being on track.

Choice of destination was now about freedom. It was yet another step in accepting the wonder of me and the possibility of the magnificence of life itself.

For years I had been reading list books. And somehow I had been using all the things I should be doing as a benchmark to judge myself as to whether or not I was doing enough. My dreams or desires had become lost in all I thought I needed to do. And more times than not, I found myself lacking. Even when I was applying what I knew, I had a little voice inside telling me I wasn't doing enough.

The experience that night of moving to being whole, moving to what I did want and how that experience excited me, how it empowered me and inspired me, led me to seek what was next with joy and anticipation. Soon I was going to be able to go to the bathroom the way I used to go to the bathroom. And life was good!

CHAPTER 21

CHOICE OF ACTION

Some of what I wanted to accomplish from my dream list was easy as far as figuring out what needed to be done on my part to accomplish the things I desired. For example, I would be upbeat and present when my girls came to see me. But there were other areas where I was unclear. And I came to be glad that in the area of having surgery to reverse my colostomy, I didn't have a clue as to where to start because I had never really explored within myself what the idea of choice of action was about, and now I had to.

What part did action play in my ability to create what I wanted? There were thousands of "to do" books that addressed all the right things that had to be included if one was to produce the results they wanted. But I wasn't into taking on what someone else found to be true for them. I wanted to find out what was true for me. I wanted to seek within myself and find what I believed regarding action and the part it played in my creative process.

It wasn't that I didn't find some good things to do within what I studied. From my perspective, there were many worthwhile principles to pay attention to, such as diet and nutrition, exercise, and attitude. These were important, but I didn't think they were the most important in getting my colostomy reversed. I wasn't looking for a magic pill or the latest secret of the ages that had been discovered by some seer or something channeled by the latest wise entity who came to show the way, although some of that material I found interesting and refreshing.

I was looking within myself for how I was going to accomplish this thing I wanted when the evidence around me said it wasn't going to happen.

I went again to pen and paper to write down my ideas. I wasn't writing paragraphs and paragraphs on every action that might be taken, I was just trying to get my thoughts organized and find out what I believed needed to be done. Mostly as I listed the various actions I thought needed to be taken, I was aware of how I felt about the actions. For I knew it would be my feelings and beliefs about the actions that would give them power.

Much of what I wrote in the beginning came right out of what I had read, what I had heard, or what others had done. And at first, part of me wanted to grab onto those ideas and start doing something. I found it somewhat disconcerting and unsettling that I did not know what I thought needed to be done. It was like being lost and not knowing which direction to go, and part of me wanted to be out of the lost feeling and just go with what others believed. But I continued to remind myself that it was not the action that held power; it was my belief in the action that gave it power.

I wanted and needed to be able to put together this concept of being at choice in my actions in such a way that my actions gave me the same positive feeling as when I reworded my goal and stated it in such a way that it moved me to it. I had to feel that the actions I was going to take would get me to what I wanted. So I continued to go within, writing down my thoughts and ideas so the next ones could come up. It took awhile. I made some starts in various directions that petered out, and when that happened, I got discouraged and frustrated with not knowing what to do. Then I would try to remember to get back in touch with "you don't have to figure it all out right now."

Each day before lunch, I made a point to find a quiet place where I could sit for a few minutes to acknowledge that I was not alone, that Providence was moving in support of what I wanted. I would read the Commitment quote and focus on the meetings and material assistance that were coming my way. And there were days when I put it all away and said, "Screw it."

What I was after was a map that I believed would get me to where I wanted to go. I believed if I got this, it would be easier to keep my focus on the goal because I would know what I would be doing to get there. I had the destination, the street address if you will. What I wanted was a detailed plan of action that showed me how to start where I was and take individual steps that I believed would get me to my destination. I wanted to create something that would give me confidence that I could do what needed to be done to create the miracle I wanted.

I needed this as part of feeling it was going to work, that soon I would be able to go to the bathroom the way I used to go to the bathroom. I didn't want a list that I hoped might work; I wanted a list that jumped out at me, filling me with "I can do this and it will work!"

Again I had a lot of trouble here with the "let go and let God" model of life, the "give no concern about tomorrow" model, the "don't limit God" model. From my point of view, those ideas did not guarantee me getting what I wanted, and I was looking for a guarantee. And I thought part of that guarantee would come with me believing in what I was doing.

I didn't rush myself in this aspect of figuring out choice. Yet at times I got discouraged because this part didn't come as fast as choosing my destination. But I continued to write out my ideas and did have a sense I was getting closer to what

I was looking for.

As I reviewed what I was getting down on paper, it became apparent to me that most of the ideas I was writing about revolved around the application of spiritual thought force, the focused, intentional prayer area, what I was calling "woowoo." But I honestly didn't think that using mental work alone would be enough. I didn't think one day I would wake up with my colon put back together. I thought it would have to be cut off of my abdomen where it was attached and sewn back together.

As I thought about that, the "what" I needed to do became obvious; I needed to get Dr. Yelton, the head of the General Surgery Department, to agree to do that. He was the one designated by the insurance company to have the final say on abdominal surgery. The problem was that he was the one who told me that it was highly unlikely my colon would ever heal.

Now I was closer; I had a game plan. But how would I get him to change his mind?

Dr. Yelton was a great surgeon, yet he had a lousy bedside manner. He didn't like it if I asked too many questions or when I was doubtful about the direction he wanted to take in my treatment. And he really didn't like it if I made suggestions. From his point of view, I was to keep quiet and follow directions. He was the doctor and I was the patient.

We had had many confrontations, especially when I wanted a more aggressive approach to the debridement surgeries. He was the first one to call me knife-happy. So initially when I realized that he would have to be the one to agree to sew up my colostomy, once again I felt that I had run into a brick wall.

After a few days of "poor me, why all these roadblocks," I got out my pen and paper and started writing out my ideas on how to get him to agree. Again and again, I tried to go back to the experience of me being more than the problems I was encountering, in an attempt to rekindle the momentum, the joy of going after what I wanted. For it was very evident that if I continued to spend my time in the story, the drama of this challenge, I would never get it done. But this time I got stuck in my doubt. I got stuck in my disbelief.

I had become so immersed in the doingness, finding the right action, I couldn't get the feeling back. My dream that someday it will be different was buried in all my thoughts and beliefs about what I could or couldn't do, what I should or shouldn't do to make my dream come true. My vision of what I was going to create had gotten lost in all I thought I would need to do to make it happen. And all my writing about what I needed to do or thought I needed to do just compounded my hopelessness.

For a few days, I couldn't get out of my lost and confused state. Even though I was attempting to believe that all things were possible, I was stuck in my inability to figure out how to get the doctor to change his mind and do what I wanted him to do. And the idea that had assisted me earlier regarding "it's only a belief" was of no help. Writing out what I thought I might need to do so I could get underneath that idea and come up with other possible actions I might do was of no help either. I think this was the first impasse I couldn't get past with my shear force of will using the "I control the Power" model. And what came in as soon as I acknowledged I was at an impasse, or that I might not be able to do enough or do it right, were all the Perhaps Models.

It wasn't like these limiting ideas bombarded me with "I told you so." They came in softly as if to give me some comfort, some direction. And I did find comfort and a kind of peace while entertaining them. They got me out of the fight; they gave me something positive to focus on instead of feeling lost in the futility of trying to manipulate form when I didn't know how to do it.

This time as I explored the Perhaps Models and how they pertained to me not getting what I wanted, I didn't feel the anger and resentment that I had felt before when they confronted me and my dreams. Understanding that the Universe just says "yes," and realizing that all models could be validated and proved, I no longer had to be as immovable in my denial, my "well, it's not like that for me" stance. I found I could not get as worked up around these limiting ideas being wrong in support of what I wanted to believe being right.

I thought the Perhaps Models were inherently limiting in that they usually inferred that the desired result might not be attainable. But they were positive in their reference that something good would probably come if I shifted my priorities or what I was committed to. These models were in many of the great books I had read and were certainly an accepted way to do life. I wouldn't be wrong for accepting one of them as my standard. Perhaps the healing I was looking for might not include the perfect healing of my body.

I think part of me was afraid to find out what I believed. It was one thing to explore the freedom of choice in theory, but to apply it meant that I would have to confront my own beliefs and what I held to be true. I knew that some of my resistance to pursuing my train of thought about getting the head of general surgery to change his mind was my fear that he would get me to change my mind. Although the psychiatrist had brought up the idea that my colon would not heal and I would probably have the colostomy for the rest of my life, the surgeons had never been that explicit. They had expressed reservations, they had inferred, they had suggested, but they had not said never.

My belief around having the infection in my spine forever or the idea that it was not curable had come from my exposure to many subtle and not so subtle beliefs from others. And part of me was afraid that if I cornered Dr. Yelton regarding my colostomy, he might influence me in such a way that I would end up believing my dream of "going to the bathroom like I used to" was just a dream, an unreachable dream.

And the impasse persisted. So I decided to focus on something else.

CHAPTER 22

CHOICE OF MENTAL ENVIRONMENT

F rom the very beginning of my study, through my exposure to the book Psycho-Cybernetics, I had read about
the power of affirmations, the concept of choosing my
own self-talk and how through choosing my mental environment, or the thoughts and ideas I allowed my mind to dwell
on, I could influence my attitudes and beliefs. It made sense to
me that if I controlled my thinking, I would control how I was
feeling, which would greatly influence what I was doing. And
the theory behind affirmations was to do just that: control
your thinking and thereby control or influence what you believe and act upon.

But I had a problem with how most authors explained affirmations, because I was supposed to be saying things to
myself that just weren't true. For example, some authorities
said affirmations should be in the first person, present tense,
stated positively as if the thing desired is already a reality.
Now imagine an affirmation like "I am completely healthy"
when I was lying in bed with tubes down my nose, gaping holes
in my body, knowing I was scheduled for surgery the next
morning, and then saying things like, "I, Terry McBride, am

now perfectly healthy." When I said or wrote affirmations like that, my mind immediately responded, "Get a grip!"

Even if I did those kind of affirmations from that place within me where I could experience myself as more than just the things that were going on around me or the things that were happening to me, when I came back to the form of my life and the pain and drama of yet another surgery, my mind would automatically discount that my wants and desires were a reality now.

So even though I read what others said about the power of affirmations and tried them for awhile to stay positive, I really didn't explore within myself how I could get them to work for me to create reality itself. But now that I was playing with the idea that the power of the Universe was backing me up in my beliefs, I was again drawn back to the concept of somehow getting control of my thinking and thereby gaining some control over my beliefs.

I still found affirmations and affirmative prayer somewhat elusive as far as how they were going to work for me in getting what I wanted. But like the other tools of choice, I knew for me to continue to figure out how to create reality, I would have to gain control over the thoughts, ideas and beliefs I held to be true. And affirmations or the idea of choosing what to think about seemed to be a very important aspect of this control.

I knew I had to change my thinking. I knew my current habits of thought did not support me in getting what I wanted. My problem was how to do it, where to start. But one thing I knew, if my affirmations or the new mental environment I was trying to create were too far away from what I currently held to be true, I would just disregard those thoughts and positive statements as wishful thinking.

So I decided to use the idea of consciously creating my mental environment in a way that would allow what I was currently thinking and experiencing to be there, and at the same time inspire and encourage me to keep moving forward toward the reality I wanted to create.

As I mentioned earlier, I had set up within myself what I called a "negative monitor," a part of my awareness that was to keep watch over the thoughts that were flowing through my mind. Any time I started to think negative thoughts, my negative monitor would make me aware that my thoughts were negative. It wasn't a right or wrong thing. I did not have to change my thoughts. It was not a Pollyanna—aren't all things great—type of thinking I wanted to move to. I just wanted to be aware of the thoughts that dominated my mind. Then I would ask myself if what I was thinking was what I wanted to think about.

Much to my disappointment, I found that the majority of my thinking was negative. Oh, they weren't "all things are going to hell in a hand basket" kinds of thoughts, but they certainly were not what would lead me to having the type of life I wanted to have.

Even on a good day, the majority of what I considered to be my positive thoughts revolved around how I was dealing with the problems in front of me. This realization about all the habits of thought I would need to change took the wind out of my sails, and I found myself wanting to give up all over again. But I didn't give up. I started writing out my ideas around changing my thinking and found I had no choice but to continue.

If there was any truth that we become what we think about, I had to be willing to make changes in how and what I thought. And while making these changes, it had to be okay for me to notice my negative thought patterns and at the same time still be able to continue to explore how affirmations could work for me.

My greatest discovery around affirmations was when I decided to focus my mental environment not on the goal I wanted, but what I needed to think about regarding my plan to get there.

It did me no good to lie in my bed and think that I was perfectly healthy. But when I would spend time thinking that I was going to find a way to convince my doctor to explore with me the specifics that would need to happen before he would consider sewing up my colostomy, I could feel my energy again moving to what I wanted. So regarding Yelton, I let go of my focus on what I would need to do to get him to change his mind and just chose thoughts that supported me believing that I was going to find a way to do it. I began to understand that I could use affirmations on what was next for me.

Sometimes I would spend time thinking that the answers I was looking for were coming. I told myself I did not have to have the answers right now, which allowed me to be comfortable in my not knowing and at the same time gave me some confidence that I wouldn't be stuck there forever.

Other times I would state what I wanted to create as if it was a reality now, such as when my daughters were coming to visit me in the hospital. At times like these, I would build a mental environment that revolved around the great time we would have and how much fun it was going to be to play with them. Before surgeries, I would write out thoughts about how inspired the doctors were going to be, how careful they would be so that they would not damage any nerves, how my body would handle the procedure well, and how I would come out of the anesthesia easily without any of the usual nausea.

I began to understand that the game of choosing a mental environment was unique to everyone based on what they believed they needed to do in the area of their thinking. So I began to choose what I would allow my mind to dwell upon, based on what I wanted to believe or what I wanted to begin to believe regarding the specific thing I was doing affirmations on. It took some discipline on my part to be consciously aware of what I thought I would need to think about in any given area because part of me wanted to have pat answers on affirmations and the other tools of choice that were always the same: sit this way, breathe this way, eat this way, think this way, and so on. But when I tried it like that, it didn't work because then I was so focused on "the right way," I didn't have the option of discovering how affirmations or the other tools could work for me.

However, when I took the time to explore what I wanted to create in relationship to my current belief about creating it, I found that I did know how to use choice of mental environment to create thoughts, and if not new beliefs right away, I could create the *possibility* that what I wanted could happen. And much to my amazement, as I consistently applied the idea of affirmation to my daily life, I started to notice changes in my attitude and follow-through that I knew were directly caused by my change of thinking.

One day, Karen said to me, "Do you realize that you're studying a little bit everyday now? You don't wait 'til the night before the test like you used to."

"Yeah, thanks for noticing. I decided that this stuff isn't just about changing my mind about being sick. I'm using it on some of my personal stuff too."

As time passed, I was less and less judgmental about all of the negative thought patterns that seemed to be ingrained in me, even though it was almost comical how many negatives I could come up with.

Based on how aware I became of all of my limiting thoughts and habit patterns, I could understand where others might believe there is something inside us that wants to limit us. But I knew different. These negative and limiting thoughts were just habits of thinking, and we can all change our habits. It was difficult for me to change my thinking all at once, but gradually I was doing it, and I knew it was working.

Slowly as I persisted in exploring choice of thoughts, I moved away from "I have to be in charge of my thoughts or else" to "I am in charge of my thoughts, and it's making a positive difference in the quality of my life." Again, I noticed that feeling of freedom I had felt earlier and knew it was because I was moving to something instead of moving *away* from something. And affirmations, or choosing my mental environment, became something I looked forward to instead of something I had to do.

≈ ≈ ≈ ≈

As the tools of choice began to come together through choosing my destination, choosing my action, and now choosing my mental environment, I began to experience even more times during my day when I was confident, or at least more assured and more at peace—times where I really got: "I am not my stuff; I am capable. I can accomplish what I want."

And right behind that, I wondered, How am I going to get my doctor to agree to sew up my colostomy? Sometimes I'd think, Here I go again, I'm right back in the middle of the fight. And other times it was more like, Okay, so now that I'm on a hot streak, how do I change his mind?

One of the biggest barriers to "getting to go to the bathroom like I used to go to the bathroom" was that I held a belief Dr. Yelton wouldn't support me in the reality I wanted to create. So I decided to change that belief.

Don't get me wrong. Dr. Yelton was a dedicated physician and a great surgeon. I'd like to give him the benefit of the doubt and think that perhaps he just didn't want to give me false hope, because as I mentioned, he had never said never. Perhaps he was unwilling or unable to openly explore the possibility of my colon healing because it was such a long shot. But I don't think it was only that. He had a lousy bedside manner, and he didn't like being challenged or questioned.

I did not believe that he would simply change his mind one day and enthusiastically support me in discussing the possibilities of reversing my colostomy and what would need to happen before my bowels could be sewn back together. So I committed to finding a scenario where we could come together and I could get what I was looking for—the road map I could follow to create the reality I wanted—and he could still be the opinionated S.O.B. I thought he was.

I began to choose my thoughts and daydream that he and I would come together, and he would tell me what changes needed to take place in my body before he would consider doing the surgery. I wasn't sure at first what I was looking for. But I consciously chose to think that the answer was coming. I didn't believe it at first, but as the days went by, I found the feeling of impasse was no longer overwhelming. There were even times when I smiled and was at peace about finding a way to get him to have the discussion.

Then one day it just came to me. I'll go in and ask him what needs to happen before he will agree to sew up my colostomy. Then he will get mad like he always does and remind me that he is the one to make those kinds of decisions. And while he is telling me the way it is, he will inadvertently give me what I am asking for.

As I thought about that scenario happening, my mind could get it as a possibility. Quite frequently Dr. Yelton would say things like, "I'm not going to do this until . . ." or "We won't let you go home until . . . ." So I was going to get him to say that same kind of "not until" statement regarding the surgery I wanted.

I began to have conversations with myself where I would go into his office and open a dialog with him. He would say something like, "I'm not going to consider reversing your colostomy until . . . ," and what would follow would be the list (the road map I was looking for) that he considered necessary before he would operate and sew up my bowels.

It was a long shot, and at the same time it was a possibility. Now it was up to me to make this possibility a probability.

As I sat there unsure of how to get Dr. Yelton to have the conversation I wanted, I started into "why me?" again. Then I remembered that just a few short weeks before I had been willing to give up.

I had been actively thinking that one of the Perhaps Models might be the way to go. But now I was going to get what I wanted. As I heard a small voice say, "You can do this," a smile came over my face, and my chest filled with joy. At first I thought this voice came from outside of me, and then tears filled my eyes as I realized it was actually me talking to me! I wasn't consciously choosing what to think, and it wasn't an affirmation. It was simply my spontaneous thought, "You can do this."

But thinking something could happen and really believing it is going to happen can sometimes be miles apart.

CHAPTER 23

CHOICE OF EMOTIONAL ENVIRONMENT

Throughout my study of the different disciplines that assist one to create what one wants, I had come to think that the most powerful tool was using one's imagination to see and feel something, and thereby create it.

In many of the ancient cultures, the effect of mentally visualizing or picturing a thing was considered magical. It was the tool of the masters. The great ones I had read about who were supposed to have been able to create reality didn't set goals, they didn't lay out plans, they didn't choose their thoughts; they simply knew that the reality they desired was the way it was now.

All that is well and good if one is sitting around reading for enjoyment. But I wanted to know how to do it myself. I wanted to know how to create reality. So when I would read and re-read the articles and materials on using our imagination to create what we desire, I was always seeking the answer to "how do I do that? How can I use my imagination, my ability to create mental images and have those images become the way it is?"

Dr. Maltz wrote: "The nervous system cannot tell the dif-

ference between an imagined experience and a real experience." But reading and thinking about applying my imagination to create something did not give me the ability to do it,
because when I tried to imagine things differently than they
were now, I would immediately slip into wondering, "Well, how
is it going to get done?"

I just couldn't keep my thoughts in line long enough to get
a clear image of what I was trying to imagine. To make matters
worse, I didn't see in my mind's eye with pictures. When I day-
dreamed, I didn't create mental images in my mind; I talked or
thought myself through my daydreams. It was more of a men-
tal/verbal process. I just wasn't a visual person as far as how I
used my imagination. And most of the stuff I read on visualization said I had to see in pictures.

I could daydream with the best of them, but when I tried
to use the same process of imagining something by choice,
something that I was trying to create for real, my mind seemed
unable to stick with the process. I would get caught up in my
thoughts about whether or not I would do enough or follow
through enough to really get the thing I desired.

Daydreams were easy because I let the daydream take me
wherever it would go, and there was no investment on my part
to make the thing I was daydreaming about a reality. But using
my imagination as one of the tools of choice to create something, now that was a different matter. And as with affirmations, I had given up on figuring out how I could use this magical tool.

But now as I approached visualization as it related to getting my doctor to give me the information I wanted, I found I
could do it much better, and that was because I was imagining
the plan instead of the goal.

Most of the information I had read on creating feelings
through mental imagery insisted that I visualize the goal as
complete, such as imagining my colostomy already put back
together and my bowels working normally. I was supposed to
do this with implicit faith that it was the way I imagined it

without concern about how it would come to be. When I tried this, I would get caught up in "yeah, but how is this going to happen?" But now that I had a plan that I thought might work, I found it relatively easy to daydream or imagine that the plan, my conversation with my doctor, would work out the way I wanted.

It was not that all of a sudden I believed. It was more that I could spend good quality time using my imagination and pretending the conversation was going to go the way I wanted it to go. And the more I did that, the more I thought this might work.

Sometimes during my visualization or conscious daydreaming, I would get ideas about how to proceed in the conversation that I thought were brilliant. And there were also times when my imagining wouldn't go well, and I would be discouraged. But all in all, I was becoming more and more excited about the tools of choice and how I could use them together to create the belief I wanted.

It was much like the map example I used earlier. If I only had an address of where I wanted to go with no clue as to where it was, it was very difficult for me to spend time imagining myself already there. But if I had a map with good directions that I thought would get me to the address, it was easy to imagine following the map, taking the turns, watching for the signs, and ultimately arriving at my destination.

So again I found for visualization to be effective for me, I had to apply it to the next thing I thought I had to do based on my belief about action. If I believed I needed to study to pass a test, it was much easier for me to visualize myself passing if I started with imagining I had studied. If I tried to visualize passing it without studying, my mind would remind me of what I hadn't done, and I wouldn't be able to concentrate on holding the imagined outcome. I knew it was only my belief about action that made action as important as it was to me, but that's how I believed. So I continued to use the tools of choice within a framework I believed would work for me.

I know it was arbitrary to divide choice into these neat categories of destination, action, mental and emotional environments. But doing that greatly assisted me to get a handle on what choice was about for me. And as I coupled them together, the whole idea of choice finally began to make sense. Many of the books listed one or two of the tools of choice as the most important factor in the creation of results. And there were phrases within the study of each tool that addressed the importance of the tool, for example: if you are not achieving what you desire, it is simply because your goals are not clearly defined; follow-through of appropriate action is the sole determinate of success; or you become what you think about or whatever you can imagine you can achieve.

But as I persisted in using each one of these concepts on one specific desire, I began to understand that when I used them together, I could create feelings, attitudes and even beliefs that I couldn't create when I used one or two of them separately.

Perhaps the most amazing thing that was going on in this process of understanding choice was about what I would call "knowing." Underneath the tools of choice and achieving success or obtaining results, there is an inferred or subtle reference to knowing. It's like the scripture, "Know the truth, and the truth shall set you free." Although most of the books I had read had not talked openly about creating knowing, I thought that was where the real power was.

In the beginning as I used the tools of choice, it was still the idea of doing enough, being specific enough in the goal, having a plan I thought would work, and having thoughts that supported me in following through with the plan. But even with these, I still had the possibility of not doing enough or not thinking the right thoughts enough. So it was still me pushing myself to get to where I wanted to go. It was as if these first three tools could allow me to create my reality differently if I used them. And that was a big "if."

But as I was able to use my applied imagination better

because I had these other choices in line, I found I began to believe that the thing I desired was going to happen, and as I continued to visualize, I began to know it was going to happen.

It seemed I had created a different reality for myself. And as this different reality, this knowing increased, I found I no longer had to push myself toward the thing I desired. I was being pulled to it, and what I needed to do as follow-through or what I needed to think was just a natural part of who I was.

It was quite a big deal for me. I had started with, "Well, why not give this stuff a try on something that's important?" and through simply persisting in finding out how choice worked for me and then using it, I was able to create a "knowing" about something that only a few months before had been a hope.

Would I have bet my life on knowing that I would have a conversation with my doctor where he would give me what I wanted? No. But I would have bet my best fly rod, and I loved my best fly rod.

As these tools of choice came together, it seemed that I was discovering for myself how through what I did, I could create faith. And it was said that faith could move mountains. Although I wasn't sure about the exact relationship between belief, knowing and faith, I had a feeling that I was playing with choice in a way that was truly leading me to the "freedom" part of "know the truth, and it shall set you free."

It was all mixed together, and I didn't really have a complete handle on how it worked, but I was playing in an arena that seemed to give me glimpses of something that was even bigger than making my dreams come true. And I was a little nervous about what that bigger thing might be; I just wanted to stay focused on using choice to get things.

So I spent quality time every day for the next few weeks becoming even more sure. Every day I would take a ten-minute walk and imagine in as much detail as possible going into my doctor's office, being with him, and opening the conversation.

I imagined him getting huffy and what he might say, how I was going to respond, and then ultimately hearing him give me the changes that would need to take place before he would consider sewing up my colostomy.

Sometimes I would come out of those visualizations smiling and feeling confident, and sometimes I would feel afraid. But I kept at it until it was obvious to me I was avoiding the issue. Finally, my desire for the meeting overrode my hesitancy, and I set the appointment.

Even though I had some doubts and fears that our talk might not go the way I wanted it to, I knew I was really on track, using the tools of choice as I understood them. I remembered the Commitment quote. And I believed that Providence was going to back me up, especially in the specific mention that meetings would occur to help me.

I didn't think it was a coincidence that the first real test of my power to create something was a meeting, when the cornerstone of my new reality was the Commitment quote. These ideas (coupled with making sure I was choosing what to think about and using my imagination in a positive way) allowed me to keep my doubts and fears within tolerable limits.

But I had one last thing I was wrestling with. And it was the idea that to be really effective in the application of spiritual thought force, or my "woowoos," I needed to give up my attachments to specific outcomes. There were so many references to that idea in the materials I was reading and essentially agreeing with, that I found it difficult to simply ignore this concept. I felt I needed to reconcile the idea of giving up attachments with my other beliefs, otherwise I might be scattered or unsure in my mental intention during the meeting.

I was unable to bring together the ideas of giving up my attachment, my connection and emotional involvement to something with the idea that when I am committed, then Providence moves too. It seemed to me that if I was not attached to a specific outcome, I would not be committed to it either. So I started using affirmations on how those two ideas could work together and finally came up with: "I will give up my attachments to the fears and doubts that the meeting might not go the way I want it to go."

It was so simple and yet so profound. Even in the middle of all my positive thoughts and feelings, my model of how the world worked still contained: "Well, things don't always work the way you want," or "You shouldn't put all your eggs in one basket." And because of these types of beliefs, I was afraid to totally commit to something, because if it didn't work, I didn't want to be devastated. But I knew I needed to reconcile this.

So I decided to take my best shot at including in the new model of how my life worked the thought that I would give up my attachments to any idea other than that things would work the way I chose for them to work. I decided to give up my attachments to ideas such as failure being part of the learning and growth process I was committed to. I also decided not to tell people about how I viewed giving up attachments. It seemed there were lots of teachers out there attached to the idea that I should give up my attachments.

Finally the day came, and as I drove to the hospital, I was excited, nervous, and sure. I had thoughts like, "By God, I am going to have it the way I want it, and there is no room for anything other than what I have been declaring." And then I had thoughts like, "I hope this meeting works, and Dr. Yelton gives me what I have declared I want."

When I got into his office, Dr. Yelton was busy and a little perturbed that I was bothering him. He said brusquely, "What do you want, Terry?"

I took a deep breath and began. "I'm trying to come to grips with my colostomy, and I'd appreciate it if you'd tell me again what would need to take place before it might be possible to reverse it."

Almost right on cue he became defensive. Turning a little pink, he seemed to grow larger as he leaned forward and boomed, "I'll be the one to decide what surgeries are needed! I'm the doctor, you're the patient."

For a moment, I felt my heart hammering in my chest, but instead of coming back with my usual angry response, I slid into a groove, and said, "Yes, I know, I was just wondering . . ."

"Wondering what?" he cut me off.

"Well," I said in a respectful voice, "you had mentioned before there was a possibility, maybe someday, and I was just wondering what it might take . . . ."

Even as I was speaking, I was silently declaring that everything was going as planned and he was right on track. It was not something I had to concentrate on, it was just what I observed I was doing.

And then he moved right into the "not until" section of our talk that I had rehearsed so often.

"There's no way I can see the colostomy being reversed any time soon," he went on, "there's just too many things that would have to change."

"Like what?"

I could tell he was getting annoyed with me, but all the practice was paying off, and I was being better with him than I could ever remember being with anyone in a confrontive situation.

"There's no way until at least four major changes take place," he went on, "First, we won't even consider reversing your colostomy unless we are certain your colon has healed."

I had my workbook with me, a small three-ring binder where I wrote out my thoughts, goals and daily schedule. I was so amazed at how well it was following what I had imagined that I almost missed the first specific item he mentioned.

I nodded my head vigorously as I began taking notes and said, "Okay."

"Next, we will not open up your abdomen while you have a draining sinus on your back from the infection in your spine. If we did that, we could cross-infect into your belly, and then you'd be in real trouble again."

"I understand."

He glared at me, then went on, "We won't do an elective

surgery while your white blood cell count is skyrocketing because of your infection, because that indicates your body is already in trauma, and we won't give it more to deal with."

"All right," I said, "but what does the blood count have to be?"

"In the normal range."

When I asked the question, I noticed I didn't feel like a frightened patient pleading with a doctor. I was powerful and in control of the situation. Oh sure, he was doing almost all of the talking, and he was talking down to me, but at the same time, I knew who was controlling that conversation; I was.

"Finally," he concluded, "you have to be healthy, with no surgeries in the previous few months. Your frequent surgeries require that we give you more and more anesthetic to get you under, which causes you to struggle for days to come out of your anesthetized state. And we're concerned that if we give you too much, you might not come out of it at all."

"Thank you, Dr. Yelton. You don't know how much I appreciate this."

There was a long silence and then he said, "I know you've been through a lot, and I also know how bothersome a colostomy can be."

"Well, thanks again for taking time to see me."

"You're welcome. Now, if you don't mind, I have work to do."

When I left his office, my body was tingling from top to bottom. I wanted to grab someone and give them a huge hug.

As I look back at that meeting, I see that that was the moment I took charge of my healing. I had been sick for almost three years and had gone through sixteen surgeries, spending a lot of time in the hospital. And finally I had the feeling of being in charge of my life and in charge of my health.

It was not the same macho talk like "kiss my ass." It was different. It was not a fight against evil, against some negative; it was embracing and experiencing: I am the creator of my life! It was an incredible feeling! I had demonstrated to myself that

I could create reality!

When I got to the lobby, I sat down and reviewed my notes on what Dr. Yelton had said to make sure I was clear on everything. In front of me, I had four distinct things that would have to happen before he would agree to sew up my colostomy.

First, I had to get the lower part of my colon to heal, the part that had been damaged from being engulfed by the infection. Second, I had to get rid of the draining sinus from the infection in my spine. The draining sinus was where the fluid from the infection drained onto the bandages I wore. Third, my white blood cell count had to be normal or almost normal. And fourth, I had to be healthy and surgery-free for the previous two months before he would consider this elective surgery.

He had also mentioned that we would need to get this done within the next two years. And I wasn't sure why he had mentioned that. But I wasn't concerned enough to ask him for clarification. I had pushed him enough, and I had wanted to get out while the getting was good.

I was ecstatic. As I walked to my car and drove out of the hospital parking lot, I was giggling like a little kid. It had worked; I had accomplished what I had set out to do. Dr. Yelton and I even had a fairly cordial parting. He didn't wish me good luck, but he did mention that I had been through a lot and he knew how bothersome a colostomy could be.

When I left, I didn't mention that I would be back when I had created what was on his list. That would have been fun, but perhaps a bit arrogant, and definitely dangerous. But getting the list was only the first step in creating the specific healing I was after. I would be coming back to see him, and he would agree to sew up my colostomy. He no longer had any choice about that.

My feeling of excitement was fairly short-lived. Even before I got the mile and a half to the freeway, I had already started thinking, "Now how am I going to accomplish the things on the list?" Yet, there was an added something in my questioning. I'm not sure I would call it confidence, but it was something like that, and I think it was because I had just experienced a big win.

As I was driving home, I got more and more into "what now?" And the joy and confidence I had experienced only minutes before seemed lost. It was getting buried under "How the hell am I going to heal my colon?"

When I pulled into my driveway, I was feeling myself becoming engulfed in the problem. I made a conscious decision to stop. Now was the time to be thankful. Now was the time to consciously and deliberately acknowledge what I had created through choice.

Yes, it was possible that I may have had the same results without using the tools of choice and my commitment, and part of my thoughts started to go there. But I wanted to continue in the creation of my new field of reality. And in that field, it was my consciousness that created what was going on in my life. My beliefs determined my experience, and they also created the things, the form, and the results I had.

If I was going to take responsibility for the problems and challenges in my life, I also got to take responsibility for the successes, the wins and the triumphs. Right there I decided I would spend time basking in the glory of winning a big one. And I decided to use affirmation and visualization, not to create something that was yet to be, I was going to use them to validate and re-experience the wonder of myself as the one who had taken charge of creating what I wanted to create.

CHAPTER 24

CREATING REALITY

One of the things I noticed in creating the meeting with Dr. Yelton was that as I completed the work I thought I needed to do, I experienced a sense of what I called faith. But it wasn't a faith that something was going to be; it was more a sense of acceptance that the way I wanted it was the way it was. It was elusive, but I thought it had to do with eliminating the effort and struggle of "doing enough" by simply accepting that the things I desired would be a natural aspect of how my life worked.

When I started the process to create the meeting and get what I wanted out of it, it seemed to revolve around "if it's to be, it's up to me." I thought I would have to stay on track exploring and mastering the tools of choice to create a new belief and thereby create the reality I wanted. I believed that Providence was supporting me, I had the assistance that the Commitment quote spoke to, and I knew I wasn't alone. But I felt that to continue to receive that assistance, I would need to keep my part of the bargain of commitment, and for me that revolved around the choices I was making.

Toward the end of the process of creating the conversation I wanted with my doctor, as I did my part, it felt like I was being pulled to that which I desired. And in that pulling, I no longer felt the same need to do enough of something in order to move toward the objective. It was as if I could relax and simply allow the reality I wanted to come into being. And if there was something for me to do, I would do it as a natural part of who I was and what I was doing. There were still things for me to do, but I did not feel the same old pressure. The doing just got done.

It became like a game I was playing. Yes, there were things to do and experience, objectives I wanted to accomplish. But in the framework of the acceptance I was feeling, I found that I had more enjoyment in who I was and what I was about. I was no longer just focusing on becoming something I wasn't.

I wanted those feelings of joy and faith now. I wanted to be relaxed as I moved into my new priorities. I wanted to feel as if my life and who I was were pulling me to my desires. I did not want to get drawn back into the game of struggle and effort.

But as I reviewed the list in front of me, I did not feel any faith that it was going to happen the way I wanted.

As I recalled the conversation with Dr. Yelton about what would need to occur before he would consider reversing my colostomy, nothing in his attitude inferred that he believed the items he listed would happen in the natural course of events. In fact, his attitude suggested that at the very best, each of the changes needed was a long shot, and with all of them needing to happen together, it made the outcome even more improbable. So there I was again, feeling the weight of "if it's to be, it's up to me," and the pressure of having to do enough began to get me down.

I spent the next few days attempting to hang out in the feeling of winning a big one. As the days wore on, I realized that part of my resistance to starting was my belief that the process of creating the things on the list would be far more difficult than getting Dr. Yelton to have an informative conversation with me.

Finally, I got off it and started using choice again. I decided not to start with what I would need to do, instead I started with a review of the Commitment quote and what it meant to me. I wrote out affirmations and consciously chose to remember, and lock into my thoughts and feelings that I was not alone, that there were unseen forces supporting and assisting me. I wrote out one primary affirmation I called my "Statement of Being." It went as follows:

Statement of Being

As I move into this time of creation, I feel the power of something bigger than me, moving with me, supporting and empowering me. I know all things are possible. And as I explore how I am going to create the healing I desire, I will notice this support and acknowledge it. I know that I do not have to figure this out all at once. All I have to do is begin right where I am and consciously choose to move toward what I want. My life is not one problem after another; it is right now a time of discovery and creation, and out of my own being I feel the joy and freedom that comes with knowing I can create reality.

I put this statement on a five-by-seven index card and put clear tape over it as if to laminate it. I read it several times a day and made an agreement with myself to start and end my day with these thoughts. What I was attempting to do was give myself a frame of reference where I could be positive and begin to feel joy in my now without tying my positive attitude and joy to any specific short-run outcome.

During the process of creating the meeting with my doctor, I seemed to be constantly looking for results. Minute by minute, I was judging and evaluating, looking for some proof from the objective world that what I was doing was working. Was my attitude always positive? Was I always consciously moving to or was I fighting something? Were other things in my life all working the way I wanted?

When I did not get feedback that indicated I was on track and everything was working fine, I would become discouraged and not continue in using choice. Sometimes I would get off track for days. And I knew it was not effective to use choice for a few minutes a day and then spend the rest of my time doubting and wondering if I was really making progress. The Statement of Being I created was my attempt to use choice to create a mental environment so that the same thing would not happen in this next phase of creating the things I wanted.

Yes, I wanted specific results within a certain time frame. I also wanted to begin to feel more joy and wonder about my life in general. I did not want to always be focusing on what was next to create, next to change. I wanted to experience more peace while I was creating the reality I desired. I wanted to play at my life instead of work at it. I wanted to experience my life as a dance and not a war to be won or something to be overcome.

As I explored this mental state I wanted to create, I was again brought back to the idea of choosing what I was thinking and feeling. And I began to realize that the concepts of choosing my mental and emotional states affected much more than just moving toward creating the health I wanted in my body. Affirmation and visualization were the acts of creating a new truth within my own thoughts and feelings. And what I wanted to be true for me was to have a mental and emotional state of mind that allowed me to feel joy and wonder as I was saying "yes" to being able to create the kind of life I wanted.

Using the concepts of affirmation and visualization was more than reviewing positive thoughts and spending time using mental imagery each day. Affirmation and visualization were about being at choice regarding what I was thinking and feeling all day long. They were also about noticing: "Are my thoughts and the things I am imagining or daydreaming about supporting and validating the reality I want or are they negating it?"

I also realized that most of the thoughts and feelings I had during the day were not a result of my written affirmations like my Statement of Being. They came from the things I was doing, what kinds of movies was I watching, what kinds of books was I reading, what kinds of songs was I listening to, what kinds of conversations was I having with myself and others, what kind of environment was I placing myself in. All of these interactions created thoughts and feelings on their own. The question was "Are the things I'm doing inspiring and supporting me to think and feel the way I want, or do they again immerse me in struggle, learning lessons, and the challenges that come with change?"

I wanted the kind of feelings and energy I felt when I moved from "the hell I can't" to "yes, I can." I did not want to start this next phase feeling that I had a lot of work to do and lots of changes to make for this healing to occur. I didn't want the pressure of how I currently held "if it's to be, it's up to me," because within that, there was a real possibility that I might not do enough or do what needed to be done correctly.

This time I wanted to start from the idea of being pulled to what I wanted rather than waiting until I had done enough in order to prove something to myself, as had happened with the meeting with my doctor. I wanted to start with faith; I wanted to start from the knowing I had felt just before the actual meeting took place. And that all revolved around my mental and emotional state of mind.

I didn't think I would get to "I'll bet my best fly rod on this one" by mental work alone, because I believed in action. But I did think I could eliminate much of the pressure I was feeling by starting with solid work in my mental and emotional states. And this is where I brought in thanksgiving.

In much of the material I had read and especially in the spiritual arena, there was a fairly constant theme regarding thanksgiving. It revolved around the idea that when I prayed or affirmed, I should give thanks for having the result I wanted before it was in fact there. I had never gotten that idea to fit into my logical thinking. It was like how I had held affirmations about me being perfectly healthy when in fact I was very sick. But now as I thought about the idea of giving thanks first, I began to understand how I could use it to assist myself to start from faith and knowing.

In my life, I experienced the feelings of thankfulness when I was sure something was true or was going to be true. It was like the faith and knowing about my meeting with Dr. Yelton; I only experienced that faith and knowing after I had enough proof in my own mind that it was going to go the way I wanted it to go. I felt thanksgiving only after I believed. And it came to me that I could turn that around and use thanksgiving to help myself believe.

Since my mind only felt thanksgiving when I believed something to be so, then if I used my imagination to feel thanksgiving about something, my mind would take that feeling of thanksgiving to mean that the imagined something was in fact so.

What a great idea! I could use my imagination to daydream something I desired as being real right now, in as much detail as possible for me at that moment. And when I got it as real as I could in my own mind, I could shift to giving thanks for it. The act of giving thanks for that specific desire as mine now would record that reality in my mind as true. It was still in the same ballpark as affirmation and visualization, but thanksgiving brought a whole new twist to creating things in my mind first and then stepping into the process of doing from a knowing state of mind.

And now I had an even better grasp on how to make my Statement of Being true because with the piece that thanksgiving brought to managing my mental and emotional state, I felt I could move away from using the tools of choice to stay focused, be on purpose, or be disciplined, and move into embodying what I wanted as part of what I believed to be real.

There were still things to do, but now I could move into finding what I thought would work from a place where I believed I would find them. And as I integrated these ideas, I noticed a new gentleness in my approach to creating things differently. It was almost as if I could feel the desires of my heart pulling me to them. At first I did not feel a strong faith or knowing, but for sure there was much less pressure from the "it's up to me" belief.

At times it was difficult for me to be thankful because behind my thoughts and feelings of thanksgiving would come all my doubts or "yes, but's": "Yes, but are you going to stay on track?" "Yes, but are you going to follow through and do what you need to do?" "Yes, but are you going to stay at choice?" And I would recall my Statement of Being and say, "Yes, I am."

As I used my statement for a few days and concentrated on beginning my day with my combination of affirmation, visualization and thanksgiving, I really got that the most important thing for me was to know that what I was doing was working, or at least it was going to work. Because from that knowing, it would be much easier to be finished with my confusion, done with my depression, and I would quit validating my concern that it might not work and start creating a reality where it was working.

My greatest joy during this time was noticing that I was creating "knowing" before I had started any "doing." Again, I wouldn't have bet my best fly rod on the outcome, but choosing my state of mind first allowed me to move into the next phase of creation with much less doubt and anxiety about whether or not I would be able to get done what I wanted to get done.

≈ ≈ ≈ ≈

The first item on my list was getting the lower end of my colon to heal. In an attempt to get clear on what I wanted as my mental framework, I started writing. If my mental environment was the key to playing this game with some sense of joy and purpose rather than struggle and effort, then the place to start was in my mind.

What I ended up getting down on paper was not so much the overall statement I was looking for, like my first Statement of Being. What did show up in my writing was what I believed about my colon and whether or not it would heal. Again, what I found was that I did not believe it would not heal. It was kind of a backdoor approach to "Yes, it can heal." I had never had anything that hadn't healed. I thought that's just what the body does. So all I needed to do was influence my colon to go ahead and heal, and although I started to stumble again and worry about how I was going to do it, I stopped myself and continued writing.

I made a list of what I might do to facilitate my body's natural healing process. It was a fairly long list that included ideas from many different disciplines. At that time, I wasn't trying to "know" what to do, I was just brainstorming within myself and writing out ideas that came to me without judging or evaluating them as good or bad. Daily I would set aside time to write on my list; and again I was looking for something that grabbed me, something that spoke to my own beliefs as a possibility. Within a few days, I noticed I kept coming back to the idea of directing my body to heal through the use of mental imagery.

Over the years, I had come across many articles and books that said I could use the power of my imagination to influence my body. This information said that if I got a vivid mental image of how I wanted my body and held that image long enough, my body would recreate itself in that image.

I hadn't paid much attention to that information because I didn't understand how it could happen within the body. It wasn't that I thought those who attributed their healing to this technique or the authors wrong. I didn't think they were stretching the truth as they knew it. I just didn't understand within myself how it could work for me. But now that I had the meeting with Dr. Yelton under my belt (and knowing my imagination had played a huge part in that meeting happening the way I wanted it to), the idea of using mental imagery to create something held a possibility it had not before.

So I reviewed the notes I had taken from some of the books I had read and went through my file of articles. I found six articles that dealt directly with using imagination in healing. I reread them and selected four that made sense to me. I decided to read each of the four articles once a day for a week and hold the possibility that I would find something I could use in them.

Now, it was my belief that most books and articles are written to infer that the authors have hit on something, with the underlying purpose to convince those who read the material to agree with them. And that's what I wanted to do. I wanted to believe like the authors did, and I wanted to believe in the testimonials they included. I wanted to begin to believe that using mental imagery was a profound and beneficial healing technique that I could use.

It wasn't that I was trying to create something that wasn't real; I believed my body was built to heal. I simply wanted to give some direction to the healing and get it to happen now. And I chose to learn to use mental imagery to do that. I knew my environment and the things I exposed myself to greatly influenced my beliefs and what I held to be true. So I consciously chose to read, reread and study the things I wanted to believe in. I also used affirmation and thanksgiving to validate the idea that mental imagery could create healing. And before the week was out, I began to think this could work.

Next, I got a picture of a healthy colon from a magazine, cut out the lower part, and put it in my workbook with the intention of looking at it twice a day for ten minutes or so and pretending that this was how my colon looked. I also kept reading the articles and using affirmation, prayer, and thanksgiving to believe what I was doing was making a difference. But no matter how much I tried to believe my colon would end up like the one in the picture, every time I looked at the bright pink, healthy colon, I thought, There's no way!

For days I tried to hold the image that my colon would recreate itself to be just like the one in the picture, and all I got was, "This is bullshit. It's never going to happen." But rather than get frustrated and discouraged, I kept reading my Statement of Being and holding the belief that I was on track finding what was going to work for me.

Then one day, I smeared the picture with pencil lead so it wasn't so healthy pink; it was now more gray than pink. Then I drew lines on it and put hatch marks on the lines to make them look like scars. Finally, I placed three bandages on the picture. It ended up looking like a picture of a colon that had been through a war. But there were no holes in it. It wasn't as good as new, but it looked like it would still work.

I continued using affirmations and thanksgiving along with my mental imaging, and the more I looked at that old beat-up colon, the more I began to think my body could heal to that level. My colon might look like hell, but it could still work without leaking. It took weeks, but through the choices I made, I began to feel really excited that I was on track with healing my colon.

My greatest discovery in this imaging process was realizing that I did not have to use the concepts I was studying exactly like the authors or teachers said they needed to be used. Once again I appreciated at a gut level that I could tailor the ideas of choice any way I needed to so I could make them work for me. I could alter any concept I was studying until it worked the way I needed it to so I could believe what I wanted to believe.

≈ ≈ ≈ ≈

The next item on the list was eliminating the draining sinus in my back. I had been thinking about how to do that ever since my doctor said it was one of the prerequisites to sewing up my colostomy. And I was no closer to knowing how to do it than I was in the beginning.

The infection created a great deal of fluid, and when the drainage wasn't good, the fluid would build up and the pain would become unbearable. Therefore, I always had to have good drainage. I figured the only way to eliminate the drains was to get rid of the infection, and when I thought about that, I immediately ran into my belief that I was going to have this infection for a long, long time. And I knew the "long, long time" was just my mind's way of saying I would have it forever: it was the "this is not curable" part of my reality.

While I was focusing on getting on track in the healing of my colon, the impasse around my draining sinus was always in the back of my mind. But I kept telling myself, "I'll get to that." And now it was time.

In the weeks it had taken me to get my plan together for healing my colon, I was also working on my mental and emotional state regarding the sinus from the infection. But I kept my main attention on the colon because I wanted to handle the items one at a time. I wanted to figure out what I was going to do on each item before going on to the next one. I chose to do it that way to make sure that I didn't get overwhelmed and go into "poor me" again. And it worked.

As I sat down with pen and paper to get my thoughts organized about the sinus track, I felt good about the process. I didn't exactly feel joy, and I didn't have a clue as to what I was going to do. But I was confident and excited about using what I knew to explore this area of creating the reality I wanted. Sometimes I would start down the "ain't it awful" road, yet the vast majority of the time, I stopped before letting any negative mindset get its own head of steam.

I continued to use my Statement of Being every morning and evening. I used my imagination and pretended that I would find a way to get this part done too, and then I would use thanksgiving to lock that image of success into my mind as a real possibility. After many days without any progress or good ideas, I became very frustrated.

One evening I was about to go into a full-blown tirade about not finding the answers I needed. It was a lot like evenings I had had so many times before: a time of blame and anger, where I played the victim. But this time as I started down that path, I told myself to stop.

I felt like I was watching myself have a conversation with myself where I knew the "poor me" stuff wasn't true any more. And it was silly to even go there. In my inner dialog, I could hear myself restating my Statement of Being, and I felt like it was a true statement about how my life worked. I could feel a new truth, a new reality in my statement, and I knew I was supported, I knew I was guided and I was not alone. It was only a matter of time until I would figure out how to do even this seemingly impossible task. I would be able to keep my belief about having the infection for a long, long time, and I would figure out how to eliminate the draining sinus.

It was amazing to hear the conversation I was having with myself. It was as if I had discovered a very wise person inside of me, and it was actually me! Sure, this new self I found was just feeding back the ideas I had been working on programming into myself. But observing my own inner dialog, I realized I was believing what was addressed in my Statement of Being. I was changing and becoming the person I had always wanted to be. I was in charge of my life and I knew it. All I needed to do was continue to use choice as best I could at any given time.

Sometimes it was only mental and emotional work; sometimes there were things for me to do, actions for me to take. And my most important job was to know, to accept that it was all working toward the outcome I wanted no matter what was going on around me now.

I found it almost comical that in the middle of discovering the new me, I had to be readmitted to the hospital to have my drains reopened. Although they hadn't closed completely and there was some drainage, other areas of infection had closed off, and those pockets were causing pain. So the surgeons had to go in and open up the whole area again.

I always knew a week or so before any surgery that I would be going in again because the pain would start. At first I could manage it with aspirin, then as the pressure would build, I would go to codeine and then to stronger pain medication. About the time the pain would become unmanageable at home, the doctors would schedule surgery to reopen the entire drainage area. I no longer argued with my doctors to be aggressive in their approach. They simply weren't interested in doing the extensive debridement surgeries where they tried to cut out all the infected material. Their only intention was to keep the drains open, and that's all they would do.

When I went into the outpatient clinic to report the pain and start the process for another surgery, I also went to the orthopedic floor to tell the nurses that within a few days I would be coming back in. This was my seventeenth surgery, and for the most part the same nurses were there who had cared for me since I had first come to the University of Washington Medical Center.

Many of these nurses were the ones who gave Karen a baby shower when Sheri was born. They were the ones who held me when I threw up. They changed my bandages and helped me go to the bathroom when I couldn't do it alone. And they held my hand all the way into the operating room, telling me they would be there when I came back from recovery. They were my friends, and I never had to pretend with them. They took care of me when I couldn't. We were family.

If possible, they would schedule me the biggest private room and the only one with its own bathroom. It didn't always work out that I would get that one, but it was always worth the effort. And it was good to check in with these friends and chat for awhile.

Three days after my clinic visit, I was admitted for surgery. When I arrived on the fourth floor, the nurses had arranged it so I got the big room with the private bathroom. I was glad for that, and I smiled at my good fortune.

As I was getting settled, I began to laugh at the thought of being glad that I was in the same room where I had experienced so much pain, so much depression. But it was also the same room where the mother of that very sick boy gave me back my Bible and told me I was right, that all things are possible if only you believe. I remembered it was her comment that stirred me to find the idea that the power of God was always backing me up.

That afternoon was like so many others before a surgery. An orderly shaved my back and upper buttocks. An IV was inserted into my arm, and as all this was going on, I could feel the tension start to build within me.

Like always, a relatively new intern came in to take my medical history and check my vital signs. As he went through the endless list of the same questions I had answered so many times before, I wanted to scream and tell him to look at my goddamn records and quit bothering me. As that thought surfaced, I could feel the old anger and frustration starting to get its own head of steam. I didn't say anything to him, but I think he could sense what was going on. Or maybe he saw the tears starting to well up in my eyes, because he stopped and sat silently for a few moments while I gathered myself together and took some deep breaths.

"Thanks," I said. "You can go on now."

"I'm sorry I have to get all this information again. I know you've been through a lot." He paused and looked at his chart. "I just have a few more questions, then all I have to do is take your blood pressure and check your heart and lungs. Is that all right?"

"Sure," I said, still concentrating on my breathing.

After he left, I lay there looking at the same walls I had stared at for so many months and tried to get myself together to do my mental work.

But I didn't do mental work on healing my colostomy; I was facing more immediate problems now. Like so many times before, I did affirmations that no nerves would be damaged. I imagined handling the anesthetic well, and I reassured myself that I wouldn't get sick and throw up after I came back from the recovery room. I affirmed that I would have very little blood loss and would not require any blood transfusions. I told myself that I would be able to empty my bladder before they needed me to, so they wouldn't catheterize me after surgery. It was like the old times, fighting to stay calm and focusing on using what I knew to get out of this one whole, when they were preparing to cut me open one more time.

Just before the dinner cart arrived, Karen, Kris and Sheri came in after they said hello to the nurses they had come to know. Setting my fears aside, I began to play with my girls. We decided to eat in the cafeteria because Kris and Sheri liked the great selection of puddings, pies, and cookies. We always had great fun picking out which ones we would have for dessert. After we ate our dinners, we shared our goodies with each other so we all had a bite of a variety of great stuff. When we got back to my room, I told the girls a few stories. I knew by their quietness they could tell their daddy was worried. When it was time for them to leave, Kris told me she was sorry I was sick again, and I said, "Me too, baby, me too."

Both my little ones hugged me good-bye, but Sheri didn't want to let me go. She didn't talk in full sentences yet, but she communicated from her soul. She was very wise, and she held on to me as if to give me something of herself. She was making sure I knew she was with me. Kris was so proud and watched as her little sister loved on me. Then she put her arms around us both and said, "I love you daddy, I'll take care of Sheri."

After they left, I got a tranquilizer and a sleeping pill and drifted in and out of sleep, trying to focus on my Statement of Being. But my mind wouldn't cooperate. I kept coming back to, "They're going to cut me open again." And the fear and depression that came from thinking that these types of surgeries were going to go on for the rest of my life started to get the best of me.

I told myself to stop focusing on negatives, and I listened for that wise voice within for some guidance, but I heard nothing. I said it again, "Please stop," but if that voice was there, I couldn't hear it. Finally I turned on my light and got out my Statement of Being and read it aloud over and over. And still I couldn't get into feeling there was any truth in what it said.

I wanted to believe. I wanted to feel the hope and joy my statement spoke to, but all I felt was my sadness about having another surgery. And like so many times in that very room, I cried myself to sleep—not so much from the fear of having another surgery, not from the idea of being in the hospital again to take care of the infection—I cried myself to sleep because I couldn't find the truth I had created and felt just a few days before.

The evidence around me—the room, the preparation for surgery, the IV needle in my arm, the sting of my back where they shaved me, the sterile hospital smell, the constant beep-beep sounds of the monitoring equipment, the hospital announcements over the intercom—all this brought me back to where I had been. And once again, I was engulfed in disease and sickness.

CHAPTER 25

MAKE-BELIEVE

W hen I awoke from the surgery, the first thing I noticed was how much pain I was in and that they had catheterized me during surgery. These were not the signs of a routine drain opening.

As I became more awake, the resident who had been part of the surgical team came in and told me the surgery had been more invasive than they had anticipated. The part that wasn't draining was mostly in the front of the spine, which they had thought was probably the case. But they had elected to go in from the back because getting to the spine from the abdomen posed a much greater risk of nerve damage. So they elected to come around my spine from the back, which meant they had to chisel even more off of my sacrum (the lower end of the spine where it flattens out just before the tailbone). They cleaned out the areas in front as best they could, then put drains in and attached a small vacuum pump to them.

The surgeons had also reopened a six-inch portion along both sides of my spine above the sacrum. The resident said they had excised some tissue and cut away more of the spine, which was clearly infected. They inserted drains into that area also. These drains were hooked up to another small vacuum pump. The tubes and pumps made it difficult to move or to lie comfortably. Again I was heavily medicated, and for the first two days, I drifted in and out of a drug-facilitated sleep.

I dealt with this whole experience pretty much like I had the other times when I had bad news and my body was more beat up than I was prepared for. I was stoic and courageous when other people were around, bitter and resentful when I was alone.

Even after the pain subsided and they reduced my pain medication, I found myself trying to sleep and ignore what was going on in my mind. I didn't even work on creating a better attitude or pick up my Statement of Being for another day. When I did read it on the morning of the fourth day after surgery, there was absolutely no truth in it for me. I had fallen into the rhythm of being sick again, and I was feeling very sorry for myself. The evidence of disease and sickness was just too overwhelming for me to believe in anything else.

I knew I needed to do something to gain some control of myself and step into the "if it's to be, it's up to me" part of my belief, for I still believed that for Providence to move too, I had to be stepping up as best as I could. It was the old "God helps those who help themselves" idea. I had to somehow get out of where I was and start back to owning the new reality I was trying to create.

I had been mentally beating myself up since the night before surgery because I hadn't been able to move into feeling any truth about my Statement of Being. And now my mental problems seemed to be compounded.

First, I hadn't been able to get myself out of the mental slump I was in, and second, I was berating myself for not being able to get out of it. My mind was going in circles. I couldn't remove myself from thoughts of disease, sickness, and "here I go again."

Finally, I got out my trusted pen and paper in an attempt to move on to other thoughts and stop the cycle I was in. The first things I wrote down were about what I had been stuck on: the surgery being more invasive, the prospect of being in the hospital much longer than anticipated, the sickness and disease thoughts that were right in front of me. And like so many times before, once I got those thoughts on paper and acknowledged they were legitimate thoughts—and certainly one way to perceive what was going on—I was better able to focus on other thoughts. Of course, what came around naturally was the result of the work I had done on my attitude with my Statement of Being. And once again, the answer was fairly simple. I needed to stop feeling sorry for myself and quit focusing on being sick.

I had been up the day before, but it was only to sit in a chair for awhile, and after they removed the catheter, I stood up to empty my bladder in a container they gave me. But now I decided to get up and go for a walk.

Getting out of bed was more than just getting up. If I was going to believe that my Statement of Being was true, I needed to start taking care of myself and stop acting sick. I needed to get up and brush my teeth and shave every morning. I needed to shampoo my hair so it didn't look so funny. I needed to take a sponge bath and put some smell-good on. I needed to take an active role in something that indicated to me I was on the road to regaining my strength and health. Sure, I still had my colostomy, and now I had vacuum pumps attached to new drains, but the pumps would only be there for awhile, and in a week or so I would be back home and be able to pick up where I had left off.

I called for a nurse. Ruth, a feisty redhead whom I adored, answered the call. When she came in, I announced, "Ruth, I'm going for a walk!"

"Great, Terry, good to see you feeling better."

"Yeah, it's about time. I think I'll walk down to the end of the hall and back."

"That might be a bit far for the first time."

"You think so?"

"How about I walk beside you. Then I can steady you if you need it," she suggested. "And I can take a wheelchair along in case you run out of gas."

"All right, if you think so."

"Why the sudden inspiration?" she asked.

"I want to stop lying here feeling sorry for myself and start doing something to get stronger."

"That makes sense."

Oh, how I loved these nurses. They really did care.

"We'll need a rolling IV stand to hang the vacuum pumps on. I'll go get one."

While Ruth got the pumps and tubes organized on the IV stand, I put on my robe. I began to feel overwhelmed trying to figure out how I could wear my robe and cover my bare butt because the robe got hung up on the tubes. My shoulders sagged, my hands fell into my lap, about to give up.

She saw my distress and grabbed my arm, "We can do this," she said softly, "And if your butt shows, we've all seen it before!"

I laughed. "Boy, that's the truth."

"So, it looks like we're ready," she said, and we started for the door.

I made it to the end of the hall but about half way back, I was feeling a bit woozy, so I sat down in the wheelchair. Ruth pushed me back to my room.

After she helped me onto the bed and hung the pumps and tubes back where they belonged, she said, "Way to go, Terry. I'll go get you a pain pill," and she left.

As I waited for her to return with the medicine, I lay there catching my breath. But even before she got back, I noticed I was feeling better. It wasn't the pain—I still wanted a pill—but I felt better in my mind.

For days, I had been attempting to shift my mental state by trying to control my thoughts and feelings. And now my mental state had changed fairly easily, not through mental work, but through the action I had taken. It was a small thing, walking to the end of the hall and part way back, but I had done something that demonstrated I was taking an active role in getting to where I wanted to be. As I lay there exhausted, catching my breath, I was no longer lying there "being sick." I was on my way to regaining my strength and my independence. And I felt as if I had turned yet another corner.

When I was lying in my bed absorbed in being sick again, I couldn't get my mind to accept the idea of my Statement of Being by my mental work alone. There was just too much evidence of my sickness. But when I started acting differently, acting as if I was moving toward health, my mind responded easily, and I felt better about myself and the direction I was heading. Once again, I realized the importance action plays in attitudes and beliefs. For me to really believe something, I needed to support my mental work with appropriate action.

The specific action wasn't the important ingredient. I had only decided to brush my teeth, shave, and take care of some personal items. And I hadn't even done any of those things yet. All I had done was walk to the end of the hall and part way back, but the impact on my mental state was enormous. In that moment, I realized that I could act myself into right thinking.

And my appreciation for the tools of choice grew. I already had the piece that I could think and feel myself into right action, and now I "owned" that I could act myself into right thinking. I was still in the same bed, the same room, still in pain, knowing the doctors had again taken part of my spine; yet I sat there smiling, feeling as if I was in control of my life.

I was either really dumb and in total denial, or I was really smart and on my way to making all of my dreams come true. I wasn't sure which, but I was smiling.

When Ruth came in with my pain pill, she saw me grinning and said, "That walk did you some good, didn't it?"

"You have no idea."

After I took the pill, I decided to do some mental work before I became sleepy from the narcotic. I retrieved my Statement of Being from the drawer of my nightstand and read it. The first time I went through it fairly quickly, and mostly I observed myself as I read it to see if I was connecting with it better than I had a few short hours before—and I was! I could feel it. Reading it now did not fill me up as it had at home when I first wrote it, but certainly I could feel the truth it spoke to. I was so thankful to have that feeling back again, and I thought, So why not give thanks?

The second time, I read it aloud, consciously saying the words and imagining the truth they addressed. When I was done, I closed my eyes and as best as I could, I imagined the Statement as the reality of what was going on within me. And when it was as true as I could get it, when I could feel it, I gave thanks. My intention was to spend thirty seconds giving thanks that what I was feeling and thinking was true. I gave thanks to God, I gave thanks to myself, I gave thanks to the Universe. And even though I found it difficult to continue for the thirty seconds, I kept at it.

I wasn't giving thanks for being perfectly healthy now. I was giving thanks that I was on track to create the reality I wanted to create. I was going to make believe and through my make-believe, Providence would have to respond and support me. When I was done, I felt the essence of thankfulness, or at least that's what I took the fluttering in my chest to signify. Shortly after that, the pain medication started to take effect, and I went to sleep thinking about the interplay between how I was acting, what I was thinking, what I was feeling, and how I could use all of them to create a new reality where what I chose to believe became the way it was.

I slept for about an hour before they woke me for lunch. After I ate, I decided to get out of bed on my own and walk around the room, but trying to get the vacuum pumps and tubes organized on the IV stand was too much trouble. Finally, I sat down in the chair next to the bed and turned on the television. I watched for awhile, but I wasn't into the soap operas and kept changing channels. I settled on a program sponsored by one of the local news broadcasts. The woman who was the co-anchor on the six o'clock news was hosting a special about the flu that had recently come through the Seattle area. It had caused widespread absenteeism in the work force and schools because it was highly contagious.

This particular flu bug only took hours to incubate and cause symptoms, and then those who got it were sick for three days. The special centered on four married stay-at-home mothers who all had children in grade school. Their stories were all similar. Their children were exposed to the flu at school and brought it home where mom, dad and the other children in the family were exposed. Within a day, everybody was in bed with the flu—everybody except the moms.

Each of these women told her own story in her own way, but they all had essentially the same thing to say. They simply couldn't be sick when everybody else was because they had to take care of their children and husbands. But after the family got well and returned to school and work, each woman then got the flu.

There were also two doctors on the show, and after the women told their stories, the doctors were asked if there was any medical reason for the difference in the incubation periods of the flu between the family members and the mothers. Both said there couldn't be a difference. One doctor said, "Women and mothers have been doing this forever. They tell themselves, 'I can't be sick now,' and they make an agreement to get sick later."

There was some debate about whether or not they consciously agreed to get sick later, but all the women agreed that they had declared in some fashion, "I can't be sick now." And if they started to feel sick, they ignored it and did what they had to do as the family care giver. One woman even said that she had conversations with the flu bug and told it that it would have to wait to make her sick.

It was a fascinating show, and I was glad others were exploring the idea of telling their bodies what they will and will not do.

It was the first time I had ever seen that kind of material discussed in person or on television. And it made more of an impact on me when I could see people who had some degree of success in doing what I wanted to do for myself. They didn't have an incredible healing like many of the stories and testimonials I had read about in my books and articles. But these were real people just like me, and they had somehow applied the principles I was exploring and accomplished what they had set out to do. They had taken control over illness.

After the show was over, I tried to find something else to watch, but nothing interested me. I finally turned the TV off and got out my pen and paper to write out some affirmations.

I began by reading my Statement of Being a few times and trying to feel what it addressed, reminding myself that all of what I was going through, all that I was experiencing right now was just part of my overall life. It didn't mean that the way it was now would be the way it would be forever. I remembered my anger at the psychiatrist when I thought he was using my past as the predictor for my future, and I realized that when I took the drama of my now and extrapolated it into my future, I was doing the same thing.

Nothing had to change in the outside world for my Statement of Being to be true right now. It was like the realization I had when I understood that I could pretend that my life was like a movie that I had watched before. And even though the current scene was not how I wanted my life to be, I could hold in my imagination that this movie, my life, would turn out the way I wanted because I had choice. I could know how the movie would end.

My Statement of Being was about the process of my life, the journey I was taking, and in that journey, I could feel joy now, freedom now, because I was discovering how to create reality.

I never did get to writing specific affirmations, but I seemed to have a much broader feeling of what I was creating by rereading my Statement of Being. When I had written it at home and used it, it seemed to stand alone. It was as if those few sentences were the only thing that stood between the way I wanted to feel and the anger and frustration I felt toward the constant problems I encountered. But this time, sitting alone rereading it again and again, I got that all the work I had been doing, all the realizations I had, all the pieces of creating a new model of how I wanted my life to work were in fact coming together.

Many of my individual insights, which momentarily shifted my attitude, seemed to be fitting together within a framework that gave me an overall perspective about life (and how it could be played) that was freeing. And even as I was feeling that freedom, I began trying to figure out how it all tied together, and the feelings of joy and freedom began to get lost in my analysis. But this time I noticed the pattern, and I quieted my mind and went back to reading my Statement of Being and feeling the truth of what I had written.

After a few more minutes of feeling the wonder of what was going on, I got back into bed and gently congratulated myself for all I had accomplished. I drifted into sleep, repeating to myself, "As I move into this time of creation, I feel the power of something greater than me moving with me, supporting me, and empowering me." And I went to sleep in peace.

When I awoke from my nap, I was still in a great mood, and I found there was nothing I needed to do. At least there was nothing for me to do like I had been approaching it just a few short hours before when I couldn't get the truth from my Statement of Being. I still wanted to be at choice, but as the afternoon wore on, I found that I was automatically doing what needed to be done.

There were opportunities for me to get upset. There were opportunities for me to go into "poor me," but I didn't go there. I really felt as if the concepts I had been working on for all these months were sinking in and becoming more natural.

Karen and my girls came to visit around five that day. As

Kris and Sheri climbed up on my bed all smiles and ready for play, Karen noticed something.

"You look good, honey, she said. "You seem in a much better mood."

"I walked today!" I said with a proud grin.

"Good for you."

"Yeah, Ruth helped me. All those things we've talked about are starting to come together."

We had a great evening. Karen had mentioned that the children missed me a lot when I was in the hospital. We decided to make some recordings of us playing together that they could listen to. I told the girls stories that we recorded on my small cassette recorder, and I got their giggles and questions on tape.

Once, after we were done with the stories, Sheri got tangled in the tubes going to the vacuum pumps. I began getting angry at the inconvenience of this disease and started to go down the "poor me" path, and then I noticed it simply wasn't appropriate to go there. After they left, I lay in my bed smiling, and the memory of how sweet it was to not go down the negative path gave me even more joy. I felt as if I was playing the game of my life differently even though most of the circumstances surrounding me were the same as they had been for some time. I was just reacting differently, or perhaps more precisely it seemed I was no longer reacting to those circumstances; I was acting on them. I was coming from that place where my current circumstances didn't seem to have the same control over me. I couldn't get my mind or thoughts completely around what it meant, but whatever it was, I liked it.

When I got my pain and sleeping pills, I decided that before I got ready for sleep, I would consciously spend a few minutes practicing the thanksgiving process I had discovered. I wanted to record in my mind the happiness and joy I was feeling regarding the changes I had made. I started with my Statement of Being and read it over, pretending it was true:

Statement of Being

As I move into this time of creation, I feel the power of something bigger than me, moving with me, support- ing and empowering me. I know all things are possible. And as I explore how I am going to create the healing I desire, I will notice this support and acknowledge it. I know that I do not have to figure this out all at once. All I have to do is begin right where I am and con- sciously choose to move toward what I want. My life is not one problem after another; it is right now a time of discovery and creation, and out of my own being I feel the joy and freedom that comes with knowing I can create reality.

When I got to the part where it stated "I feel the joy and freedom," I talked myself into pretending the feelings even big- ger. And when I got them as big and as real as I could, I moved into giving thanks that they were real.

After a few moments, my thoughts started to drift, and I gently brought them back to giving thanks. As I continued to focus, I found myself drifting in and around joy, in and around freedom. I experienced goodness and peace. It wasn't only a mental thing; I felt it. I could feel my body relax as my mind was quiet in the wonder of now.

It was one of my best-ever meditations or times of mental imagery. When I was done, I noticed I had been in that state for almost forty-five minutes instead of the ten minutes I had planned, and that excited me even more.

I decided to use the small basin I had to brush my teeth while sitting on the side of the bed. I sat up, and as I was get- ting my toothbrush and toothpaste out of my nightstand, I heard within my own mind, "Go make friends with the bug that causes your infection."

At first I wasn't sure what that thought meant, but as I let it roll around in my mind, I realized I was thinking about the mothers who had chosen when they would get the flu. I was thinking that I might be able to use that same idea and make a deal with my body and the E. coli bacteria that caused my infection. If I could somehow gain control over how my body responded to having the bacteria, I might be able to have some control over my draining sinuses.

Even though I did not believe I could eliminate the infection without the doctors doing a more aggressive surgical approach, through watching the TV special, I did have a simple model where I might be able to choose how the infection and my body would interact. I wasn't sure I believed it. Certainly I didn't know how I would do it, but it was a possibility that excited the hell out of me.

I put down my toothbrush and picked up my pen because I wanted to get my thoughts down while they were still fresh and exciting, before the "yeah, but's" came in.

As I was writing, I realized I didn't have to believe that making a deal with the infection would work. I could start with this idea just as I had started with healing my colon through mental imagery. I had an approach that I thought might work. Perhaps there was a way for me to still have the infection and yet not have a need for a draining sinus. Just as I had done things that increased my own belief about the power of mental imagery and the role it could play in healing, I could do other things to create a belief around making a deal with the infection and what that would bring.

As I thought about what I might do to create a belief that I could control how my body and the infection interacted, I realized that I might also be able to control how my immune system, namely my white blood cells, reacted to the infection. If I could do that, I might be able to have a normal white blood cell count even though I still had the infection. I didn't think there was any medical or scientific basis supporting this concept of choice, but there was no scientific basis for the mothers being able to choose when they would be sick with the flu. They just made it up that way.

I felt a tingling start from my heart and move out until my

whole body was involved. I knew I was experiencing a huge revelation within myself, and I started to smile. There I was, sitting on the side of my bed with my bare butt showing. I had tubes coming out of my body, and pumps sucking out vile-looking fluid, and with all that, I was thinking I had finally figured it out. Then I started to laugh.

With all of my study, with all that had transpired in this very room where I now sat, I knew my whole life was going to be about make-believe

CHAPTER 26

MAKING IT UP DIFFERENTLY

The next morning as I tried to convince myself that it was possible to make up or choose how my body reacted to the infection, I ran into a huge roadblock.

I didn't have any books or articles to use as a reference to support that something like this could be done. All I had was the TV show about the mothers who waited to get the flu. And the doctors on the show had no "logical" explanations for how one could do that. Even the one doctor who made the comment that mothers had been doing this kind of thing for a long time could not explain why or how one could choose the way his or her body dealt with illness.

It wasn't the same process as having the picture of the colon. With that technique, I had articles where experts explained how that creative process worked. And there were testimonials from those who had used this technique and created their bodies differently by using it. I had read and reread these articles and testimonials as a means of creating the belief I wanted. But now, I had no experts to help convince me of what I wanted to believe. I only had the desire to choose how my body reacted to my infection.

I was frustrated that again there didn't seem to be a pat answer. The idea of creating a new belief still involved something I could do, and the concepts of choice that I could use were the same. But how I could use choice in this particular situation was unclear.

Part of me wanted it to be simple because it was hard to figure out what I was supposed to do. I think at some level, I wanted someone else to tell me how to do it. But if I was to be really free, I knew I needed to come up with the answer myself. Otherwise, sooner or later I would run into the limiting beliefs of the ones I let do it for me.

So I began to write down my thoughts and kept reminding myself that there was a way for me to create the belief I wanted. Even though I wrote out that I controlled the power of Creation Itself, I did not believe at that point that I could just choose what to believe without any concern about whether or not it was true. I needed some sort of middle ground where I could allow myself to have my current beliefs and still be moving toward changing them.

I knew that all methodologies have proof that they work. Those who write or teach always have testimonials and experts to validate the specific list of things they're promoting as what needs to be done. But I had already concluded that belief in a methodology was the main ingredient that gave power to any specific methodology. And I didn't like that I still thought I needed to have someone else or something outside of myself validate what I wanted to believe. But, I did.

I knew that consciousness creates reality. I knew that as you believe, so shall it be done unto you. I knew that the real power is in belief, but I couldn't "own" that I could just make up my belief. I couldn't get my mind around the simplicity of that idea. I still wanted some support from outside of me.

I kept affirming, imagining, and giving thanks that I could simply make up what I wanted to believe, and I continued to read my Statement of Being, reminding myself that I didn't have to figure it out all at once. Then one day it came to me: "Why don't you pretend you have the support you need?" And as I played with that, I began to think, this might work.

It was the same realization I had with the picture of the healthy colon. I hadn't believed in that technique all at once. It started with a hope. And through the choices I made, it moved to a believable hope, not something that I would bet my life on, but something I thought might work. So I began to pretend.

I made my memory of the TV show more specific. I pretended that the doctors were more thorough in their explanations of what these mothers had done. I began to selectively remember articles and other information I had read in a way that supported what I wanted them to say. If it was all about make-believe, why couldn't I do whatever I thought I needed to do to believe?

At times it was almost funny. I would catch myself remembering what I had read or heard that absolutely supported or justified what I wanted to believe, and then I would wonder if the article really said that or was I only choosing to remember it that way?

At first when this happened, I would lose my justified position. But after awhile, by focusing on my make-believe theory, it didn't matter whether or not I had really read it from some knowledgeable source; it was what I thought, and that's what was important.

Again, I wasn't sharing this process with anyone. I imagined what it would be like if I told the psychiatrist what I was doing. My bet was it would just give him more fuel to validate his position that I was living in a dream world.

It took several weeks before I felt as good about making a deal with my infection as I did about healing my colon through mental imagery. And I kept using the tools and actively looking for ways to support myself in believing that what I was doing was working.

As always, the commitment principal was working for me. As I shifted my commitment and chose to focus on the part the mind plays in the healing process, I began to have meetings, material assistance, and events that supported me in my new focus. A whole new batch of articles came into my life. Some were sent to me, some I found. Some were cover articles that jumped out at me while looking at magazines at a newsstand.

I also changed my actions. In the mornings when I irrigated my colostomy, I no longer griped, complained, or played the "ain't it awful" conversations in my mind. Instead, I talked to my colon and praised it for healing. I looked at the picture of the beat-up healthy colon and felt the joy of being in the middle of creating that for myself. I changed the bandages on my drains four times a day instead of only twice so I would see less discharge. And each time I changed them, I would acknowledge that there was much less drainage than usual and thank my body for the way it was dealing with the infection.

At first when I changed the bandages, I would think, Sure, there's less drainage, but that's only because you just changed them a few hours ago. And I would counter that with, It doesn't matter when I changed the bandages; there is much less drainage, and what I am doing is making a difference. After awhile, when I changed them and noticed less drainage, I would feel joy and believe that what I was doing was working.

One of the most memorable things that happened during this period occurred one morning while I was praising my colon for healing. I had been doing this for several weeks, and as the process began to feel more natural, I wasn't as concerned with the specific words or thoughts I used. Then this particular morning, I really felt the praise; I felt the love and acknowledgment I was giving to my body.

I was no longer pretending to get my body to do what I wanted. I was praising my body for the actual healing that was taking place. And my body was responding to my conscious acknowledgment of its magnificence.

The only experiences I could equate with what I was feeling were the times when my daughters would come to me scared or hurt, and I would hold them and tell them how much I loved them and that everything was going to be okay. I didn't try to convince them of anything about the event that hurt or scared them. I just reassured them of my love and held them, and they responded by being more at peace.

It was that same type of experience that morning. I was mentally holding a part of my body and telling it how much I loved it, how much I respected it, and I felt my body love me back. I felt myself relax, and yet it was more than just relaxing. It was as if my body was empowered by me simply loving it, and I felt that the empowerment was assisting my body to heal.

I had read and heard that there isn't anything that love can't heal. But I had never understood what that idea meant. However, the experience that morning gave me a framework for what it might mean, and I decided to incorporate that technique into my healing practices. As time went on, I gained such benefit from loving and holding my body that I consciously started every morning and ended each evening with loving myself.

I would lie in my bed and touch my body, especially the areas that were in distress, and as I stroked my skin, I would talk to my cells, tissues, and organs and tell them they were wonderful and how much I appreciated them.

I took time every day to have a dialog with my body and the E. coli bacteria. I talked to my white blood cells and told them what I was doing. I pretended these cells were intelligent and understood that I didn't want them to have such a violent reaction to the infection. I talked to the E. coli and told it that I didn't want it to spread. I told the infection that my cells wouldn't attack it if it would just settle down. I created a pretend model where my body and the infection could live together without the acute distress I had experienced in the past. I imagined my body and the infection living in peace together.

Some days I was very specific in my self-talk and daydreams. Other days I simply had loving conversations with my colon, the infection, and my white blood cells.

In this creative process, part of me wanted a huge revelation, a significant event where bells would go off and I would feel transformed in that instant to perfect health. But that didn't come. And after awhile, it was okay, for I began to understand that it isn't a matter of success or failure, it's simply a matter of picking an idea and sticking with it until it becomes a tangible reality.

≈ ≈ ≈ ≈

About three months after my meeting with Dr. Yelton, I had to go into the orthopedic clinic for a general evaluation required by the industrial insurance. It included a battery of tests that usually took three to four hours. I had the normal blood work done, a complete physical, and this time they did a colonoscopy, a visual exam of the lower colon from the inside. To my surprise, the resident who was doing the exam said, "This doesn't look inflamed. It's healing quite nicely."

I thought about it for a moment and asked, "Does that mean it's healed enough to sew it back together?"

"We won't really know if it's healed completely without opening you up and examining it first-hand."

"Will Dr. Yelton get a copy of this report?"

"Yes, he'll be notified."

Two days later, I went back to the clinic so they could review the results of the tests with me. Because this whole process bored me, I was glancing at a magazine and only half listening as the intern explained the test results—until he said, "I'll be darned. That hole in your back isn't growing any bugs."

"What'd you say?"

"The hole in your back isn't growing bugs. You still have the infection; it's just not draining. The drain has closed off in the middle."

He brought up his open hand and closed his fist as if he was squeezing shut a hose. When he did that, I almost wet my pants, because that gesture was the same one I was using as a visual example of what my body was doing.

I regained my composure and asked, "Could you tell me what my white blood cell count is?" As he looked through the results of the blood work, I prayed.

"Not bad," he said. "It's up a little bit but not that much. It looks like your body and the infection have moved into a state of homeostasis.

"What's that?"

"It's sort of where the body and the infection get used to each other."

I sat there looking at him, barely breathing, afraid to ask him anything else.

"Are you okay?" he asked. "You look a little pale."

"Yeah, I'm okay. Could I have a copy of the report that says I don't have a draining sinus, and also the one that says that my white blood cell count is almost normal?"

"Why do you want them," he asked.

"Because Dr. Yelton is going to sew up my colostomy!"

"Boy, I'll bet you're glad about that."

I smiled to myself. Yeah I am, but Dr. Yelton doesn't know it yet.

≈ ≈ ≈ ≈

When I left the orthopedic clinic, I was dazed. I was happy, excited and confused. I sat down in the waiting area and began to chuckle. I felt like a dog that chased a car and caught it, and I wondered, now what do I do? After a few minutes, I went outside behind the hospital where its property bordered the waterway that connected Lake Washington with Lake Union. I sat down on a bench to collect my thoughts and plan my next move.

In making friends with the infection, I still believed I needed to have a place for the infection to drain. So my goal had been to have a two-week window where I could still have the infection yet not have a draining sinus. I wanted to slow down the production of fluid so the drains could heal and the fluid buildup would be so minimal that I would not need to have the drains reopened for two weeks. And now it had happened. What was next was to get Dr. Yelton to agree that this was the time to sew up my bowels.

Part of me was eager to walk up to his office and say, "Let's do it." But I didn't think that would work. So I sat on the bench and systematically created a movie of how I wanted our next conversation to go.

First, I got specific on the results I wanted and ultimately settled on Dr. Yelton agreeing to do the surgery the next day. Then, I role-played how I would approach him and what I would say. I rehearsed and revised my conversation until I was satisfied. Would I have bet my life he would agree to what I wanted? No, but again, I would have bet my best fly rod on it. And that had become my benchmark for when it was time to move. As I walked back to the hospital, I wasn't scared or confused any more. I knew what I wanted, and I would not be denied.

When I went into Dr. Yelton's outer office, I could see past his secretary's desk that he was in. Good!

"Ma'am, the orthopedic guys wanted me to come see Dr. Yelton."

Without her relaying the information, Dr. Yelton looked up and said, "Come in, Terry. What do they want?"

I took a deep breath and went in. "Remember when we talked about reversing my colostomy . . . ?"

"Listen, Terry," he interrupted, "I thought we went over this before. I've already told you I'll be the one to decide when and if that will ever take place."

He went on for a few more moments in that vein. When he was finished, I let the room fill with silence, then said, "I am sorry I've caused you so much pain over these past years."

He stopped cold, his brow wrinkling. He looked like he was trying to figure out if I was mocking him or serious. While he was in that confused state, I handed him the report and said, "The orthopedic guys want you to know I don't have a draining sinus."

He took the report from me and read it. When he was finished, he looked up. "You know you still have the infection. Your drains have just healed up in the middle." Then he made the same gesture of closing his hand. When he did that, I thought, I Own You! And that statement wasn't from anything other than I was the one controlling where our conversation was going.

Next, I handed him the report on my white blood cell count. As he read it, I said softly, "I think this is the opportunity you've been waiting for." Then I shut up and consciously filled his mind with the thoughts I wanted him to think.

After what seemed like an eternity he said, "You could be right. I'm in clinic next Tuesday. Go down and make an appointment, and we will discuss this then."

"Thank you, Dr. Yelton. I knew we were going to come to agreement on this today."

His forehead furrowed over darkening eyes. Before he could say anything, I added, "If we wait till Tuesday, the sinus could open up again."

"Are you saying you want me to do this surgery today?"

"No, I was thinking we could do it tomorrow."

In the heavy silence that followed, I filled his mind with the answer I wanted. I wasn't being arrogant, and I wasn't afraid. I was simply consciously manipulating his thinking so he would do what I wanted.

Finally he said, "Okay, go home and get your stuff, and I'll call Admitting. You can come in tonight, and we'll do the surgery in the morning. But you're going to think you drowned, because we're going to flush you from both ends till you've got nothing left inside you."

I damn near fainted when he agreed. On the way out through the lobby, I stopped at a pay phone and called Karen to give her the news. We celebrated briefly, and I told her I'd be home in about a half-hour.

When I got to my car, I was so filled with emotion I couldn't drive. Sitting in the parking lot composing myself, I heard myself say out loud, "Soon I'm going to go to the bathroom like I used to go to the bathroom."

After a short while and some deep breaths, I got myself together and drove home, breaking into laughter from time to time. When I opened the front door, Karen was there with tears in her eyes. She leapt into my arms and covered me with kisses.

"You did it!" she whispered in my ear.

We had a wonderful celebration dinner—Karen, Kris, Sheri, Karen's parents and me. After dinner, I sat down with the girls and explained why I was going to the hospital.

"Daddy isn't sick this time," I said. "This time, the doctors are going to fix my tummy so I can go to the bathroom the regular way."

"Do we get to come to the hospital again?"

"Sure, Mommy will bring you in a few days." They burst into smiles and hugged me.

When Karen and I left for the hospital, they waved and said, "We'll see you in the hospital, Daddy."

As I went through the admission procedures, I was already busy creating my reality for surgery the next morning. I was excited and nervous all at the same time, especially when I remembered the trouble I had had after they first did the colostomy. So I focused on talking to my body and reassuring myself that I would handle the surgery well and that when they opened me up, they would find my colon healed.

After Karen left, as I was congratulating myself for creating the exact surgery I wanted, I tried to remember when the shift had taken place, when I knew for a certainty I was going to get my colostomy reversed. And I could find no single event where all of a sudden I believed. It was a step-by-step process of staying focused, where I slowly began to think that what I was doing was working and what I wanted to happen was, in fact, going to happen. It was more than just positive thinking. I had used choice and had created a new reality for myself.

In the beginning, I thought I needed to force what I wanted into my life. But as I continued to stick with the ideas I wanted and used choice to reprogram my beliefs, I really began to experience that all I had to do was allow what I wanted to be so. I had read about allowing and accepting the desires of our hearts and minds, but when I was stuck in my disbelief, I couldn't get my mind around what that meant.

As close as I could get to when I began to create this new reality for myself was when I first wrote out my Statement of Being. With that statement, I accepted what was going on in my now, and at the same time declared that it was not going to be that way forever. Then I coupled that declaration, that hope for my future, with the power of Providence backing me up.

I think if I had stopped there, I would still be hoping things would change. But what allowed me to really know that I was going to get what I wanted was when I continued doing what I thought I needed to do. Sometimes that "doing" revolved around actions I took, sometimes it was thinking certain thoughts and sometimes it was consciously using my imagination. I thought I had succeeded where others might have failed because I had persisted in integrating my choices into one workable model that allowed me to believe.

As I drifted into sleep, I once again found I was busy trying to figure out how I could use what I was learning to get even more of what I wanted. But this time, there was also a deep sense of wonder along with the knowledge that I didn't have to figure it out all at once. Tomorrow I would get my colostomy reversed, and that was good enough for now.

CHAPTER 27

YES, I CAN!

A s always, Karen was there beside me holding my hand when I awoke from surgery. I smiled at her and said, "We did it!" and immediately drifted into a peaceful sleep.

Later, the resident who actually did the cutting and sewing told me that overall the surgery was uneventful, which was nice to hear for a change. He said the lower part of my colon was beat up and scarred, but intact. And they were quite optimistic that my bowels would soon be working fine. He said I would probably have some trouble having bowel movements regularly because of the scarring and where it was now sewn back together. He also mentioned that I should expect some pain when the peristaltic action moved through the reconnected portion.

For the next few days, they only gave me liquids to eat and drink. But I wasn't concerned about my diet; I was ecstatic to finally be rid of the colostomy.

I was in the hospital for eleven days for that one, and I spent most of the time sitting on the pot trying to go to the bathroom. It turned out that the scarring was more troublesome than they thought it would be. When the peristaltic action moved through where they had sewn my bowels together, I experienced a great deal of pain. If I ate breakfast soon after I woke up, the peristaltic action would have such force that the cramping and pain would double me over, and I would have to lay in bed in a fetal position.

Even using the positive-thought techniques I knew, I couldn't help but feel discouraged and wonder if I would ever be healthy and whole again.

Five days after the surgery that reversed my colostomy, Dr. Greenlee opened the area in my back where the sinus had closed and inserted a rubber tube so the incision wouldn't close. And I was back to having a draining sinus and changing my bandages twice a day.

About the time I was released, I had figured out how to deal with the scarring on my colon and what precautions I needed to take as to what and when to eat. And even though I really wasn't back to going to the bathroom like I used to, I was thrilled to no longer have the colostomy.

I was now only a month and a half away from graduating from college and the preparations for finals and on-campus job interviews took up most of my time. I was still using the techniques of choice, but mostly I focused on the things that were of immediate concern, like graduating and getting a good job. The drains I had were no longer much of an inconvenience. Apparently the work I had done on getting my body and the infection to coexist was still working, because even with the new drains, there wasn't much fluid coming from them. Once in a while I would get worried that there might not be good drainage, but I didn't have the kind of pain that was associated with pockets of infection.

I thought about healing the infection with the same concepts that I had used to heal my colon and get my colostomy reversed, but it was not something that was a priority. In fact, I didn't even write about it to see what might be done. I had a belief that I would have the infection for a long, long time, and

I had other matters to attend to.

After I graduated, I got a job with a national certified public accounting firm. I bought two new suits at Penney's, borrowed $1500 from my brother Gerry for a down payment on a three-bedroom house in Mountlake Terrace just north of Seattle, and before I knew it, I was working long hours and traveling throughout the northwestern states as an auditor.

When I was in school and sick, I seemed to have more time to devote to my use of the tools of choice. Even having the colostomy gave me that hour in the morning to do my work. But now that I had a job and a house and my family to take care of, I just didn't seem to find the time to practice creating the reality of perfect health. I still used my Statement of Being once in a while, but even in that, I was focusing on things other than healing the infection. I was studying for the CPA exam and focusing on becoming proficient as an accountant. I really thought I would get back to using choice to create the health I wanted when I had more time.

About four months after starting work, one of the partners in the firm suggested I join the Jaycees, an organization for young men between the ages of eighteen and thirty-five, and I did. Their purpose is to do community service projects and through that develop leadership skills. Two years later, I was appointed Treasurer for the Washington State Jaycees.

As a state officer, I was required to speak at local chapter meetings, so I took the four-week speaking program the Jaycees called Speak Up Jaycee. I also took several of the personal-development programs offered on how to plan a successful project. Much of the material was similar to what I had been studying while working on getting well, and I took to it like a duck takes to water. Soon I was promoting the various personal-development programs to chapters throughout the state.

I had a couple of minor surgeries in the two and a half years since graduating but nothing very invasive, and I was only in the hospital for a few days for Dr. Greenlee to reopen the drains. During one of the drain surgeries, Dr. Greenlee did another of those X-ray procedures where they inserted a small tube into the sinus track and pumped in the special dye that showed up on the films. The X-rays showed that the infection had settled in the front, lowest part of my spine, where the major nerves for the legs come out of the spinal column. He said it would be virtually impossible to go in and scrape that area without damaging the nerves, so again I was left with chronic osteomyelitis.

≈ ≈ ≈ ≈

The whole purpose of the Jaycees was to assist its members to gain the skills that would allow them to achieve their personal life goals. And the more I taught the fundamentals of successful living, the more I became aware that I was not using the tools I knew to eliminate the infection. Sometimes when this happened, I would get on track for a while and start focusing on that specific objective. But my determination and focus never lasted very long. I was too busy to make my own dreams come true. I was hoping that something would change, but I wasn't using the tools of choice to create the change I wanted.

Finally, three years after the colostomy was reversed, I had two surgeries back to back and was in the hospital for nineteen days. The infection had spread into the tissues around my lower spine, and again Dr. Greenlee was concerned that it might be moving to my hip joint. He said that if that happened, I could lose the use of my leg. While hospitalized for those surgeries, I really got that I could not expect to have the infection without the possible catastrophic complications it could bring. And I decided it was time to get healed.

I got out my Statement of Being and started writing about how I was going to approach ridding my body of the infection.

The first thing I decided was to develop a system that would be easy to use and would allow me to stay on track in using choice every day to move toward my own personal desires no matter how busy I was. I made some cassette tapes to listen to, which spoke to the ideas I wanted to focus on, and I developed a workbook where I recorded my progress in doing what I said I was going to do.

Getting focused and staying on track turned out to be easier than I had imagined. Before, when I was using choice on a daily basis, I had a great deal of discretionary time throughout my day. I had things to do such as study, go to class or lay around my hospital room, but other than going to class, I could choose when to do what needed to be done. So I really didn't organize the time to do my creative work other than loving my body when I woke up and when I went to bed, and the work I would do while taking care of my colostomy.

Now that I developed a schedule and a plan for when I would use the tools of choice, it was easy to use my scheduled time to support following through with my plan by using affirmations and visualizations. I learned that I could use the tools to support myself using the tools. And once again, it became like a game, and I made an agreement with myself to spend ten minutes a day using one of the tools or a combination of them on my specific desire to eliminate the infection. Listening to the tapes didn't count in the ten minutes because I listened to them in the car when I was driving.

The tapes I made for myself were also a huge benefit. I had acquired motivational tapes from other people, but I found that too many times the authors of the tapes were just telling me what I should be doing or believing based on their own agendas. On the tapes I made for myself, it was more like having a fireside chat, reminding myself of the basics of choice and encouraging me to continue using them. On some of the tapes, I talked about the benefits of doing certain actions such as writing out my thoughts or using affirmations to support me in following through with my actions. Other tapes addressed the benefits of using thanksgiving as a means of creating belief, or how visualization becomes easy when you have a plan you believe in. As I continued to make different tapes, they became like an ongoing dialog with myself that assisted me to continually explore how I might use choice to get more of what I wanted.

On my tapes, I had specific suggestions on how the individual concepts within choice worked, but I did not become dogmatic about how each of the principles should be used. I wanted them open-ended so listening to them would get my mind thinking about how I might apply the concepts to the individual desire I was concentrating on. The more I used them and followed through with the actions, affirmations, and visualizations that pertained to each goal I was going after, the more ingrained the ideas became. Although I wasn't getting any clear specifics on how I might heal the infection, I was on track in many other areas through using choice consistently. And again I knew that in any particular endeavor, it is not a matter of success or failure, it is simply a matter of picking an idea and sticking with it until it becomes a tangible reality.

The only way I could imagine eliminating the infection was to kill the bugs with an antibiotic. So I talked Dr. Greenlee into admitting me to the hospital for intensive antibiotic therapy. I was in the hospital for twelve days while they administered various antibiotics with IV drips and shots. During that stay, I got acquainted with the doctors who specialized in dealing with infections.

I was released after two weeks, but the infection persisted. Only a month later, I knew the infection was pocketing because of the pain, and I would need to have my drains reopened. But I had some ideas on what I wanted done.

Through my discussions with the infectious disease specialists, I had been formulating a game plan. When I went in to see Dr. Greenlee in the clinic to talk about opening the drains, I had a written plan of attack.

After he examined me and agreed that the drains would have to be opened, I asked him, "Do you think we will ever beat this thing?"

After a long pause he replied, "No, Terry, I think you will

always have this infection."

"Then you can't cut on me any more. I'll need to find another doctor."

Leaning forward, his jaw dropped. "What are you talking about?"

"I'm unwilling to have this for the rest of my life. I don't care if we win this time, but I do care whether we believe we can win. I care that we approach each surgery with the possibility that it will be the last."

Dr. Greenlee's face softened with a smile. "You've got a plan, don't you?"

"Yes, as a matter of fact, I do. Want to hear it?"

"Of course I do. I've always said you know more about what's going on with your body than we do."

"Well, when I was talking with the infectious disease guys last month, they said that the reason they only allow people to take this antibiotic for two weeks is that it has the potential to damage the inner ear. It's a reaction within the body that raises something within the blood that destroys bone, and the most delicate bones that are damaged first are the small bones in the inner ear. They said some people can be on the antibiotic longer than others, but everybody can be on it for two weeks without concern about ear damage. That's why they limit the antibiotic treatment to fourteen days.

"I asked them if a blood test could tell whether the dangerous chemical was getting too high, and they said 'yes.' So I suggest I get on the antibiotic now, and then after the surgery, I can have a blood test every two weeks to see if I need to stop."

Dr. Greenlee said, "Are you sure it works like that?"

"Yes, I am. Call and ask the infectious disease guys."

He did, he picked up the phone and called the head of infectious disease, and they had a conversation.

"You're right," he said. "Okay, what's the rest of your plan?"

God, I loved this man! I just smiled at him, remembering that day in the hall when he took me in, when no one else seemed to care any more.

"When we've done these debridements before, we only had one incision site, and when we tried to flush it out with saline, the water just squirted back out. Why don't we go down to the infected part of the spine from two directions? Then when we flush the wound out with saline, the flow of the water into one hole will flush out the wound completely with the waste coming out the other hole. It could be like running water through the wound to really clean it out. And let's put antibiotic in the water we flush with."

"I've never heard of doing that," Dr. Greenlee said.

"Me neither, but why not? Let's saturate the area with antibiotic. And most importantly, we need to go in from the front. The infection is in the front of the spine, and we have to get that area flushed and saturated with the antibiotic."

"No, Terry, we can't go in from the front and get all the way to your spine; it's too risky with all the nerves in your pelvic area."

"Not if we start wide."

"What do you mean?"

"Let's start from my hip bones and follow the pelvic girdle down, then we won't even have to go through the belly; we'll go around the nerves."

Dr. Greenlee sat there looking at me, and I could tell he was giving my idea real consideration.

To help convince him, I added, "Would you want to live the rest of your life with drains and surgeries, or would you want to take your best shot at getting rid of the problem? The risks are minimal, and it's the only thing left to do. What do you say?" In the silence, I filled his mind with the thoughts I wanted him to think.

After a moment, he said, "Okay, we'll do it! I'll talk with the infectious disease department and bring one of them in on this, and we'll see what happens. And you know, Terry, this could work."

"One last thing," I said, "let's use big hard drains so the

incision sites won't close. I want them to stay open for months so my body can kick out the bugs."

"Sounds like you really thought this out, Terry," he chuckled. "And I think using the hard drains is a good idea."

When I left his office, I went up to the fourth floor and told the nurses I would be coming in on Thursday. The large room with the private bathroom wasn't occupied, and they said they would put a "reserved" sign on it for me. Then I went back to work to tell my bosses I would be going into the hospital again.

That night I was scheduled to speak at a Jaycee chapter meeting about thirty miles from downtown Seattle. It was in the opposite direction of my home, so I stayed downtown and had dinner at a local restaurant. It was good to have time alone; I needed to think, I needed to plan. More than that, I needed to believe this new approach was going to work. As I reviewed my notes for the talk I was going to give that evening, I knew that I was standing on the threshold of having what I wanted regarding my health, and I was a bit frightened. It had been five years since my fusion, and this coming surgery would be my twenty-first major surgery. But as I sat there a little afraid, I knew there was nothing to do other than use the tools of choice as best I could.

It was late when I got home and Karen was asleep. The next morning when I told her about my talk with Dr. Greenlee and the plan we had made, her face lit up in a radiant smile.

"You healed your colon and got rid of your colostomy. I'll bet you can do this one too."

My heart opened. What a gift she was! "Thank you for believing in me." Her simple statement reminded me again that it is not a matter of success or failure, the really important thing was to stick with an idea and hang onto it until it blossomed into reality.

For the next two days, I was very busy at work finishing up the summary of an audit I had just completed. And in my spare time, I wrote down my thoughts and ideas about how I was going to stay focused and create this final healing. It had been almost three years since I had healed my colon, and although I was using choice on a consistent basis and teaching the basics of choice two or three times a week at Jaycee meetings, I hadn't been using choice or my mind on healing. So I was a bit rusty at first. But as I wrote my ideas down, the subtleties of how I had used choice before came back, and I found myself excited about this opportunity I had to completely heal my body of the infection. Once and for all, I had a chance to demonstrate to myself that I could create the reality I wanted.

When I packed to go to the hospital on Thursday morning, it was like the first time I was admitted to the University Medical Center. Again I felt like I had a new savior, except this time it was ME!

When Dr. Greenlee came in that afternoon, we discussed what was going to be done and the types of drains he was going to use. I really appreciated the way he let me have input with regard to what I saw as the overall purpose of the surgery. It was more than simply opening drains. Together we were creating a surgical strategy to work in conjunction with an extreme antibiotic regimen; this combination held the possibility of eliminating the infection. And I think at some level, he was as excited as I was. Although he wasn't into the "woowoo" stuff like I was, when he left he said, "I'll do my part, you keep your fingers crossed." I suppose that was the best he could do as far as encouraging me. But I knew there was a lot more to do than just crossing my fingers and hoping.

The rest of the afternoon was taken up with the standard preparation work. I was shaved, had some blood drawn, and, of course, the old standby—an intern came in to give me a physical and ask me the same old questions. And I smiled through the whole ordeal. When Karen, Kris and Sheri came in, I was in a great mood, and we headed off to the cafeteria.

The surgery went as planned. It was a little more uncomfortable than some because there were two surgical sites and three hard half-inch rubber drains in each that went into my right and left hips all the way to my spine. The first day or so

I was heavily medicated with morphine but as soon as I could, I shifted to a milder painkiller because I wanted my mind clear. I wanted to continue talking to my body and to encourage both my body and my mind to work together in the various facets of creating the reality I wanted.

I used all of the tools to keep focused and work on the specifics in my plan. Daily I reviewed my written goal and the plan I had to attain it. I used affirmation, visualization, and the thanksgiving process to make sure that the specific steps in my plan were working. I directed how my body reacted to the antibiotic with the intention of staying on it for months without any bone damage. I pretended that I could determine how the antibiotic would finally destroy the infection.

I saw and felt in my imagination how the infected area was washed clean by the three flushing procedures that were done each day. With the resident who was an expert in infectious disease, I explored how with long cotton swabs and a special solution they made, I could keep the incisions open. And I imagined the antibiotic from my shots moving through my blood system and into the infected area, there combining with the antibiotic from the saline flush, eliminating all bacteria.

I made cassette recordings of my own voice talking me through what was happening and how all the facets of what I was doing, thinking, and feeling were coming together easily and naturally so I would be infection-free. And boy, I got into it! I redid the tape a couple of times, and with the other work I was doing, I could feel the truth of what it spoke to.

I was in the hospital for seventeen days. We did the flushing with the antibiotic solution three times daily, and I received a shot of the antibiotic twice a day. At first, with the help of the resident and then on my own, I kept the drains unclogged with the swabs. On the fifteenth day, they drew some of my blood and tested it for whatever it was that could damage the inner ear. Dr. Greenlee got the results and said I was tolerating the treatment fine; and when I was released, I was given a two-week's supply of the antibiotic and needles. He wanted me back in two weeks for more blood work and then he would decide whether or not to continue.

With the system I developed to support myself, it was easy to stay on track in using choice every day to create the reality I wanted. Each time they tested my blood, I was allowed to continue with the antibiotic regiment. I was able to keep the hard rubber tubes in for almost three months and even when they came out, I kept the drains open for another two months. I stayed on the antibiotic for another month after the drains closed, and then we decided to stop. In all, the drains had been open for five months, and I had taken the antibiotic for six months.

≈ ≈ ≈ ≈

After the drains closed, there was nothing to do but wait and see. I continued using choice every day and kept my mind focused on being infection-free. After another three months with no indication of pocketing, Dr. Greenlee said he thought the infection was in remission. I didn't like that word because to me remission means its coming back. But he couldn't talk about being cured; it just wasn't in his mental framework. He believed in chronic osteomyelitis.

At times, I would get concerned when I felt a pain or discomfort in my lower back, and I would start to think, *What if it's the infection?* and I would immediately use choice to think about something else before the negative train of thought got rolling. Sometimes I would get frustrated with my belief that I needed to use choice every day to make sure that my life was going the way I wanted it to. But I realized that I didn't grow up with the belief that life was easy, where we automatically get what we want. So I knew in order for me to make my dreams come true I would have to change my internal program about life, and that revolved around choice.

About a year after the surgery, I left the public accounting firm and went to work for a large truck manufacturer headquartered in Bellevue, Washington. By then I had been elected

Executive Vice President of the Washington State Jaycees, and I was even more involved in teaching the principles of choice as they pertained to project management within our organization. And the more I taught the principles and witnessed people changing their lives through using choice, the more I knew that's what I wanted to do as my career.

Six months after starting with the trucking company, I had my first performance evaluation. I had been doing well, and my boss said I could look forward to a long and rewarding career with the company. I was to get a substantial raise in salary, which would help pay for the new car Karen and I were thinking about buying.

That night I drove to the southern part of the state to speak at the Vancouver Washington Jaycee meeting. During the two-plus-hour drive to and from the meeting, I was listening to some of the tapes I had made for myself, and I realized that if I didn't get out of the corporate world now, I would be stuck there for the rest of my life.

The next morning, I reviewed my plan with Karen and went to work. I finished the project I was working on, and when I took it into my boss, I told him I was leaving. I needed to get out before my salary and perks locked me in. He understood what I was getting at and suggested I give a two-week notice or I would burn some bridges and not be able to come back if I wanted to. I said, "I don't want any bridges to go back over; I only want to move forward." I packed my personal possessions and was gone before noon.

Within the week, I had rented office space in an old warehouse in downtown Seattle, and I opened my own company. I dabbled with a few ventures and finally settled on teaching and consulting in the personal-growth industry. I named my company McBride Enterprises and chose the letters ME as part of my logo to remind myself that all things are possible if I believe. In other words, "If it's to be, it's up to ME."

≈ ≈ ≈ ≈

Three years later, I had to go back into the hospital because the old colostomy site became infected. There were some scary times at first, because the tests showed the infection was the same E. coli bug I had had in my spine. However, after the surgery, Dr. Greenlee assured me the spine was not involved. During the next year, I had two more surgeries before they eradicated that infection, and while in the hospital for the last one, I really got that for me to have perfect health, I would have to be at choice on an ongoing basis to create it. To support that, I made a major decision.

From the same hospital room where I fought for my life on a circle bed ten years earlier, I called my office and told my secretary and partner I was closing the company. I was going to write a training course that I could use for myself and offer to others that would assist me and others to understand and use the tools of choice on a daily basis. It took a year to write the course, and when it was done, I sold the first twenty-three programs to the CPA firm where I had worked previously.

It was another four years before I really believed I was done with the infection. And I knew without doubt that I had created that reality. Over the years, I have had three plastic surgeries to repair the scars on my abdomen and bring together the muscles in my back.

Since going to work for myself, I have been teaching and inspiring others to know and use the tools of choice. I have been witness to even more incredible success stories than mine over the years. Through it all and through using my own program, I know that when confronted with what seems like impossible odds, I no longer have to start from "the hell I can't." I now start from "yes, I can!"

P.S. *There are still times when people get in my face and insist that I accept my human limitations. When that happens, part of me wants to tell them to kiss my ass. But that's just the facet of me that still thinks I need to be the toughest guy in the valley.*
    Go make your dreams come true!
                                    —Terry McBride

EPILOGUE

I had my first surgery, the spinal fusion when I was twenty-three. The last one dealing with the infection was eleven years later. In all, I had twenty-seven major surgeries, including three plastic surgeries to clean up my scars, and I spent 281 days in the hospital.

At the writing of this book, I am just days away from turning sixty, and I do not have a bad back. I am not recovering from a bad back and I have none of the limitations, pain or complications the experts said I would have.

Some say I was lucky to come out of my health challenge completely whole, but luck had nothing to do with me getting well. I healed my body and created the magnificent life I have because I accepted responsibility for what I wanted and used choice to create it.

It's so easy in our cultures to get caught up in the drama of life as it has been taught for generations. Daily we are bombarded with all the things that aren't working, the problems we must deal with, and the challenges right in front of us. Because of this, it can be difficult to stop thinking about problems and focus on solutions. But I believe this is the single most important aspect of having the kind of life you want.

I know the idea of living life as if we are in a playground where we get to make our dreams come true is almost too much to imagine. But if we do not imagine, if we do not hope, if we do not step forth and finally say "no" to suffering, separation and disease, we leave ourselves and our children fighting the same problems we have faced. But saying "no" to the old way is not enough. We as individuals and societies must begin to say "yes" to what we do want.

Take time for your dreams.

—Remember—

You are magnificent and the rest you get to make up.

FROM THE EDITOR

I met Terry McBride two years ago when I attended his two-evening workshop. One of the first things I noticed about him was his enthusiasm for life. It was obvious that he experienced his life and what he was about as a joyous adventure.

Having been involved in my own personal development through workshops, books, and various trainings for over twenty-five years, I understood the basics he was teaching. At the same time, his approach was unique. As he explored choice and how it can be used, he allowed each of us to find our own way. And he inspired us to focus on what we did want, instead of simply using the principles and techniques he was teaching, to deal with the challenges we faced.

As he talked about how he discovered the power of choice when he was healing himself, I knew that if I paid attention to the choices I was making in my life, I too could have the dreams of my heart and mind.

At the end of his workshop he offered the Everybody Wins program, his nine-week, take-home training. I decided to invest in it, not because he sold me—that's not Terry—he just showed how the daily use of his tapes, workbook and text could be beneficial and asked, "What would your life be like if you had a method to assist you to use the tools of choice to get what you want?"

I got the program so I'd have a support system and specific tools to help me focus on getting what I truly wanted. And, it really worked!

Using Everybody Wins took only minutes a day. Within a short time, I witnessed wonderful changes in my life. I was more on track, and I was having more fun. As I completed the training, I realized I was creating the life I always wanted. And I'm excited to go through it again because, through using this program, I will continue applying choice to my new dreams.

Working with Terry on his book has changed how I view myself and how I approach living. And through having the Everybody Wins program as a resource that I can use again and again to remind and assist me to use what I know, I too see my life as a joyous adventure.

Note: I wanted to share this with you because the Everybody Wins program has made a big difference in my life. If you would like to have the program to support yourself in using the tools of choice, you can use the order form on the following page, or you can order on-line at www.terrymcbride.info.

—Leslie Petrovich
Editor, The Hell I Can't!

THE EVERYBODY WINS PROGRAM
ORDER FORM

For immediate processing, order additional copies online at:
www.terrymcbride.info

To order additional copies by mail, simply copy or detatch the following form, fill in completely and mail to:

McBride Enterprises
2753 E. Broadway, Suite 101-313
Mesa, AZ 85204

☐ Please send me_____copies of the *Everybody Wins Program*.
    Internet and Book Special: U.S. $185.00 (normally $225.00)

Sales Tax: Add $12.09 sales tax for products shipped to Florida.

Shipping & Handling: Add $12.00 U.S. for each program

Shipping/Contact Address - Please Print Clearly:

First Name: _____ Last Name: _____

Email Address: _____ Phone Number: _____

Address: _____

City: _____ State/Province: _____ Zip Code: _____

Payment Type:
☐ Check   ☐ Money Order   ☐ MasterCard   ☐ Visa

Credit Card Information - Please Print Clearly:

☐☐☐☐ ☐☐☐☐ ☐☐☐☐ ☐☐☐☐

Card Expires - Month: _____ Year: _____

Name On Card: _____

Billing Address: _____

City: _____ State/Province: _____ Zip Code: _____

Signature: _____

BOOK ORDER FORM

For immediate processing, order additional copies online at:
www.terrymcbride.info

To order additional copies by mail, simply copy or detatch the following form, fill in completely and mail to:

McBride Enterprises
2753 E. Broadway, Suite 101-313
Mesa, AZ 85204

☐ Please send me_____copies of *The Hell I Can't!*.
   Internet and Book Special: U.S. $19.95 (normally $23.95)

Sales Tax: Add $1.30 sales tax for products shipped to Florida.

Shipping & Handling: Add $5.90 U.S. for each book.

Shipping/Contact Address - Please Print Clearly:

First Name: _____ Last Name: _____

Email Address: _____ Phone Number: _____

Address: _____

City: _____ State/Province: _____ Zip Code: _____

Payment Type:
☐ Check   ☐ Money Order   ☐ MasterCard   ☐ Visa

Credit Card Information - Please Print Clearly:

☐☐☐☐ ☐☐☐☐ ☐☐☐☐ ☐☐☐☐

Card Expires - Month: _____ Year: _____

Name On Card: _____

Billing Address: _____

City: _____ State/Province: _____ Zip Code: _____

Signature: _____